D0358789

Collins
tracing your
family history

How we are related

		GREAT GREAT GRANDFATHER great great grandson	=	**GREAT GREAT GRANDMOTHER** great great grandson	
	GREAT GRANDFATHER great grandson	=	**GREAT GRANDMOTHER** great grandson		**GREAT GREAT UNCLE** great great nephew
GREAT UNCLE great nephew	**GREAT AUNT** great nephew	**PATERNAL GRANDFATHER** paternal grandson	=	**PATERNAL GRANDMOTHER** paternal grandson	**THIRD COUSIN TWICE REMOVED** first cousin twice removed
SECOND COUSIN ONCE REMOVED first cousin once removed	**FATHER** son = **MOTHER** son = **STEPFATHER** stepson	**AUNT** nephew	**UNCLE** nephew		**THIRD COUSIN ONCE REMOVED** second cousin once removed
SECOND COUSIN second cousin	**SIBLINGS** Brother	**ME**	**HALF SIBLINGS** half brother	**FIRST COUSIN** first cousin	**THIRD COUSIN** third cousin
SECOND COUSIN ONCE REMOVED third cousin once removed	**NEPHEW/ NIECE** uncle	**SON** father	**HALF NEPHEW/ HALF NIECE** half uncle	**FIRST COUSIN ONCE REMOVED** second cousin once removed	**THIRD COUSIN ONCE REMOVED** fourth cousin once removed
SECOND COUSIN TWICE REMOVED fourth cousin twice removed	**GREAT NEPHEW/ NIECE** great uncle	**GRANDSON** grandfather	**HALF GREAT NEPHEW/NIECE** half great uncle	**FIRST COUSIN TWICE REMOVED** third cousin twice removed	**THIRD COUSIN TWICE REMOVED** fifth cousin once removed

MY RELATIONS' RELATIONSHIP TO ME IS IN CAPITALS – ie, 'THEY ARE MY XXXX'
my relationship to my relations is in lower-case – ie, 'I am their xxxx'

Collins
tracing your
family history

Anthony Adolph

 Collins

'who begot whom is a most amusing kind of hunting' Horace Walpole

For our friends' daughter Kim Van Trier, who completed her journey from conception to birth in marginally less time and with considerably less fuss than the writing of this book, and for Scott Crowley, whose quiet support and encouragement throughout have been unfaltering.

First published in 2004 by
Collins, an imprint of
HarperCollinsPublishers
77–85 Fulham Palace Road
London W6 8JB

This new edition published in 2008

The Collins website address is www.collins.co.uk
Collins is a registered trademark of HarperCollins Publishers Ltd

11	10	09	08
4	3	2	1

Text © 2008 Anthony Adolph

All rights reserved. No part of this publication may be reproduced, stored in a retrieval system, or transmitted, in any form or by any means, electronic, mechanical, photocopying, recording or otherwise, without the prior written permission of the publishers.

Editor: Emma Callery
Art Editor: Ruth Prentice
Design: Hannah Attwell/Bob Vickers
Picture Research: Suzanne Bosman

**A catalogue record for this book is available
from the British Library**

ISBN 13 978-0-00-782909-5

Printed and bound by Leo, China

CONTENTS

INTRODUCTION

Long before there were computer programmers and engineers, blacksmiths or even farmers, our ancestors told each other stories of who they were and where they came from. Over time, as other subjects became more important (or at least seemed to be), our ancestral tales began to take a back-burner, the older ones blurring into creation myths but the more recent ones remaining important to their tellers and listeners.

❛ The rise of written records heralded a gradual erosion of oral traditions. ❜

▽ My great-great-grandparents, Albert Joseph Adolph and his wife Emily Lydia, née Watson. When I started my research, they were as far back as my grandfather's memory stretched.

When memories started to be written down, one of the first things to be recorded were ancient genealogies, linking the living to their ancient roots. It is for that reason that we can trace the Queen's ancestry back through the Saxon royal family to their mythological ancestor, the god Woden. Yet for most, the rise of written records heralded a gradual erosion of oral traditions and, in medieval England, memories tended to grow shorter in proportion to the proliferating rolls of vellum and parchment recording our forbears' deeds, dues and misdemeanours. And then, just as it became apparent to our ancestors that they were losing touch with the past, it crossed people's minds that these self-same documents, compiled for no better reason than to record land transfer, court cases or tax liability, could help us retrace our past and discover the identities of our forgotten forbears.

This, the act of tracing family roots through both remembered stories and written records, is genealogy, the subject that has preoccupied most of my life, first as an amateur and later as a professional ever since, as a child, I encountered the pedigrees of elves and hobbits at the back of *The Lord of the Rings.* And it has been my good fortune that the past few decades have been ones of exceptional growth in genealogy as a pastime across the world, from a minority interest with snobby overtones in the 1960s to a mainstream activity, contributing significantly to the tourist industry and constituting one of the principal uses of the internet. In recent decades, it has broken through, too, into the media.

▽ The author presenting BBC1's 2007
Gene Detectives with Melanie Sykes.

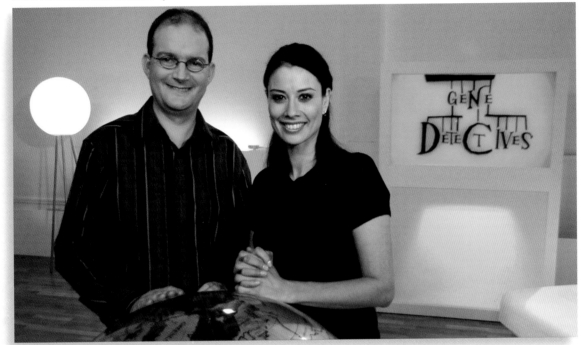

FAMILY HISTORY is enjoying an extraordinarily dynamic phase and much is changing. In the last few years, internet companies have realised the profits to be made by setting up pay-to-view websites, especially covering the two great building blocks of 19th-century family trees, General Registration and census records. The small amounts paid by users fund further indexing work, thus bringing yet more records within far easier reach of more people than ever before.

These sites have truly revolutionised searching. When I wrote the first edition of this book, I would only have sought people in the 1871 census (for example) if I had a precise address, or had no alternative choice. Now, I can search the entire 1871 census online in seconds. I would make one plea, though: if you are new to this, please don't take these new developments for granted, or grumble at the relatively very small amounts of money being charged. You are at a vast advantage over genealogists in previous generations. Equally, however, pre-internet genealogists did have to get to grips with and understand how these records worked in far more detail, and this tended to make them very good researchers. So, having saved a lot of time thanks to the internet, why not use some of it to read the relevant chapters of this book, so that you can form a more rounded picture of how the original records were created, and where the originals may be found? This edition is as up-to-date as it can be — yet improvements in accessibility occur almost monthly. These are exciting times indeed.

NEW EDITION

△ My mother's great-grandfather, Rev. Patrick Henry Kilduff – one of a treasure trove of old photographs I was given by a distant cousin whom I had traced in the course of my research.

❛*Millions of people are now actively investigating their origins, or at least thinking about doing so.*❜

The first year of this millennium saw two series appearing on national television, BBC 2's *Blood Ties* and my own series, *Extraordinary Ancestors*, on Channel 4. These were followed by further series with which I have been privileged to be involved, particularly Living TV's *Antiques Ghostshow* and Radio 4's *Meet the Descendants*, which have continued to tell stories of genealogical investigation and discovery.

Millions of people, including you, are now actively investigating their origins, or at least thinking about doing so. This complete guide is intended to cover all the topics you will need to know about to trace your family tree. You can start at the beginning, letting it guide you through the process of getting started and working back through the different types of records which should, given time and patience, enable you to trace your family tree back for hundreds of years. Or, if you are already a genealogist, you can use it as a reference book to identify and learn more about the vast array of different types of source that may be available for your research.

In some respects, this book follows the standards already set out by its predecessors, and I fully acknowledge my enormous debts to genealogical writers who blazed the trail before me, not least Sir Anthony Wagner, Mark Herber, Terrick FitzHugh, George Pelling, Don Steel, John Titford and Susan Lumas. In other respects, and within the parameters set by what is expected of genealogical reference books, I have tried to add to this my personal perspective, not least by drawing on my experiences in translating genealogy into radio and television.

A NEW BOOK FOR A CHANGING WORLD
In this book, I have tried to reflect the extraordinary changes that have recently injected new life into this most ancient of subjects.

DNA technology
DNA technology has escaped the confines of the laboratory and become readily available to anyone with even a modest research budget. Do not be deceived by the relative brevity of my chapter on the subject; its implications for genealogy are vast.

Multi-cultural roots
Although Britain has always been a multi-cultural nation, a barrage of prejudices and phobias meant that we have only recently started to uncover the full extent of our global roots. Only in the last two decades have the many white families with black or Asian ancestors been able

to start investigating such connections. Only recently have they been permitted by society and, in some cases, their own attitudes, to look on their connections with other continents with fascination rather than shame. Equally, thanks to the post-war mass immigration of black and Asian families, there are now a very great number of British families with roots exclusively from overseas. But by far the greatest trend, resulting from relationships between the different ethnic communities in Britain, is the rise of generations with roots both in indigenous white Britain and in other continents.

Other genealogical writers have not ignored this fact, but nor have they addressed the issue in any depth. I felt that, in writing a book for genealogists in modern Britain, it was appropriate to broaden its scope to acknowledge the vast number of readers whose ethnic English blood – if they have any at all – is only a small proportion of their total ancestral mix. I have not attempted to write a worldwide guide to tracing family trees but, while the focus of the book is on research in England, I have tried to show and remind readers how the same or similar sources can be located and used in the rest of the British Isles and in countries all around the world. Please note that, when I refer to records outside Britain, I do so by way of example: the absence of a reference to a type of record in a certain country does not mean that records are not there. The volume of material available for America requires a separate book and has therefore been omitted almost entirely.

△ Shilpa Mehta (on the right) with her father, Shailendra, and brother, Shayur, in Zambia before her family settled permanently in England (see page 248).

▽ The Genes Reunited website home page: www.genesreunited.co.uk

The internet

The internet has changed genealogy by making different types of records more easily searchable and by creating new resources that never existed before, such as the GenesReunited website. If you are serious about tracing your family tree, I recommend you either acquire a computer, find a good library or café providing internet access, or are very, very nice to someone who is already connected to the web. While you should never trust anything on the internet without checking it in original sources, the amount of time you can save using the resources available online is enormous.

On a daily basis, new indexes and resources appear, change, grow or, in some cases, disappear from the great information super-highway that is the worldwide web. Website addresses are so helpful and important that I have provided the ones that are most useful at the time of writing, and made them an integral part of the text. However, the rate of change inevitably means that, by the time you read this book, some things will have changed and proposed new legislation even threatens to restrict access to some of the records described here. In most cases, though, change will only have been for the better in terms of more records becoming more easily accessible via index and databases.

PROFESSIONAL HELP

I became a professional genealogist in 1992 after several years studying at the Institute of Heraldic and Genealogical Studies. During most of my career, first working for a well-known firm of genealogists and latterly with my own freelance business, I have spent more time establishing what sources are available to solve particular problems and commissioning record agents to search them, than actually being in archives myself.

This is a course of action I wholeheartedly recommend to all readers of this book. Many people say, 'But I want to do it all myself.' Fair enough – and use this book to acquire a detailed knowledge of the sources and their whereabouts. But there are many cases where paying a record searcher in a different county (or on the other side of the world) for a couple of hours' work can save a vast amount of time, travel and accommodation costs, especially if the source you identified turns out to have been the wrong one. Receiving positive results by post (or email) may not be quite as exciting as turning over a dusty page and finding an ancestor's name but, frankly, most records

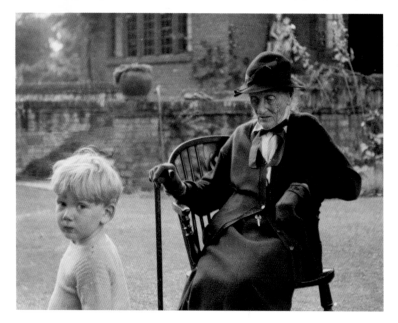

▽ Connections between the past and present. My great-great-aunt Louisa Havers (1832–1937) at Ingatestone Hall, Essex, in 1917, with her young cousin Philip Coverdale who, as an old man, took me under his wing and taught me how to trace family trees.

are now searchable only by microfiche in record offices anyway. The time you will have saved having the search done can then be spent visiting the place where you have discovered your ancestor once lived. If you really want to do it yourself, though, don't let me stop you. I merely offer a piece of personal advice.

GETTING TO KNOW YOUR ANCESTORS

Throughout this introduction, I have referred to genealogy. There's also a subject called family history. Essentially, genealogy is tracing who was who – the nuts and bolts of the family tree – while family history is more about finding out about the ancestors themselves, exploring their lives and working out how they came to do what they did and be who they were. That in itself then merges into the subject of biography. Once you have researched your family history in depth you will, in effect, have researched mini (or not so mini) biographies of your ancestors. Most, if not actually all, of the sources used by biographers are described in this book. Getting to know your ancestors can be a fascinating experience even if you do not (as people who have seen me in *Antiques Ghostshow* will know) want to roam into the world of psychics.

But, in investigating your family tree, please bear in mind there is a real distinction between your ancestors and the records in which they appear. I have known people to cherish birth certificates as if they were the spiritual embodiments of their forbears. They are not. Think of when you last looked at yours and what a nuisance it is when you generate records similar to those you use for tracing ancestry. Obtaining passports and driving licences is a chore: dealing with banks, lawyers, the Inland Revenue and social services is tiring and invariably annoying. Often, when you encounter an ancestor in a record, they, too, were probably vexed and annoyed through the making of it. Equally, useful though they are, many modern genealogy programs and charts require you to focus so much on dates of birth, marriage and death that you can easily forget that the people concerned actually had lives in the intervening years. The real ancestors stand back behind the dates and records they generated: bear that in mind and you won't go far wrong in learning to understand them.

△ Filming the story of *EastEnders'* convoluted family tree on location at Elstree, 2000.

▽ The author filming ITV's *Lost Royals* at the College of Arms with former BBC Royal Correspondent Jenny Bond and Norroy and Ulster King of Arms.

PART ONE

Tracing family trees is mainly about seeking records, but before you do that, there's a great deal you may be able to learn from your own family – close as well as distant relatives. And whatever you find out, don't forget to write it down. Start properly and avoid tears later!

CHAPTER ONE
ASK THE FAMILY

With very few exceptions, nobody knows more about your immediate family than your immediate family. Yet the first steps in tracing a family tree are often ignored or skipped over in the headlong dash for illustrious roots and unclaimed fortunes.

Most people reading this will probably have made at least some sort of start at researching their family tree. This chapter gives structure to your first steps and, I hope, to all your research over years to come.

STARTING OFF

However old you are, the very best way to start research is by writing down your own essential details, which are:

➤ **Date and place of birth**
➤ **Your education, occupations and where you have lived**
➤ **Religious denomination**
➤ **Anything interesting about yourself, which future generations may be glad you took the trouble to record**
➤ **Date and place of marriage, and to whom (if applicable)**
➤ **Date and place of children's births and marriages (if applicable)**

Then repeat the same process for your siblings, parents, their siblings, your grandparents and so on, adding details of when and where people died, if applicable.

One of the key elements here is write it all down because all this work will be to little avail if you do not record your findings.

Besides information on the living, you will soon start to record information on the deceased, as recalled by their children, grandchildren and so on. This is oral history – things known from memory rather than written records.

THE ORAL TRADITION

Originally, all family trees were known orally. In Britain, there are a handful of pedigrees of the ancient rulers of the Anglo-Saxons, Vikings, Britons, Gaels and Picts, which stretch far back into the past, and which are known now because they were later written down. They contain some palpable mistakes and grey areas, but they are greatly valued because they are pretty much all we have left. Sadly, cultures such as Britain that adopted widespread use of written records tend very quickly

△ Family papers: a letter to my great-great-grandmother from her husband's cousin, Mrs Dorthea Boulger (1908), concerning their family history.

JUST BECAUSE very few written records were made in pre-colonial Africa does not mean that family trees cannot be traced. Benhilda Chisveto of Edinburgh knew her father was Thomas Majuru, born in 1953, and that his mother was Edith, but that was all. She then made enquiries about her family from older relatives still living in her native Zimbabwe, and was told the following family tree, dictated orally and perhaps never recorded on paper before.

Thomas Majuru was son of Mubaiwa, son of Majuru (hence the modern surname), who lived near Harare, and who was apparently the only survivor of his area when British forces invaded in 1897. He buried the dead and then sought refuge in Murehwa, where the family now live. He was son of Mukombingo. Before Mukombingo, the line runs back, son to father, thus: Kakonzo; Mudavanhu; Mbari; Taizivei; Barahanga; Jengera; Zimunwe; Katowa; Mhangare; Maneru; Dambaneshure; Chihoka; Chiumbe; Musiwaro; Mukwashahuue; Makutiodora; Diriro; Gweru; Makaya; Chamutso; Guru; Waziva; Misi; Chitedza otherwise called Chibwe Chitedza; Nyavira also called Nyabira; Mukunti-Muora.

A FEW FACTS

The only dates in the oral history were for Mbari, who was chief of his tribe from 1795 to 1797, and Katowa, who was chief 1450–97. The earliest ancestor, Mukunti-Muora, supposedly lived 4000 years ago. One thousand would be more realistic, and to get back from 1795 to 1450 in five generations is stretching it. There may, then, be some omissions of generations, or misremembered facts, but that makes this no different to the earliest oral pedigrees of the British Isles, which stretch back to Arthur, Brutus of Troy and the god Woden. This does not detract from their immense value because they undoubtedly do record the names of ancestors who really lived, and who are not recorded in any other fashion. Lose the oral history and these ancient memories will vanish irrevocably.

to lose the oral history that has been accumulated over the centuries. For much of the Third World, and the native cultures of the Americas and Australasia, this invasion of literacy has happened much more recently, and oral traditions are still strong. With the spread of literacy, though, oral history is under threat and will probably disappear altogether very soon; hence the need to write it down and make it available on websites such as Genes Reunited.

Such traditions should be treated with the greatest respect, but it is unrealistic to imagine that they can be strictly accurate. When using oral history as the basis for original, record-based research, you mustn't be surprised if you find names, dates or places are given slightly (or sometimes wildly) inaccurately. I sometimes get my own age wrong by a year (I certainly can't remember my telephone number all the on the 20th February by the Revd. J.Y. Brampton, Godfather Matthew Mason, Godmother, Julia Mason.

Michael John Mason born 26th March 1823 baptised by Revd. J.Y. Brampton 31st March 1823. Godfather John Morgan Godmother Rebecca Jackson, died 27th March 1824, buried in Vault at Moorfields Chapel. —

Rosina Frances Mason born 12th November 1824 baptized by the Revd. Thos Doyle. Godfather John Morgan, Godmother Frances Ralph.

Michael Thomas Mason born 12th March 1825. baptized by the Revd. Thos Doyle, Godfather, Thomas Ralph, Surgeon Godmother Anna Mason

Certificates of Baptisms may be obtained at St George's Catholic, Chapel, London Road, Southwark, Surrey

△ Family papers: lists of children's dates of birth and baptism were often kept by families, especially before the start of General Registration in 1837.

time), so you should be prepared for this and, if you do not find what you are looking for under Thompson in 1897, see if what you want isn't listed under Thomson in 1898 instead.

In fact, you can't trace a record-based family tree properly without developing a healthy scepticism for anything you are told, or indeed anything you read. There are deceptions and lies, of course. One family I helped, who were called Newman, discovered their ancestor had faked his own suicide and started a new life – as a 'new man', his original name having been something completely different.

More often, though, discrepancies and inaccuracies arise through simple mistakes or lapses of memory. 'Granny would never lie,' said one client of mine, 'so that birth certificate must be wrong.' No, Granny didn't lie, she just got her age slightly wrong. There's a real difference.

Indeed, recording oral history often relies on interviewing the elderly. Sometimes, it's the only time very old people have any proper attention paid to them, so be indulgent if they don't reel out exactly what you want in ten minutes flat. Letter, telephone and email can all help you gain valuable information from your relatives, but if you can visit them, so much the better. It may seem a bind, but it's often worth it and will become part of your store of memories to pass on to later generations. I once went all the way to Tours in France to visit Lydia Renault, a cousin of my mother's. I arrived at 11am and, whereas her English relations would have offered me tea and some ghastly old biscuits, Lydia suggested whisky and Coca-Cola, which we drank on her balcony, overlooking the Loire, while she regaled me with tales of her family at the start of the 20th century.

ELICITING THE PAST

That was an exception. If you get tea and stale biscuits, receive them with as great a semblance of delight as you can muster. If you are approaching someone you haven't met before, make every effort to write and telephone in advance and make it absolutely clear you are after their invaluable knowledge, rather than their (usually less valuable) purse. Write down (or tape record) everything they say, as the seemingly irrelevant may later turn out to be the main clue that cracks the case. If they have difficulty remembering facts, ask them to talk you through any old photographs they may have – that often stimulates the synapses – and sometimes you may get more from them if you allow them to contradict you.

> ❛Write down everything your interviewee says, as the seemingly irrelevant may later turn out to be the main clue that cracks the case.❜

FOR EXAMPLE:

'What was your grandfather's mother called?'

'Oh, I don't know.'

'I think it was Doris.'

'No, no, Doris was his sister. His mother was Milly!'

Another tip: if they can't remember a date of, say, when someone died, try to get them to narrow down the period in which it could have happened.

'When did your great-grandmother die?'

'I don't know.'

'Well, do you remember her?'

'Oh yes, she was at my wedding.'

'So she was alive in 1935. And was she at your first child's christening in 1937?'

'Oh no, she died before then.'

▽ My grandfather's air raid warden card. Note that he had been appointed before the war, in 1938.

Be sensitive, too, to changing social attitudes. Fascinating though it may be to you, the very elderly may not want to talk about their parents' bigamous marriage, so if you want any information from them you must tread very carefully. One man's black sheep, after all, is another's hero.

THE POWER OF PAPER

Don't forget, though, that younger relations of yours may have been told things by much older relations who are now dead. Equally – and here we leave the realms of oral history and move on a step – they, like the elderly, may have family papers and heirlooms. These come in so many forms: letters, school reports, memorial cards, passports, vaccination and ration cards, and so on, all crowned by the queen of all family papers, the family bible.

Some bibles can be centuries old, faithfully recording the births, marriages and deaths of each member of the family. The tip to finding family bibles is to trace down the female-to-female line of the family, as they are often passed from mother to daughter. Lost or unwanted ones (how can anybody not want a family bible?) often end up at car boot sales and genealogical magazines have been known to publish letters from well wishers who have found such a bible, describing its contents and volunteering to return it to the right family.

Whether it's a family bible or a 70-year-old funeral bill, write down all the salient details (or, better still, photocopy everything) because such papers may contain clues that will only become useful to you long afterwards. Ignore such advice at your peril and, if you have to go back all the way to Wigan to have another look at your cousin's grandmother's address book you didn't bother with ten years ago, don't blame me.

Actually, the real prize transcends even that, because sometimes you will find that an ancestor will already have tried to trace the family tree. One of the things that really encouraged me to pursue my own was

△ Pages from the Fairfax family bible, which even includes an extra newspaper cutting.

▽ Family reunions: a family photograph showing the Adolph, Mitchiner and Gale families celebrating the 80th birthday of my grandfather Joseph Adolph in 1990.

△ www.genesreunited.co.uk

AN OUTLINE OF THE MAIN SOURCES

PRELIMINARY RESEARCH

☑ **Make notes on what you know**

☑ **Constantly update your notes**

☑ **Ask immediate family**

☑ **Network with remoter family**

☑ **Register with www.genesreunited.co.uk (see page 31) and other 'contact' websites**

☑ **Update your entries as you learn more**

BASIC RESEARCH

☑ **General Registration (from 1837) (see page 44)**

☑ **Censuses (1841–1901) (see page 66)**

☑ **Wills and administrations from 1858 (see page 124)**

MORE IN-DEPTH RESEARCH

☑ **Unindexed censuses, using directories (see page 82)**

☑ **Parish registers (from 1538) (see page 96)**

☑ **Bishops' transcripts (from 1598) (see page 114)**

☑ **Manorial records (see page 118)**

☑ **Wills and letters of administration (before 1858) (see page 124)**

☑ **Gravestones (mainly from 17th century) (see page 138)**

☑ **Newpapers for obituaries, etc. (Mainly from 18th century) (see page 144)**

☑ **Electoral registers (see page 164), etc. to find addresses**

☑ **Parish chest and poor law material (mainly from 17th century) (see page 166)**

☑ **Occupation records (especially army and navy, mainly from 18th century) (see pages 176 and 190)**

☑ **Legal records (see page 222)**

☑ **Education records (see page 236)**

☑ **Printed pedigrees, heraldic records, etc. (see pages 290 and 298)**

AND, IF ALL GOES EXCEPTIONALLY WELL ...

☑ **Medieval tax lists and land records (from 1086) (see page 212)**

☑ **Early university and school records from Middle Ages (see page 236)**

☑ **Ancient oral pedigrees now in print**

being given a Harrods' carrier bag full of 'the family papers', which turned out to be my great-great grandmother's notes, showing her attempts to trace her family tree between 1880 and 1920. Sadly there was no sign of her finished family trees – if there ever were any – and nor have they ever turned up. However, the bag did include replies to letters she had written to her second and third cousins, thus filling out my own family tree before I had ever set foot outside my front door.

CHARTING CONVENTIONS

= Indicates a marriage, accompanied by 'm.' and the date and place

—— Solid lines indicate definite connections

… Dotted lines indicate probable but unproven ones

∿ Wiggly lines are for illegitimacy and 'x' for a union out of wedlock – important on old pedigrees but less relevant today

– – Loops are used if two unconnected lines need to cross over

⊠ Wives usually go on the right of husbands, though only if that doesn't interfere with the overall layout of the chart

⊠ Conventionally, surnames are put after men's but not women's names, but again this is becoming a bit old fashioned

COMMONLY USED ABBREVIATIONS

b. born	d.v.p. or o.v.p. died before father	m.i.w. 'mentioned in the will of'
bpt or c. baptised or christened (same thing)	ed. educated	followed by f. for father, gf. for grandfather and so on
bach. bachelor	fl. lived ('floreat')	MI monumental inscription
bur. or sep. buried	inft infant	spin. spinster
coh. coheir(ess)	k.i.a. killed in action	temp. in the time of
d. or ob./obit. died	lic. marriage licence	unm. unmarried
d.s.p. or o.s.p. died without children	m. or = married	wid. widow or widower (as appropriate)
	m. diss. by div. marriage dissolved by divorce	w.wr./pr. will written/proved

Possible Father BLOGGS
of Pedigreesville
=
Possible Mother

Mystery BLOGGS
wit. to m. of E.C.A.
BLOGGS

Earliest Certain Ancestor BLOGGS
Yeoman of Pedigreesville
(?bpt 1 April 1546, Pedigreesville)
wr will 2 August 1600
will pr. at Treetown 3 September 1603
=
Ancestress MATERNAL
m. (banns) 4 March 1567/8
Treetown
wits John MATERNAL and
Mystery BLOGGS

Widow MISERY
m. 8 April 1634
Genesville
d.s.p. 4 October 1637
bur 6 October 1637
Genesville (M.I.)
=
(1 Forbear BLOGGS 2)
lawyer of Genesburg
bpt 5 February 1570/1
Pedigreesville
m.i.w.f. 1600
to be father's exor.
will wr 1 November 1635
d. 6 January 1635/6
bur 7 January 1635/6
Genesburg (M.I.)
will. pr (Treetown)
8 January 1635/6
=
Goodwife MOTHER
m (lic.) 7 September
1599
Genesburg
bur. 8 November 1606
Genesburg
m.i.w.f-in-law 1600

Blacksheep BLOGGS
Sailor
bpt 25 October 1574
Pedigreesville
m.i.w.f. 1600 'to have
a shilling'
d.v.p. unm.
bur 2 March 1602
Elsewheresville
X
Lucy LOOSE
servant of
Elsewheresville

Sloth GLUTTON
Earl of Greed
bur. 10 May 1690
Richville
=
Heiress BLOGGS
bpt 2 November 1601
Genesville
m.i.w.f. 1635/6
m. 28 June 1625
Debston
bur. 9 May 1689
Richville

Notsolucky BLOGGS
bpt 3 May 1603
Genesville
ob. inft
bur 7 July 1604
Genesville
M.I.

**Lovechild Blacksheep
LOOSE alias BLOGGS**
bpt 1 March 1601
Elsewheresville
m.i.w. Forbear BLOGGS
1635/6

Equally, there are no rules about what you can or can't include on a family tree. Put in as much or as little as you want and include as many families as you want, though beware of cluttering. I would recommend a minimum of full names, dates of birth or baptism, marriage and death or burial, where those events took place, and occupations. If your chart lacks any of these, it will be of little use to other researchers and, more importantly, it will be boring. If you know someone was crushed to death by a bear or invented the casserole dish, for goodness sake put it on the chart!

There are some sensible conventions and abbreviations, which you'll need to know both for compiling your own charts and understanding other peoples'. These are outlined opposite.

EXPANDING ON THE BASICS

When it comes to writing up the family history, you can, again, decide what to say and how to say it, and you can get ideas from the examples in this book and the many published family histories and articles in family history journals and magazines.

It's a good idea to try to relate the events in the family to the world around them:

➢ **Who was on the throne**
➢ **What wars and plagues would have concerned or affected them**
➢ **What the places where they lived were like at the time**
➢ **What their occupations entailed.**

This is a valuable exercise, which might actually help you find out more about them, or highlight inaccuracies or even mistakes in the family tree. It is also a good reminder that these were real, breathing people who existed in the world, not as pale shadows on old, dusty records. Indeed, if you think your ancestors only existed within the confines of parish register entries and, now, the forms generated by genealogical computer programs, it's unlikely you will gain very much from family history, or that other people will enjoy and benefit from your hard work. The more you can think of and convey the idea of your ancestors as real human beings, the more fun – and success – you're likely to have.

△ Marriage bond for John Nursey, surgeon of Coddenham, Suffolk.

KNOW all Men by these Presents, That We William *Revil of Coddenham in ye County of Suffolk, Surgeon, & John Nursey of ye same place, Surgeon* ———

are holden and firmly bound to the Worshipful FRANCIS FRANK, Batchelor of Laws. Commissary in and throughout the Arch-deaconry of Suffolk. lawfully appointed: in the Sum of Two Hundred Pounds of good and lawful Money of Great-Britain, to te paid to the said FRANCIS FRANK, or his certain Attorney, Successors or Assigns: To which Payment well and truly to be made, we bind ourselves, and each of us by himself for the whole, our and each of our Heirs Executors and Administrators, firmly by these Presents. Sealed with our Seals, Dated the *twelfth* —— in the Year of our Lord One Thou-

HERE IS THE SAME information about the Fairfax family, presented as a narrative pedigree, a prose account and a traditional family tree.

NARRATIVE PEDIGREE

John Fairfax, born about 1710, married Mary Hayward on 16 September 1735 at Framlingham, Suffolk. He was a draper and grocer of Coddenham and wrote his will in 1751, naming his executors as his wife Mary and brother-in-law John Hayward. It was proved 2 June 1758 (Suffolk Record Office IC/AA1/184/49). His children (details of which are recorded in the family bible) included:

1 Frances, born 24 May 1736, baptised 25 May and died 31 May, Stowmarket.

2 Mary, born 9 June 1738, baptised 26 June at Stowmarket.

3 John Fairfax, born 30 June 1739, died 15 weeks old, buried at Stowmarket.

4 John Fairfax, born 30 August 1741. Left a watch by his father. Married Penelope Wright at St James's, Bury St Edmund's, on 5 May 1770. Elected freeman of Bury St Edmunds, 1802. Death recorded in *Gentleman's Magazine* as being in a fit on 12 February 1805 while visiting 'a friend [sic], Mr P. Nursey, at Little Bealings'. He had two children:

> 1 Penelope, born on 17 April and baptised on 31 May 1771 at St James's, buried on 30 June 1787 at Bury St Edmunds.
>
> 2 Catherine, born on 6 November 1772 and baptised on 3 December 1790 at Bury St Edmunds by Rev. Mr Sharp, as is recorded in the family bible.

5 Catherine Fairfax, born 7 September 1742 and baptised by Mr Meadows. Inherited share of a messuage in Kettleburgh from cousin Katherine Fairfax in 1747/50. Married John Nursey by licence on 4 April 1764 at Coddenham, before witnesses John and Mary Fairfax; he was described as a surgeon of Coddenham and she as daughter of John Fairfax of Coddenham, a draper. Died at Wickham Market on 13 April 1827, aged 85. No will has been found in Suffolk. They had children, including the landscape artist Perry Nursey (baptised on 25 June 1771 at Stonham Aspall).

△ Catherine Nursey, née Fairfax, mother of the Suffolk landscape painter Perry Nursey. Picture owned by her descendant Mrs Nancy Bedwell

PRESENTING YOUR RESULTS

PROSE ACCOUNT

THE LIFE OF JOHN FAIRFAX

JOHN FAIRFAX was born in 1710, four years before the death of Queen Anne ushered in the reign of George I and the start of the Hanoverian period. Growing up in rural Suffolk, he was variously described as a grocer and draper in the village of Coddenham, indicating either an enterprising mind or (less likely in view of the relative prosperity of his children) an inability to find the right niche in life. He married Mary Hayward on 16 September 1735 at Framlingham, a market town some ten miles from Coddenham, and, indeed, going to market there may have been how he met her. He wrote his will in 1751, making her and her brother John his executors, and it was proved, indicating he had died by then, in 1758, two years before the death of King George II.

John's children included Frances, Mary, two Johns and Catherine, of whom Frances and the first John died young. To his surviving son JOHN FAIRFAX he left his watch 'that was my cousin Smith's' and £63 to apprentice him 'to some proper business at a fit age'. This younger John married Penelope Wright at St James's, Bury St Edmund's, on 5 May 1770 and obviously benefited from his apprenticeship, as he became a freeman of Bury St Edmunds in 1802. He died in a fit on 12 February 1805 while visiting his nephew, the artist Perry Nursey, at Little Bealings. He had two children, Penelope and Catherine.

John senior's daughter Catherine, born 7 September 1742, received a bequest of land from her father's cousin Catherine Fairfax in 1750 and, perhaps as a result of this, made a good marriage to the local surgeon, John Nursey of Coddenham. They married there by licence on 4 April 1764. She was mother of the artist Perry Nursey (baptised on 25 June 1771 at Stonham Aspall), at whose house her brother died in 1805.

FAMILY TREE

CHAPTER FOUR
BEFORE YOU BEGIN

Before starting with the main sources for tracing ancestry it is important to understand a little about how and where records are kept, starting with the main archives, and the different ways of gaining access to them. Reading this chapter now may save you a great deal of head-scratching and wasted time later on.

USING THE NATIONAL ARCHIVES

GETTING HOLD of material from TNA couldn't be easier:

⊠ You can establish what documents you want to see on **www.nationalarchives.gov.uk/catalogue** and pre-order them so they will be ready when you arrive.

⊠ You can also have photocopies made on the spot or take a digital camera with you and photograph the records you want while you are there.

⊠ Finally, you can also order documents once you are there for delivery to your home address.

ARCHIVES

There are many organisations that hold archives of records. Be aware that most exist to preserve records, and not primarily to let you finger them. Most of the help you will receive from such organisations will be provided out of kindness, not obligation. Courtesy and thanks never go amiss, whoever you are dealing with.

If you are thinking of visiting an archive to undertake some research, always make sure it will be open, find out if you need to book and also do your best to establish that the records you want to see are actually there. Remember that sometimes records are temporarily removed from their permanent homes for restoration, rebinding and other reasons. Most are free but require a reader's ticket, so if you do not have one, take some identification, preferably a passport.

THE NATIONAL ARCHIVES (TNA)

This was formed in 2003 through a merger of the **Public Record Office** and the **Historic Manuscripts Commission (HMC)**. TNA is the principal repository for British national records, which are referred to constantly in this book. Among those records that are used the most by family historians are censuses and Prerogative Court of Canterbury (see page 120) wills and records relating to soldiers and sailors.

The main task of the HMC, also called the Royal Commission on Historical Manuscripts, is to catalogue collections of records outside TNA. Its published reports cover a vast array of manuscripts in public and private hands, from the House of Lords to Longleat, and including businesses, solicitors' papers, county record offices and so on.

The indexes to the printed reports can make surprising and rewarding 'lucky dip' searches, and the HMC's on-going work is indexed centrally in the **National Register of Archives**, accessible via TNA's website. This includes a search facility for those personal names and topics that have been indexed within the records and leads direct to contact details for the relevant archive.

TNA's website provides a great deal of information about how to get to and use the archives and its records, and also enables you to download any of its many very informative information leaflets which will tell you more about many of the most commonly used records. Look at the website before you go to TNA, not least because you can pre-order the documents and have them ready and waiting for you when you walk in. The website also contains some very useful databases, particularly the main catalogue, **www.nationalarchives.gov.uk/ catalogue**, which you can use as a short cut for specific searches or as a general trawl for references to the names that interest you. You are highly likely to find them cropping up in categories of documents you never expected, or even categories of documents you had never heard of before. Stella Colwell's *The National Archives*, (TNA, 2006) is geared specifically to genealogists.

TNA also maintains **Access to Archives**, an online catalogue to material held in many British archives, including the county record offices. Once you have found material that interests you it also provides links to the **Archon Directory www.nationalarchives.gov.uk/archon**, to give you full contact details for the archive concerned.

In the old days censuses were kept at Portugal Street, and General Registration records of birth, marriage and death were kept at Somerset House, then St Catherine's House, and then the Family Records Centre. Now all are on file/fiche at TNA, and are increasingly available online.

OTHER ARCHIVES

Wales: Wales was officially subsumed by England in 1536, but it has its own archives in the **National Library of Wales**.

Scotland: Scotland's **National Archives of Scotland (NAS)**, are now part of the new **ScotlandsPeople Centre**. The catalogues of this and most other Scottish archives are available at **www.scan.org.uk**.

Ireland: Both Eire and Northern Ireland have central archives, the **National Archives of Ireland** and the **Public Record Office of Northern Ireland (PRONI)**. (Contact details for these addresses in Ireland are given in the Quick Reference panel overleaf.)

COUNTY RECORD OFFICES

Unlike TNA, county record offices are a relatively new innovation, starting from the archiving work of George Herbert Fowler in 1913.

QUICK REFERENCE

HISTORIC MANUSCRIPTS COMMISSION (HMC)
Ruskin Avenue
Kew, Richmond
Surrey TW9 4DU
☎ 020 8876 3444
www.archon.nationalarchives.gov.uk/ hmc_pubs.htm

NATIONAL ARCHIVES (TNA)
Ruskin Avenue
Kew, Richmond
Surrey TW9 4DU
☎ 020 8876 3444
www.nationalarchives.gov.uk

NATIONAL REGISTER OF ARCHIVES
www.nationalarchives.gov.uk/nra

ACCESS TO ARCHIVES
www.A2A.org.uk

ARCHON DIRECTORY
www.nationalarchives.gov.uk/archon

GENERAL REGISTER OFFICE (GRO)
Smedley Hydro
Trafalgar Road
Southport
Merseyside PR8 2HH
☎ 0151 471 4200
www.statistics.gov.uk/registration

NATIONAL LIBRARY OF WALES
(LLYFRGELL GENEDLAETHOL CYMRU)
Panglais
Aberystwyth SY23 3BU
☎ 01970 632800
www.llgc.org.uk

NATIONAL ARCHIVES OF SCOTLAND (NAS)
HM General Register House
2 Princes Street
Edinburgh EH1 3YY
☎ 0131 535 1334
www.nas.gov.uk

QUICK REFERENCE

NATIONAL ARCHIVES OF IRELAND
Bishop Street
Dublin 8
Eire
☎ 00 353 1 407 2300
www.nationalarchives.ie

**PUBLIC RECORD OFFICE OF
NORTHERN IRELAND (PRONI)**
66 Balmoral Avenue
Belfast BT9 6NY
Northern Ireland
☎ 028 9025 5905
http://proni.nics.gov.uk

ACCESS TO ARCHIVES
www.A2A.org.uk

BRITISH LIBRARY
96 Euston Road
London NW1 2DB
☎ 020 7412 7676
http://blpc.bl.uk

MORMON FAMILY HISTORY CENTRES
Hyde Park Family History Centre
64/68 Exhibition Road
South Kensington
London SW7 2PA
☎ 020 7589 8561
(Main centre – see website for
other locations)
www.familysearch.org

❛*As with the rest of this book, I use English and Welsh records as the main example, but the general principle of how to use the records can be applied to many other countries, from Jamaica to India.*❜

The county record offices grew out of the old diocesan record offices and their main achievement was bringing together many of each county's public records under one roof, and it was this that helped fuel the first boom in family history research in the 1970s. Most county record office catalogues are now accessible through **Access to Archives**. Offline, an excellent guide to the county record offices is J. Gibson and P. Peskett's *Record Offices: How to find them* (FFHS, 1996).

OTHER ARCHIVES

The best guide to specialist archives is J. Foster and J. Sheppard's *British Archives: A Guide to Archive Resources in the United Kingdom* (Palgrave, 2002). One page alone gives details of the Carpenters' Company archives in the City of London, which date from the Middle Ages; the Carlton Club, with registers of members from 1832; and Camden Local Studies Centre, whose holdings include records of the Manor of Hampstead 1742–1843 and the papers of George Bernard Shaw.

MUSEUMS AND LIBRARIES

Both are excellent for background information on what places were like when your ancestors lived there, but they can also hold extraordinary collections that may include information on your families. Foremost is the **British Library**, whose website includes its catalogue to manuscripts and printed books, enabling you to search for what you want and order it before you go.

Local museums and libraries, especially local studies libraries, hold photographic collections for the locality, and the librarians themselves are often very knowledgeable about the area, electoral registers, local maps, and so on.

MORMON WEBSITE AND FAMILY HISTORY CENTRES

With its world HQ at the Family History Library, the Mormon church, officially the Church of Jesus Christ of Latter-day Saints, maintains about 100 **Mormon Family History Centres** around the UK, freely open to the public and containing many useful genealogical resources. The church's interest in family history is religious – its aim ultimately is to identify as many people as possible, living and dead, in the context of their family relationships. To this end, they have amassed a vast collection of microfilms of original records from all over the world, including many British archives and many records described in this book. Any of these can be ordered to your local centre. The timorous should be reassured that visitors are entirely safe from any attempt to convert them – far from it: Mormons have made an immense contribution to this field, accessed for free. The Mormons' free website, **www.familysearch.org**, is described in detail on pages 110–13. Another Salt Lake-based organisation, **MyFamily.Com**, which owns **Ancestry.Com**, has a pay-to-view website (**www.ancestry.com**), which contains a great and growing number of records, especially drawn from censuses.

OTHER WEBSITES

SCOTLANDSPEOPLE

Scotland's Old Parochial Registers, censuses, testaments (wills) and much of its General Registration is online at a pay-to-view site, **www.scotlandspeople.gov.uk**.

GENES REUNITED

There are a number of websites that aim to link up family trees, but the most exciting is **www.genesreunited.co.uk**. The site allows you to enter details of your family (or upload a family tree already typed in 'Gedcom' format), building an online family tree, which is easily altered and amended.

A number of search tools then enable you to find out if surnames on your tree appear on other trees on the site. In return for a £9.50 a year membership fee, you can email the contributors of other possibly relevant names and work out if you do indeed have ancestors in common, and if so create a link between the two trees. Those with common surnames will be relieved to know that the searches can be honed, by personal name, year of birth and by place of birth.

The site was launched in November 2002 and at the time of writing has 8 million members worldwide and over 111 million names. It is therefore becoming a formidable research tool, which can already be used to localise where people with particular surnames were born and communicate with people actively researching them. The site is one of several that provides access to many important sets of data, particularly the quarterly indexes to General Registration indexes and 1841–1901 census returns.

OTHER GENERAL WEBSITES

The internet, as everyone knows, contains a great many websites of use to genealogists. There is no official central portal for these, but there is an unofficial one, **www.cyndislist.com**, which has assumed this

△ Access to Archives website home page: www.A2A.org.uk

△ Scotland's very own research website home page: www.scotlandspeople.gov.uk.

> ❝*The internet, as everyone knows, contains a very great many websites of use to genealogists.*❞

role and contains categorised links to pretty much everything that's out there.

A British version of this is **www.genuki.org.uk**, containing links to many useful websites for the whole British Isles. Genuki also hosts a plethora of newsgroups and mailing lists, searchable under areas and topics, that you can join. An overview of other important websites is given on pages 78–81.

SOCIETIES

Many countries have societies formed by genealogists to help each other. The main one in Britain is the **Society of Genealogists (SoG)**. Its library is the finest of its kind, including the Great Card Index (3.5 million slips from a vast array of sources) and a huge collection of pedigrees submitted by members, varying enormously in quality but including many of very high standard. The contents of its library together with many searchable databases are on its website. It publishes the *Genealogists' Magazine*.

A curiosity in English genealogy is the **Institute of Heraldic and Genealogical Studies (IHGS)**. It organises a graded series of courses and qualifications in genealogy. It also has a library that is open to the public for a fee and produces a journal, *Family History*.

Most counties (sometimes even parts of counties) and some specialist areas such as Catholic and Anglo-German have family history societies. They come under the umbrella of the **Federation of Family History Societies (FFHS)**. Membership includes many Commonwealth and United States societies too, and it publishes *Family History News and Digest* biannually, summarising the contents of the different journals. Family History Societies have membership worldwide and their journals include articles on relevant sources and case studies, lists of members' interests and ancestral names. Many also have their own libraries and organise projects to index records such as gravestones and censuses. It is often a good idea to join your nearest Family History Society even if you do not have any local ancestors, because many of the talks will be of more general application, and many organise reciprocal research via other societies.

MAGAZINES

There are a number of family history magazines on the market, publishing 'how to' articles, items on general and specialist sources and specific family stories, and usually including book, software and

ONE-NAME SOCIETIES

THESE SOCIETIES concern those interested in specific names, such as the Fairfax Society. Many are members of the **FFHS** and **Guild of One-Name Studies ('GOONS'!)**. Many produce journals or newsletters, and besides collecting and tracing individual family trees for a name, many systematically extract all references to the name from categories of records such as General Registration indexes, so are well worth consulting.

Large libraries, such as the **SoG**, have collections of journals from societies outside Britain. The FFHS and **www.cyndislist. com** can put you in touch with relevant societies abroad.

website reviews, question-and-answer pages, letters, news and contact details for both professional and private researchers. The main ones in Britain are *Family History Monthly*, *Family Tree Magazine*, *Practical Family History*, *Who Do You Think You Are?*, *Your Family Tree* and *Ancestors*, the latter produced by TNA. In a similar category is the *Genealogical Services Directory*, which provides up-to-date contact details for all British Isles record offices, family history societies, organisations and professional record searchers and genealogists.

BIBLIOGRAPHIES

Much research has already been published and it is always worth checking to see if your family tree is included. The main British genealogical bibliography is G. W. Marshall's *The Genealogist's Guide* (GPC, reprinted 1973); supplemented by J. B. Whitmore's *A Genealogical Guide: An Index to British Pedigrees in Continuation of Marshall's Genealogist's Guide* (J. B. Whitmore, 1953). Besides the well-known Burke's publications, heralds' visitations (see page 302) and much else, these books encompass the rich veins of material ranging from transcripts of pedigrees in Close Rolls (see page 150) to copies of memorial inscriptions in overseas cemeteries, published in Victorian and early 20th-century antiquarian journals.

QUICK REFERENCE

SOCIETY OF GENEALOGISTS (SoG)
14 Charterhouse Buildings
Goswell Road
London EC1M 7BA
☎ 020 7251 8799
www.sog.org.uk

INSTITUTE OF HERALDIC AND GENEALOGICAL STUDIES (IHGS)
79–82 Northgate
Canterbury
Kent CT1 1BA
☎ 01227 768664
www.ihgs.ac.uk

FEDERATION OF FAMILY HISTORY SOCIETIES (FFHS)
PO Box 2425
Coventry CV5 6YX
☎ 024 7667 7798
www.ffhs.org.uk

GUILD OF ONE-NAME STUDIES (GOONS)
C/o Society of Genealogists
Box G
14 Charterhouse Buildings
Goswell Road
London EC1M 7BA
www.one-name.org

❛ *Bibliographies encompass the rich veins of material ranging from transcripts of pedigrees to copies of memorial inscriptions.* **❜**

Coming closer to the present, there is G. B. Barrow's *The Genealogists' Guide: An Index to Printed British Pedigrees and Family Histories 1950–75* (Research Publishing Co., 1977), followed by T. R. Thompson's *A Catalogue of British Family Histories* (Research Publishing Co and SoG, 1980). Incredibly useful too are Stuart Raymond's *County Bibliographies* (S. A. and M. J. Raymond). These books reference published material (including family history journals) in terms of family histories and local histories, newspapers, county histories and published records of all sorts, particularly providing an overview of the publications of the county and national record societies and publications.

For Scotland there are M. Stuart's *Scottish Family History* (GPC, 1978), supplemented by P. S. Ferguson's *Scottish Family Histories* (National Library of Scotland, 1986), and for Ireland, the bibliographies compiled by B. de Breffny in 1964 and E. MacLysaght in 1982.

Many privately published and rare manuscript family histories are catalogued in the SoG's online catalogue, SoGCAT, **www.sog.org. uk/sogcat/sogcat**. Many printed family histories are digitally available in the Family History Library catalogue section of **www.familysearch.org**.

BIOGRAPHICAL DICTIONARIES

Many countries have biographical dictionaries. Britain has led the way with L. Stephen and S. Lee's *Dictionary of National Biography* (Smith, Elder & Co., 1885), which was kept up to date by a series of supplements and completely revised and re-edited to create the *Oxford Dictionary of National Biography* (OUP, 2004). It is available in print and can be searched online on a subscription basis at **www.oup.com/oxforddnb**, though it should also be available at good libraries. You can search not just under the names of the subjects, but also under any other names (such as wives, sons-in-law, and so on) appearing in the articles and also by topic. So if you want to find any biographies mentioning something like ice cream, you can.

The DNB has been fully updated by a huge team of writers, including me, and the biographies include, where known, dates and places of birth, death, marriage and burial and any known details of parents, family origins, spouses, and offspring and is thus a formidable genealogical as well as biographical source.

Many people were important or well known in their time but are not considered so by posterity. There have been many biographical dictionaries past and present, not least *Who's Who* (OUP), which has been published annually since 1897, and its accompanying *Who Was*

△ From hip to history: Linda McCartney's tragically early death means she has joined Princess Diana in the *Oxford Dictionary of National Biography*.

Who (OUP), concerning the deceased, both of which are combined on a CD-Rom version. Here you will find the great and the good, from holders of public office to captains of industry, the top brass in the armed forces, the upper echelons of the clergy, and also writers, artists, editors and a host of others. Brief details are provided of dates of birth, marriage, death, parents and offspring. It is more useful for providing a date of birth so you can seek a birth certificate than in actually providing adequate genealogical details in its own right – but, of course, the biographical information it contains is marvellous.

Besides these, there are many further biographical dictionaries relating to specific groups in society, like the armed forces or religious groups, which are discussed in the appropriate chapters.

RECORD SOCIETY PUBLICATIONS

Many county record offices and archives have published indexed volumes transcribing some of their original records. The Lancashire and Cheshire Record Society, for example, has published many of its counties' wills, royalist composition papers, freemen records and much else. Trawling through these can throw up all sorts of treasures.

The easiest way of finding out what has been published is through E. L. C. Mullins' *Texts and Calendars: An Analytical Guide to Serial Publications, Vol. I* (RHS, 1958) and *Vol. II, 1957–1982* (RHS, 1983), D. and W. B. Stevenson's *Scottish Texts & Calendars: An Analytical Guide to Serial Publications* (Royal Historical Society, London) and *Scottish Royal Historical Society* (Edinburgh, 1987). These may save you very lengthy searches through original records.

SPECIALIST INDEXES

A catch-all to the many weird and wonderful indexes out there is J. Gibson and E. Hampson's *Specialist Indexes for Family Historians* (FFHS, 1998). This covers topics as diverse as Congregational and Baptist ministers at Dr William's Library, London (see page 260); multiple births worldwide; memorial cards (1846–1980); criminal registers in TNA class HO 27 (1805–92); members of the Ancient Order of Foresters; and much else.

RESEARCH DIRECTORIES

Besides magazines, journals and an increasingly huge number of websites, many private researchers are also listed in special directories and for a small fee you can be listed too, with your name, address and the names you are interested in, with specific periods and countries, if

THE SOCIETY OF GENEALOGISTS

MANY PUBLISHED and even manuscript family histories have been deposited at the **Society of Genealogists**. Their catalogue is therefore a sort of super-bibliography of work done previously. As of 2005, the catalogue can be searched online at **www.sog.org.uk/sogcat/index.html**. Many family histories can also be seen online at **www.lib.byu.edu/fhc**.

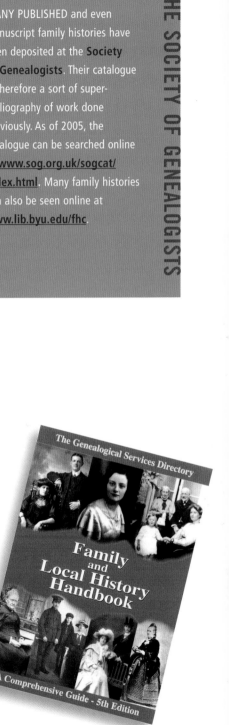

The Genealogical Services Directory

Family and Local History Handbook

A Comprehensive Guide - 5th Edition

THESE PAGES contains various miscellaneous but also very useful facts to help you in your research.

ENGLISH WORDS

⊠ You will come across lots of old-fashioned expressions and phrases, which is half the fun of exploring the past. There are some specialist dictionaries like R. Milward's *A Glossary of Household, Farming and Trade Terms from Probate Inventories* (Derbyshire Record Society, occasional paper 1). A stalwart source, however, remains the *Oxford English Dictionary*, the older the edition the better.

OLD HANDWRITING

Reading old handwriting is called palaeography. There are two sorts of problems:

1 In the past, some letters were written differently to the way they are now, so are extremely unfamiliar.

Examples of the different styles of letters are given to the right.

⊠ Be aware, too, that writers often abbreviated words using apostrophes, or sometimes apostrophes followed by the last letter or two – and sometimes the apostrophes were just missed out. 'William' was often written 'Will'm' or Wm, James as 'Jas', 'Majesty' as Maty' and so on.

⊠ Two excellent guides to old scripts are H. E. P. Grieve's *Examples of English Handwriting 1150–1750* (Essex Record Office, 1949) and L. Mumby's *Reading Tudor and Stuart Handwriting* (Phillimore for BALH, 1988).

2 Bad handwriting. However, like cracking codes, you can often work out what an incomprehensible letter is by studying its companions. For example, if you can read 'Ed-ard' then you can surmise the other letter is a 'w' – but look for the letter elsewhere to make sure you have it right: never go with an unsupported guess.

⊠ You can also see how letters are written in phrases or words where you know what the letters should be. Many wills, for example, start 'In the name of God Amen', so you can see how the scribe wrote his 'I's, 'n's, 't's and so on before tackling the will itself.

⊠ Don't be daunted by age. Sometimes a 16th-century document can be so beautifully written as to be easier to read than some modern scribble.

A	
B	
C	
D	
E	
F	
G	
H	
I, J	
K	
L	
M	
N	
O	
P	
Q	
R	
S	
T	
U, V	
W	
X	
Y	
Z	

MONEY

⊠ Besides being a 60s' drug, LSD was also the acronym for pre-decimal currency of pounds (livres), shillings and pence (dinarii). This was written in a number of different ways; for example, four pounds, two shillings and three pence ('thruppence') could be written £4-2-3 or £4 2s 3d or 4l 2s 3d or using Roman numerals – ivl iis iiid or even iiijl ijs iijd.

⊠ It is very difficult to find out how much money was worth relative to what it is today. The Bank of England has a ready reckoner and you can also study C. R. Chapman's *How Heavy, How Much and How Long? Weights, Money and Other Measures Used by our Ancestors* (Lochin Publishing, 1995) and L. Mumby's *How Much is that Worth?* (Phillimore for BALH, 1996).

DATES

⊠ Years and days haven't always been recorded the same way in every country. C. R. Cheney's *Handbook of Dates for Students of English History* (CUP, 2000) lists all old forms of dating, including by saints' days and popes' and kings' regnal years.

⊠ Years were often counted from the date of a sovereign's accession, so, for example, the first day of the first year of the reign of Elizabeth II started on 6 February 1952, the day she succeeded her father.

⊠ The book also provides a calendar for looking up which day of the week fell in what date in a given year. So, if someone wrote a letter dated 25 May 1657 saying their father died 'last Monday' you can find out that 25 May 1657 was a Friday, so 'last Monday' must have been 20 May.

OLD STYLE AND NEW STYLE

⊠ Britain and Europe used to use the old-style Julian calendar, whereby the year began on Lady Day, 25 March, not the new-style Gregorian calendar, which starts the year on 1 January. The Julian calendar started to die out among lay people in the Tudor period, and by the 18th century it is often hard to tell whether a date is being given in old style or new style.

⊠ Different countries changed to the Gregorian calendar at different times. Most of Western Europe changed in 1582, Scotland in 1600, England and Wales in 1752 and Russia and the Balkans in the 20th century. Therefore, a letter written in France on 1 February 1610 was likely to have been written just under a year before one dated 25 January 1610 in England.

⊠ It also means that dates appearing in old records need adjusting to make sense in modern terms. A baptism recorded in a PR on 24 January 1722 would, in modern terms, have taken place on 24 January 1723 because, under the old calendar, New Year's Day (25 March) had not yet arrived.

⊠ To avoid confusion, researchers tend to record the

△ A member of Pope Gregory's commission on the calendar pointing out the backslide of the Julian calendar.

date using 'double dating', recording the old-style year followed by the new-style year, i.e. 24 January 1722/3. Never, when you see this, strip out the 'old' date and just write 24 January 1723, because someone else may come along, realise that 23 January is before 25 March, not realise that you've already adjusted for double dating and write 24 January 1724 instead.

⊠ On the International Genealogical and Vital Records indexes (see page 110), dates are allegedly adjusted but without double dating. Non-conformist registers were using new-style dating well in advance of 1752.

⊠ Another difference between the Julian and Gregorian calendars was that the latter used leap years and the former didn't. By the time Pope Gregory introduced the new calendar in 1582 the lack of leap years had already caused the old-style date to lapse ten days behind the solar year, so he simply ordered ten days to be cut out off 1582, between 4 and 15 October. Because England persisted with the old calendar, it sunk increasingly behind Europe, and was 11 days behind by the 17th century. Therefore, events that share the same dates in different countries, such as the deaths of Shakespeare and Cervantes on 23 April 1616 in England and Spain respectively, actually took place 11 days apart. England and Wales cancelled the days between 2 and 14 September 1752 to catch up with Europe.

COMMON ABBREVIATIONS AND ACRONYMNS

Someone in AGRA or the SoG will know how to work back from GRO records at TNA and PPR and maybe stuff in class WO 97 at TNA (the old PRO) back via the IGI to CMBs taken from PRs or BTs on mf at CROs. I have tried to keep acronymns and abbreviations to a minimum in this book, but here are the main ones I have used together with some additional acronymns you will encounter in the outside world.

AGRA	Association of Genealogists and Researchers in Archives
BT	bishop's transcript
CMB	baptisms, marriages and burials
CRO	county record office
FFHS	Federation of Family History Societies
FHS	Family History Society
FRC	Family Records Centre
GRO	General Register Office (records are searchable at the FRC)
HMC	Historic Manuscripts Commission (now TNA)
IGI	International Genealogical Index
IHGS	Institute of Heraldic and Genealogical Studies
NAS	National Archives of Scotland
PCC/PCY	Prerogative Court of Canterbury/York
PPR	principal probate registry
PR	parish register
PRO	Public Records Office (now TNA)
PRONI	Public Record Office of Northern Ireland
SoG	Society of Genealogists
TNA	The National Archives (ex-PRO and HMC)

LATIN

⊠ Few things terrify genealogists as much as the use of Latin in old records. Sorry, but that's the way things were and we've got to live with it. If you really can't cope with basic Latin there are some very good, modestly priced translators, but often you should be able to manage, however poor or non-existent your school-book Latin. Remember, you were not alone and many of the compilers of the records had only the most tenuous grasp of the language, and therefore used it very basically and often with English rather than Latin word orders and plenty of stock phrases.

⊠ Especially in parish records, Latin is scarcely an impediment to understanding. That 'Petrus filius Ricardus et Gracia Smith' means 'Peter son of Richard and Grace Smith' will surprise few. However, just because ancestors' names were recorded in Latin does not mean they ever used them thus: when Ricardus Smith went to the pub in the evening he was plain Dick and should appear on the family tree as Richard.

⊠ Good guides to Latin include E. A. Gooder's *Latin for Local History: An Introduction* (Longmann, 1978) and R. A. Latham's *Revised Medieval Latin Word-list from British and Irish Sources* (OUP, 1965). There is also one online at **www.genuki.org.uk**.

SOME COMMONLY USED LATIN WORDS

annus	year
dies	day
est	is
filia	daughter
filius	son
matrimonium	marriage
mater	mother
mensis	month
mortuus	dead
natus	born
nuptium	married
obit	died
parochia	parish
pater	father
sepultat	buried
uxor	wife
vidua	widow

▷ The beginning of St Luke's Gospel, Lindisfarne Gospels, c.698.

PART TWO

This section covers the big records in genealogy – birth, marriage and death records, censuses, and so on. These form the backbone of your family tree and should provide you with a vastly increased knowledge of your family history.

do not search back before their ancestors would have been 18. 'Full age' means 21 or over, or under 21 but lying to avoid the need for parental consent. If ages are given, they may be inaccurate: boys who upped their age to join the army might say they were older than they really were, while the opposite was often true for older women wanting to marry nice young soldiers. If you suspect an ancestor was not being entirely truthful, it is worth checking a later census to see if they gave more accurate information later in life.

➢**Occupations.** Until the mid-20th century, even if she worked 18-hour days at a coal mine or scrubbing other peoples' doorsteps, the bride's occupation was very seldom deemed worthy of recording.

➢**Place of residence.** These are often misleading. Generally, the bride's address is likely to have been her normal address, but grooms often took up temporary residence in the parish, usually for a minimum of four weeks, in order to be allowed to

marry in the parish church. Sometimes the bride and groom will give the same address, but this is unlikely to mean they were openly sleeping together. More likely, he was her father's apprentice or lodger, or his family and hers were renting different sets of rooms in the same building.

➢**Names and occupations of fathers.** Mothers' names were not recorded. If fathers were retired, they might be rather grandly entitled 'gentleman'. Dead fathers were very often given a posthumous promotion by their proud children, such as boatswain to captain. It was normal, but sadly not universal, to state whether the fathers were alive or dead at the time of the marriage: generally, assume that the father was alive unless otherwise stated, but do not take this as absolute fact.

➢**Whether the marriage was by banns or licence.** These terms are explained more fully on page 99.

➢**Signatures or marks of bride, groom and a minimum of two witnesses.** As we have seen, marks did not always denote illiteracy. Remember that although signatures of the bride, groom and witnesses will

▽ **An Adolph family wedding in Hove, 1915.**

▷ *The Wedding Breakfast* by George Elgar Hicks (1824–1914).

appear on the original certificate, the certificates issued by the GRO are copies in the registrars' handwriting. You can apply to the relevant superintendent registrar if you want to see the originals. This is especially useful if you wish to identify someone by their signature. Witnesses were often siblings of the bride or groom; but do not make the mistake of thinking that because a favoured sibling did not witness a marriage they cannot have been present.

➤**Name of clergyman.** If the bride or groom were related to a clergyman, he might have come to their local church to perform the ceremony for them.

Marriage records are often missed because people assume their ancestors practised the rule of 'no sex before marriage'. After many years as a full-time genealogist I have serious doubts as to whether many people have ever heeded that maxim, as a great deal of couples registered the first child's birth less than nine months after their wedding day. Nor was it unknown for couples to say they were married when they registered their first child, but not walk up the aisle until a year or two later. If you cannot find the marriage before their first child was born, try looking afterwards. Equally, some people forget how large families could be in the past, and give up far too soon. It is not unusual, especially in the 19th century, to find a marriage taking place 15 or 20 years before an ancestor's birth. Sometimes, you will find out that your ancestor was older than their youngest aunts and uncles.

Genealogists were universally disconcerted by M.W. Foster's *A Comedy of Errors, or the Marriage Records of England and Wales 1837–99* (M.W. Foster, 1999), which revealed that up to 5% of marriages recorded by local registrars never made it to the registrar general's records. So if you cannot find the marriage you want in the GRO indexes and suspect you know where it took place, try the local registrar.

GENERAL REGISTRATION

⊡ If you know the exact name, date, place of the birth, marriage or death you want from 1900 onwards, you can place an order with the Registrar General at **www.gro.gov.uk** without needing to look up the index reference. Usually, though, you will need to search for the event you want.

⊡ Until 1992, the only way to seek a birth, marriage or death was to visit St Catherine's House (and earlier on, Somerset House) in London and search the heavy quarterly index volumes that weighed 25lb each. I used to spend a day a week doing it, and it was horribly hard, physical work, often with several eager searchers fighting over the same volume, or tripping over children and old ladies in the narrow aisles. In 1992, microfiche copies of the indexes were published, and these can still be found at **TNA** as well as in many archives, record offices and Mormon Family History Centres. They are far less physically demanding to search, but very hard on the eyes. For those without internet access, they now remain the only way of searching, because in October 2007 the index volumes themselves left their final public searchroom – the Family Records Centre at Myddleton Avenue, Islington, and were exiled to the Office of National Statistics' offices (Somerford Road, Christchurch, Dorset, BH23 3QA) where they are *not* available for searching. The FRC remained open for a few months, finally closing in spring 2008.

⊡ In the early 2000s, copies of the General Registration indexes started appearing online, and are now available at a variety of sites: regardless of the site, remember that they are all copies of the same original indexes. The General Register Office had grand plans (code-named 'DoVE') to make a full online index of all entries, showing additional information such as mothers' maiden names for all births, spouses' names for all marriages and ages for all deaths right back to 1837. At the time of writing plans have been completely shelved due to lack of funds, but check **www.gro.gov.uk** to see if this has now changed. Fingers crossed!

⊡ The best place to start looking is **www.freebmd.org.uk**. Volunteers are working on making a full index of births, marriages and deaths. It is not yet complete (the site includes graphs to show how complete each year is), and may never be. You will often find what is clearly the right entry, but never assume that you are looking at a *complete* index. If you are not absolutely sure you have found the right entry, you must now search in the complete indexes on microfiche or on other sites.

⊡ Next, the splendid site **www.familyrelatives.com** has full indexes for the births, marriages and deaths for the period 1866-1920, and 1983-2005. A search in these periods will return *all* the entries for the name you want, that are in the original indexes, the odd human indexing error aside. The site also has fully-indexed First and Second World War-forces deaths.

⊡ Many sites now offer access to the quarterly indexes from 1837 to the most recent available date. These include **www.genesreunited.co.uk**, **www.ancestry.co.uk**, **www.thegenealogist.co.uk** (which is actually the same as **www.ukbmdindex.co.uk**), **www.findmypast.com** (formerly **www.1837online.com**) – the latter has *all* the GRO indexes, including consular, army and 'at sea' indexes – as does **www.familyrelatives.com**. The latter has a great extra feature, whereby you can identify your connection to people named in index entries in such a way as other people who find the same entry can contact you.

⊡ Alternatively, for a fee, you can visit a superintendent registrar's office to search the indexes for that district, or request a search by post, but only do this if you are convinced that the entries you want will all be in that registration district: if not, use the national indexes.

⊡ Many one-name societies (especially members of the Guild of One Name Studies, see pages 32-3) and individuals interested in single surnames have produced exhaustive lists of General Registration references to that name. See *General Register Office one-name lists in the library of the SoG*, (SoG, 1997).

⊡ Certificates are often collected by local family history societies and archives, and others are published as 'Unwanted Certificates' in *Family Tree Magazine*, but the chances of these collections containing the very certificate you want are always going to be slim.

⊡ Several counties now have websites containing composite computerised indexes to local registrars' indexes. For example, **www.CheshireBMD.org.uk** contains a growing proportion of the Cheshire registrars' records for the period 1837 to 1950. Cambridge, Yorkshire, Lancashire, Middlesborough and Newcastle have begun similar indexing projects and other counties are likely to follow. An overview of these sites appears at **www.ukbmd.org.uk**. Certificates found through these sites can be purchased from the relevant registrar online for £7.00.

QUICK REFERENCE
See main sources in Useful Addresses, page 306

PURCHASING CERTIFICATES

You can search the indexes to births, marriages and deaths (see page 57), but to see the records themselves you must purchase certificates, costing £7 each. There are strong arguments against paying for this as they are, after all, public records and things may change, but not yet.

LIFETIMES: DEATH IN A FENCE

THE DEATH CERTIFICATE of Samuel Blain showed that he died on 19 April 1899, aged 88, and was a retired roadman. His place of death was unusual, 'The Forest, Delamere', and the cause of death was 'exhaustion the result of being suspended in a wire fence – accidental'. The certificate tells us an inquest was held by the Chester coroner on 21 April.

The local Cheshire newspaper, the *Chronicle* (examined at the British Library's newspaper library at Colindale), for 22 April gave the following report:

Mr J. C. Bate, coroner, held an inquiry to-day (Friday) at the Tiger's Head Inn into the circumstances attending the death of Samuel Blain, labourer, aged 86 [sic], who was found dead in Delamere Forest on Wednesday night. It appeared from the evidence of the widow that her husband had not been able to work for several years, but it had been his habit to go out for a walk into the Forest every morning and to come back with a few sticks for fire lighting. On the morning in question he left home but did not return.- Samuel Blain, son of the deceased said that when he came home from work on Wednesday evening his mother told him that his father had been out all day and had not returned. In consequence of this he went to search for him in the Forest, and found him fast in a wire fence, quite dead. He went for assistance and the deceased was taken home.- Having heard the evidence the jury returned a verdict in conformity therewith.

Besides the terribly sad story, note that a different age (86 rather than 88) is given for Samuel, and we learn he had a widow who survived him, and a son, also named Samuel.

△ The old General Registration
Index volumes at the now closed
Family Records Centre are gone for
good, replaced with online images.
They lived formerly at St Catherine's
House, and then at Somerset House.
Until microfiche copies were made
in the early 1990s, these volumes
were the only way to search for
births (red volumes), marriages
(green) and deaths (black) – and
they were jolly heavy!

Once you have found the entry you suspect is the right one, you can order a certificate using the Registration Online Ordering Service (ROLO) at **www.gro.gov.uk** or ring 0845 603 7788. The cost is £7 and there is usually a delay of four working days before you can collect the certificate or have it posted to you. If you want next-day results, you can pay £23 for a priority service.

A checking process is available for all GRO certificates. It is a system whereby you can provide additional information on the back of the application form about what you hope will appear on the certificate. If the information does not appear on the certificate, the certificate will not be issued and you will be refunded £4 of the £7 you paid for it. This means that if you have four possible references to an ancestor's birth, you do not have to buy all four (at a cost of £28) but you can have them checked: three negative results and one correct certificate will cost you only £19. However, the fact that you are unsure which reference is likely to be right emphasises how little you really know about the people concerned, so be very careful about what information you use as a checking point.

Occupations and addresses changed a lot, so avoid using these as checking points. The best ones to use are rough ages or parents' names but, again, be careful because the registrar general's staff have been known to be somewhat over-punctilious.

If you are seeking the marriage of someone with a father called John, and the certificate actually gives the father as John Edward, the checkers may return your application with a negative result, so make your search criteria broader by requesting a check for a father called 'John plus or minus any other names'. Equally, instead of stating the exact age that you think someone should have been, give yourself a little leeway. Instead of 'age 20', say 'age 18–22'.

Beware false economies

Because of the fees involved, some people may be reluctant to buy certificates, but not to do so is invariably a false economy. When I started tracing my ancestry, I had a rough idea of my great-great-grandmother's age, and found an index reference to someone of the right age in Shepton Mallet. I decided to save money by not buying the certificate and wasted ages searching through other Shepton Mallet records looking for her family, without success. In the end I bought the certificate only to find that the certificate belonged to somebody completely different. Faced with this frustration, it was only then that I broadened my search and managed to find the right reference, but this time it was in London. Even if the Shepton Mallet entry had been right, I still would have benefited by having bought the certificate at once. Many people are in similar situations and will often say 'I've hit a brick wall' when all they actually need to do is to fork out for a certificate.

OTHER USEFUL POINTERS

Until 1874, stillborn children did not have to be registered. When children died very young, you will sometimes find their death but not their birth has been registered.

Like other certificates, information recorded on death certificates will often be slightly unreliable, but none more so than on elderly peoples' death certificates, because the informant was invariably of a younger generation and unlikely to know all the facts for certain. Doctors, care-home workers or friends can register deaths and they may scarcely have known the deceased, but bereaved children are equally unlikely to get all the facts straight.

Do not forget that death certificates can provide information on people born long before General Registration began. The death certificate of an elderly ancestor in 1837 will provide co-ordinates on your family history back in the 18th century.

If a coroner's inquest took place, this will be noted on the death certificate. Coroners' records are closed to access for 75 years after the event and many have been destroyed. Those over 75 years old and which have survived are usually to be found in the relevant county record office, and their whereabouts is detailed in J. Gibson and C. Rogers' *Coroners' Records in England and Wales* (FFHS, 1997). A much better way of finding details of an inquest, however, is to look in the local newspaper (see page 144).

Death certificates seldom provide much useful information in themselves, but they can be helpful if you are stuck.

OVERCOMING PROBLEMS

➤**Clerical errors.** The General Registration indexes were compiled by the registrar general's clerks from copies of certificates sent in by the super-intendent registrars, who in turn were receiving information from the local registrars: at each stage of the process, errors could and did creep in. If you receive a certificate that does not say exactly what you expected,

GENERAL REGISTRATION OUTSIDE ENGLAND

A good general guide to General Registration world-wide is T. J. Kemp's *International Vital Records Handbook* (Genealogical Publishing Co., 2001), which includes details of general registration worldwide with copies of application forms and fees.

SCOTLAND

Scottish General Registration records date from 1 January 1855 and are kept by the **Registrar General of Scotland** at New Register House, Edinburgh. Booking is advisable, and you will be charged a fee of £16 per day or £60 per week for access to Civil Registration, census and parish records. You can search the General Registration indexes by computer, note down the reference number of entries that seem relevant and then examine them on microfiche. The computer does not pick up variant spellings, so if your ancestor John McDonald was indexed as John MacDonall, then you will miss him unless you search under that spelling. You can check the original records at once, at no extra cost, and it is often possible to trace back to 1855 in a day. A certificate costs £6 while a photocopy of an event between 1855 and 1891 costs £1.50.

www.scotlandspeople.gov.uk is a major development in Scottish genealogy. It includes indexes to Scottish General Registration of births, marriages and deaths from 1855 to 1906, 1931 and 1956 respectively. You can see basic details of an entry for 30p or download images of the original records for £1.20.

Microfiche copies of the records 1855–1920 are available at **Mormon Family History Centres** and the **SoG**.

You can also commission a search from the register office staff.

The **Registrar General of Scotland** also has indexes to:
- Consular returns of birth and death from 1914 and marriages from 1917.
- Army births, marriages and deaths of Scots in British bases worldwide from 1881.
- Deaths of Scots in the armed forces for the Boer War and the First and Second World Wars.
- Births and deaths of Scots or children of Scottish fathers in British aircraft from 1948.

IRELAND

For fuller details see my *Collins Tracing your Irish Family History*, (Collins, 2007). Civil registration for Protestant marriages started on 1 April 1845 and on 1 January 1864 for all births, marriages and deaths. The records and registration districts were organised as in England. The public searchroom is at Joyce House, Dublin and the records will be online soon. Births are indexed quarterly. Between 1903 and 1927 and from 1966 to 1995 they are indexed annually and include the child's date of birth as well. Mothers' maiden names are included from 1903. Marriages and deaths are indexed quarterly right up to 1965. Indexes to marriages and deaths from 1966-1995 are in alphabetical order and with precise date and surname of spouse for marriages, and precise date, age and marital status for deaths. All post 1995 records are indexed on computer and can be checked by the staff: it is believed that all indexes will soon be online. The Registrar General in Dublin also holds:
- Births at sea from 1864 and deaths at sea up to 1921
- British consular returns for Irish abroad 1864–1921.

Civil records for Northern Ireland from 1922 are kept by the **Registrar General of Northern Ireland**, which also has microfiche copies of the Irish birth indexes from 1864. Mothers maiden names are given in the birth indexes from' 1903. You can search the indexes for a fee of £8/day with extra charges depending on how many records you would like to see. Book in advance.

The Registrar General in Belfast also holds:
- Births and deaths at sea from 1922.
- British consular returns for Northern Irish people abroad from 1922.
- War deaths 1939–48.
- If you know when the event took place you can order certificates online at **www.groni.gov.uk**. It is important to remember variant spellings, not least because many Irish names are English renderings (and sometimes quite arbitrary ones) of Gaelic names. Surnames may appear with or without the prefixes O', Mc or Mac.
- Irish civil registration for births 1865—74 and Protestant marriages 1847–64 are indexed on the Vital Records index (see page 111) on **www.familysearch.org**.

CHANNEL ISLANDS

Alderney and Sark: Births and deaths from 1925 and marriages from 1919 are kept by the **Clerk of the Court** (Alderney) and the **General Registrar** (Sark). All other records are held on Guernsey.

⌘ Guernsey: Births and deaths from 1840 and marriages from 1919 are held by at **Her Majesty's Greffier**. The indexes and records are available for public searching. Up to 1949, married women's deaths were recorded under their maiden names. Occasionally, death certificates will give the maiden name of the mother. Copies of the 19th-century records are also at the **Priaulx Library**. Copies of the birth and death registers 1840–1907 and marriages 1840–1911, and indexes for births and marriages to 1966 and deaths to 1963 are at the **SoG**. During the German occupation 1940–45 a separate set of records was kept, and is now held at the General Register Office with copies at the SoG.

⌘ Jersey: Births, marriages and deaths from 1842 are kept by the **Judicial Greffe**. Only postal searches are possible, although copies of the indexes 1842–1900 are at the library of the **Société Jersiaise** and the Channel Islands Family History Society. Marriage certificates often give the spouses' birthplaces.

ISLE OF MAN
⌘ Civil Registration of births and marriages started in 1849 and deaths in 1878, and was compulsory for births and deaths from 1878 and marriages from 1884. The records are kept by the **Chief Registrar** at the General Registry, where you can search in the original registers and obtain certificates. Copies of the indexes up to 1964 are at the **SoG**.

QUICK REFERENCE
See also main sources in
Useful Addresses, page 306

**REGISTRAR GENERAL OF
SCOTLAND**
New Register House
Charlotte Square
Edinburgh EH1 3YT
☎ 0131 334 0380
www.gro–scotland.gov.uk

**REGISTRAR GENERAL OF
NORTHERN IRELAND**
Oxford House
49–55 Chichester Street
Belfast BT1 4HL
Northern Ireland
☎ 028 9025 2000
www.groni.gov.uk

REGISTRAR GENERAL OF EIRE
Public Searchroom
Joyce House
8–11 Lombard Street
Dublin 2
Eire
☎ 00 353 1 635 4000

REGISTRAR GENERAL OF EIRE
Headquarters (for
correspondence)
Convent Road
Roscommon
Ireland
☎ 00 353 90 663 2900
www.groireland.ie

For Channel Island and
Isle of Man addresses,
see page 311

SCOTTISH CERTIFICATES

ALTHOUGH THEY WERE SLOW to follow the English by introducing General Registration, the Scots made up for the lost time by introducing much more detailed certificates in 1855 (see page 105). Sadly, these were so complicated that the amount of information required was reduced the next year, though the ensuing documents are still more detailed than those found south of the border.

⌦ **Births.** Mothers' maiden names are given in the birth indexes from 1929. Certificates for 1855 and from 1861 onwards have the addition of the date and place of the parents' marriage. Those for 1855 alone also record the ages and places of birth of the parents and details of the child's older siblings.

⌦ **Marriages.** Married women are indexed under both their maiden and married names. Certificates include the names of both parties' mothers and fathers, and mothers' maiden names.

⌦ **Deaths.** Ages are given in the death indexes from 1868 and dates of birth from 1969. The mother's maiden name is given in the death indexes from 1974. Certificates for 1855 and since 1861 provide the name of the spouse and of the deceased's parents, including the father's occupation and mother's maiden name. For 1855 alone the names of offspring were recorded, and from 1855 to 1861 so was the place of burial.

WHEN MARK CURTIS and his son Daniel started having their family tree traced three years ago, they could never have predicted what a complicated story would emerge.

Mark's great-grandfather Frank was born in India in about 1884/5, son of a soldier called George Curtis, though by the time of Frank's Lancashire marriage in 1909, George had become a postman. Frank's birth and baptism were recorded twice in the Army Register Book of births, marriages and deaths, a copy of which is at the FRC, once by George's regiment and secondly by the Royal Army Service Corps, and showed he was born in Bangalore on 15 June 1885, son of George Curtis, a sergeant in the 8th Hussars, and his wife Mary Richards.

George, son of William Curtis, a labourer, and Mary married in church at Trinulghery, Secunderabad on 30 July 1884 and the marriage record showed George was 30, so born about 1853–4. However, searches for his birth or baptism either in the army birth/baptism records at the FRC, the English and Welsh General Registration records or elsewhere all drew complete blanks. A record of George's birth simply was not to be found.

FURTHERING THE SEARCH

We knew George became a postman. Postmen's records are at the Post Office Archives (see page 182) and the pension records showed only one likely candidate, whose pension started in 1919. His application told us he had joined the Royal Mail in 1899 and had served with 'diligence and fidelity'. His date of birth was stated to be 22 June 1855, a year later than the age suggested on the marriage record. But even with this new information, a record of the birth was still not to be found.

We therefore tried his army records, finding his service papers in TNA, in class WO 97. These told us masses about George, including that he was 5' 8" tall with a chest measuring 3¼' and that he had a sallow complexion, brown hair, brown eyes, a good physique and a pulse of 64 beats per minute. We learned of his travels to India and South Africa, and back, the diseases he had suffered there: like most soldiers, he caught both hepatitis and syphilis, but he continued to serve. In the end he was posted back to England, to Canterbury, not far from the Royal Dragoons pub on the appropriately named Military Road. He later suffered a riding accident while serving in Ireland, leaving the army there in 1898; his conduct had been 'exemplary' and 'temperate', which means he did not drink too heavily. For the record, his death certificate shows that he died of pneumonia and a fractured bone on 18 November 1939, aged 84, at 41 Elswick Row, Newcastle.

FURTHER DELVING

But where was he born? His army discharge papers (see page 197) stated he was born on 22 June 1855 at St Mary's, Reading. However, no birth record could be found there, nor a corresponding baptism, and neither he nor his father William Curtis, the labourer, were in the 1861 census. It turns out Reading was not his birthplace, and we still do not know why he said it was.

In fact, the 1901 census (see page 69) states his birthplace as 'Barnby', Suffolk, but in this record he is mis-entered as George Carter and, in any case, at the time the research was being undertaken, the 1901 census had not yet been released. However, his army papers also gave his next of kin as Mary and, before his marriage, as 'Mother, Harriet------ Barnaby near Beccles [Suffolk]'.

Although it is most useful for events before General Registration began in 1837, the International Genealogical Index on **www.familysearch.org** can sometimes be helpful solving mysteries after then (see page 110). There was no George Curtis entry, which was obviously right, but further searching revealed a William Curtis, son of

William and Harriet, baptised on 24 June 1860 at Barnby, Suffolk. This certainly seemed to indicate the right family – and the original entry confirmed that the father, William, was indeed a labourer.

As George was supposedly born around 1853–5, the 1861 census of Barnby was the next stop. This revealed William Curtis the labourer at Back Lane, Barnby, with his wife Harriet and children, including William's step-son George Moore, aged eight.

FOUND!

Taken aback, yet very excited, we sought a birth certificate. George Moore was born on 22 June 1852, at Barnby, as George, son of Harriet Moore, an unmarried woman from Barnby. And to seal the case we found the marriage of William Curtis and Harriet Moore taking place on 12 April 1855.

I cannot explain why George said he was born in Reading, but it seems that sometime after the 1861 census was taken, William and Harriet decided to alter George's surname and year of birth to make it fall within the year of their wedding. This made George seem like their legitimate son, or else George decided to do this himself. Illegitimacy carried some stigma at that time, and perhaps it was considered best all round if the matter was glossed over.

The moral of the story, as Mark and Daniel discovered, is that the answer to a family mystery can be found, but you must keep on seeking new information about the person you are after: eventually, with sufficient persistence, you may well succeed.

◁ The birth record of George Moore, later called George Curtis, revealed at last.

▽ Medical certificate from 1875 for George Curtis on enlistment

LIFETIMES: THE TALE OF THE NEARLY LOST SOLDIER

EXAMPLES OF GENERAL REGISTRATION IN OTHER COUNTRIES

Most countries around the world have General Registration, although relatively few have had such a system for anything like as long as Britain. Below are some details of General Registration in countries where British people may wish to do research. In all cases, you can obtain up-to-date information and advice from the relevant country's embassy in London, usually from the embassy's cultural section. Bear in mind that the primary duty of an embassy is not to help you trace your family tree, and the average receptionist is unlikely to be an expert on genealogy, so a considerable degree of polite persistence is often required to ensure you are passed on to someone who will be able to help. But, invariably, your efforts will pay off.

AUSTRALIA
Civil registration started at different times in the different states, beginning with Tasmania in 1838. Many of the records for different states are being published on CD-Rom by the Latter Day Saints in the form of pioneers' indexes: contact them on **www.familysearch.org.** Records tend to be fairly detailed, e.g. including parents' names on death certificates.

BANGLADESH
Modern civil registration started in 1960. What little has been recorded can be accessed via the **Bangladesh Demographic Survey and Vital Registration System**.

INDIA
Contact the **Registrar General's Office** or address enquiries to the 'Chief Registrar of Births, Deaths and Marriages' of the capital city of the relevant state, union or territory. Civil registration of births and deaths was introduced in Bengal in 1873 and throughout India in 1886 but outside major towns and cities compliance was very low. Registration of marriages became compulsory for some faiths by special Acts: for Christians (1872 and 1955), Parsees (1936) and Hindus (1955). In practice, the best way of finding out about a marriage is to contact the place of worship where the event is thought to have taken place.

JAMAICA
Compulsory civil registration of births, marriages and deaths started on 1 January 1878. Records are kept at the **Registrar General's Department**. Much can be accessed on microfiche through the **Mormon Family History Centres**.

KENYA
Modern civil registration of births and deaths for whites began in 1904, available to Asians from 1906, compulsory for Asians from 1928 and compulsory for blacks from 1963 (and in other states from years up to 1971). Contact the **Principal Civil Registrar** or the local district registry. White marriages have been registered since 1902 but few black marriages have been recorded. Islamic marriages are registered by the **Minister of Mohammedan Marriages**.

NEW ZEALAND
Civil registration started in 1848, first for whites only, but Maoris soon started to use the system voluntarily until it became compulsory in 1911 for marriages, and 1913 for births and deaths. Copies of the indexes to 1920 are at the **SoG** in London.

PAKISTAN
Modern Pakistan has required the registration of all over 18, and all foreigners, since 1973. Birth, marriage, death and divorce records kept by the Directorate of General Registration, which you can contact via the **Pakistan Embassy**.

SIERRA LEONE
Civil registration began in Freetown in 1801 but has never been truly comprehensive. Information is held at the **Office of the Chief Registrar**.

SOUTH AFRICA
Civil registration started piecemeal in its constituent provinces, beginning with the Cape of Good Hope (1820), while national civil registration started in 1923, with records held by the Department of Home Affairs, which you can contact via the **South African High Commission**.

QUICK REFERENCE

See also main sources in Useful Addresses, page 306

BANGLADESH DEMOGRAPHIC SURVEY AND VITAL REGISTRATION SYSTEM
Bangladesh Bureau of Statistics
Gana Bhavan Extension Block-1
Sher-A-Bangla Nagar
Dhaka 7
Bangladesh

REGISTRAR GENERAL'S OFFICE
West Block 1
P. K. Puram
New Delhi 110066
India

REGISTRAR GENERAL'S DEPARTMENT
Island Record Office
Spanish Town
Jamaica

PRINCIPAL CIVIL REGISTRAR
PO Box 30031
Nairobi
Kenya

MINISTER OF MOHAMMEDAN MARRIAGES
PO Box 45687
Nairobi
Kenya

PAKISTAN EMBASSY
Community Directorate
36 Londes Square
London SW1X 9JN
☎ 020 7664 9246

OFFICE OF THE CHIEF REGISTRAR
Births and Deaths Office
Ministry of Health
3 Wilberforce Street, Freetown
Sierra Leone

SOUTH AFRICAN HIGH COMMISSION
South Africa House
Trafalgar Square
London WC2N 5DP
☎ 0870 005 6974
www.southafricahouse.com

OTHER GENERAL REGISTRATION RECORDS

The Registrar General holds a number of civil registration records besides those for England and Wales. They contain broadly similar types of information and can be found at TNA and on **www.findmypast.com**.

➤**Consular records:** records of birth, marriage and death of British subjects kept by British consuls from 1 July 1849.

➤**Birth and death at sea:** from 1 July 1837. See C. & M. Watts, *Tracing Births, Deaths and Marriages at Sea* (SoG, 2004).

➤**Forces deaths:** for Boer (1899–1902) and First and Second World Wars.

➤**Forces births, baptisms, marriages and deaths** (except foregoing): regimental returns (1761–1924), forces chaplains (1796–1880) and returns (1881–1965).

➤**Indian service deaths:** 1939–42.

➤**Deaths in the air and missing persons:** 1947–65.

➤**Births, marriages and deaths:** in Ionian Islands (1818–64).

▽ A record of death at sea.

NA 006452

CERTIFIED COPY of an ENTRY IN THE MARINE REGISTER

Application Number Y548992

Pursuant to the provisions of the Merchant Shipping Acts 1894 and 1970 and the Births and Deaths Registration Act 1953.

186 Death at Sea on board of H.M.S. 'Adventure'

When Died	Name & Surname	Sex	Age	Rank or Profession	Cause of Death	Signature,Description Residence of Informant	When Registered	Signature of Registrar
24 July 1/63	Henry Collins	Male	31	Private 5 Co 84 Regt	Heart Disease	T B Lethbridge Commander H.M.S Adventure	24th July 1/63	T B Lethbridge Commander

I hereby certify that this is a true copy of the Minute made in the log of H.M.S. 'Adventure' on the 24th day of July 1863.
Witness my hand,this 26th day of July 1863. (Signed) T B Lethbridge Commander H.M.S. 'Adventure'
A true copy G Graham. Registrar General.

...TIFIED to be a true copy of an entry in the MARINE REGISTER OF ....DEATH.........
Given at the GENERAL REGISTER OFFICE, under the seal of the said Office, this **23rd** day of **February** , **2004** .

...ths and Deaths Registration Act 1953 (sec. 34) provides that any certified copy of an entry purporting to be sealed or stamped with the seal of the General Register Office shall be received ...f the birth or death to which it relates without any further or other proof of the entry, and no certified copy purporting to be given in the said Office shall be of any force or effect unless ...r stamped as aforesaid.

...: THERE ARE OFFENCES RELATING TO FALSIFYING OR ALTERING A CERTIFICATE AND USING OR POSSESSING A FALSE CERTIFICATE ©CROWN COPYRIGHT
WARNING: A CERTIFICATE IS NOT EVIDENCE OF IDENTITY.

03/02 SPSL 002790

CHAPTER SIX
CENSUSES

The first mention of censuses is familiar to many from the Christmas story. Sadly, Caesar's census will not help many modern family historians, but more recent ones will. Those for 19th-century Britain can provide ages and places of birth, essential information for seeking births and so identifying earlier generations.

△ **Censuses are now available online. This is a page from www.1901census.nationalarchives. gov.uk.**

Census returns used to be regarded as the second port-of-call after General Registration records. Now, with them all online from 1841 to 1901, they can often represent the first and easiest way of tracing a family tree back through the 19th century.

From 1851 to 1901, census returns provide ancestors' names, relationships to others in the same household, ages and places of birth. With good fortune, you may be able to find your grandparent or great-grandparent with their parents in the 1901 census, then seek the same family in the preceding censuses. At that point (and with good fortune still attending), you will find the names of your forbears who were born in the early 19th or even late 18th centuries, whose baptisms can be sought in parish registers.

Do not attempt to perform these genealogical gymnastics using censuses in isolation. To be sure you have traced the right line, you absolutely must use General Registration records as well. Both categories of records complement each other to help you build up incredibly detailed pictures of your ancestors' lives. Used together, they can enable you trace a fully proven family tree back to the early 19th century.

THE RECORDS

Each enumeration book (see opposite) starts with a brief description of the area covered, usually street by street, and also always includes details of the parish, town or borough. Censuses provide a splendid snap-shot of your family on a specific evening in the past showing your ancestors in the context of their family, extended family and neighbourhood. But do remember that the records are just that. If someone was away from the household, even for just that one night, they were supposed to be enumerated where they actually were, not where they normally lived.

IN ENGLAND, various population counts have taken place since the Domesday survey of 1086, but thereafter only on a local basis, such as the censuses for parts of the City of London for 1638 and 1695, held at the Corporation of London Record Office. The first national census taken in England, Scotland and Wales was in 1801. It was made in response to the threat of invasion by Napoleon and was designed mainly to ascertain how many men were available for conscription into the army. A debate had also been raging on and off for half a century as to whether the population was declining or, on the other hand, whether it could rise to an unsustainable level. The results showed a population of 8,893,000 in England and Wales. In 1811, largely because of more efficient enumeration, the number was much greater – 10,164,000 in England and Wales – triggering a genuine panic of a population explosion which would rapidly overwhelm the country.

Censuses have been taken every decade since then, except for 1941, when everyone was busy with the all-too-real threat of invasion from Germany. However, until 1841, in almost every instance, they remained mere head counts, although in some 750 happy cases enumerators chose to write down the names and sometimes even occupations (see overleaf). From 1841 onwards, when the Registrar General was placed in charge of the system, Britain has had proper censuses listing everyone together by address, with ages and occupations. Because of secrecy legislation, they are not available for public searching for 100 years, so the most recent records available now are those of the 1901 census.

COMPILING CENSUSES

To compile censuses, the General Registration sub-districts were divided into enumeration districts, which were basically the areas that a single enumerator could cover in foot on an evening. Just as now, forms were distributed in advance of census night, to be completed by each household on the appointed evening or, if everyone in the household was illiterate, by the enumerator. The enumerators copied the resulting information into enumeration books and sent them to the Registrar General for statistical analysis. This was done by clerks with blue pencils, ticking or crossing off entries as they were counted, something which newcomers to census returns sometimes find confusing. Equally, the clerks sometimes wrote general descriptions against occupations – but once you know this, the clerks' notes are easy to spot and ignore.

The original householders' forms were destroyed but, more by luck than judgement, almost all the books were kept, but scarcely very well – the returns for 1841 and 1861 were found in the roof of the Houses of Parliament, and sections of the former, particularly for parts of Kent, Essex and London (Paddington, Kensington, Golden Lane and Whitecross), have never been located. They were transferred to the Public Record Office by 1912 and it was not until much later that their immense value for family history was realised. The microfilmed copies of the books are what we use now for census searching and formed the basis for the increasing number of census indexes.

▽ Detail from *The Census at Bethlehem* by Brueghel (1525–69).

CENSUS RETURNS

⊟ The original census returns are not available for public searching. But they are available on microfilm rolls and on the internet. Microfilm copies can be searched at **TNA**, Mormon Family History Centres, and many archives and libraries have films covering their area. Full details are in J. Gibson and E. Hampson's *Census returns 1841-1891 in microform; a directory to local holdings in Great Britain, Channel islands, Isle of Man* (FFHS, 1994), 6th edition.

⊟ For many decades, family history societies worked on indexing their local census returns. Some indexes just gave reference numbers and others were almost complete transcriptions. Many of these indexes are still available in local archives, from the societies concerned (see **www.findmypast.org**) or in major genealogical libraries, such as the **SoG** and **IHGS**. They are covered by J. Gibson and E. Hampson's *Marriage and Census Indexes for Family Historians* (FFHS, 2000).

⊟ There are fiche indexes, compiled by the Mormons, to the 1881 census, and some counties in the 1851 census. They were indexed in a number of creative ways: you can scan through the index of everyone in with your surname, or you can search by birthplace, enabling you, for example, to easily pick out all the Smiths who were born in a certain village.

⊟ Firms such as **www.my-history.co.uk**, S&N's **www.genealogysupplies.com** and **www.archivecdbooks.org** sell CDs of sections of census returns, with varying degrees of search facilities. The online censuses have largely superseded these, unless you want to make an in-depth study of your ancestral village, or area, and spend a lot of time studying how all the families were interrelated, in which case they have a lot to commend them.

⊟ The first census to be indexed online was the 1881 census, which appeared on the Mormons' site **www.familysearch.org** back in 1999 – so many people logged on that the site crashed. This was the first time that the press realised that genealogy had progressed from a moderately popular hobby, to a mainstream interest. The site provides a free transcription of the 1881 census for England and Wales, but not images of the original pages.

⊟ The Mormons' success encouraged commercial firms to start indexing the other censuses. The 1901 census appeared in 2002 (with similar computer problems – so many people logged on that the site crashed and took several months to restore!). Now, you have a choice of which pay-to-view site to use to gain access to the fully-indexed censuses from 1841 to 1901, and to online images of the original pages. Foremost are **www.genesreunited.co.uk**, **www.ancestry.co.uk**, **www.findmypast.com** (1841–1891 only) and **www.1901census.nationalarchives.gov.uk/** (1901 only). **www.nationalarchives.gov.uk/census** offers access to the **www.ancestry.co.uk** censuses for a cheaper rate than the **www.ancestry.co.uk** site offers directly.

⊟ The site **www.freecen.org.uk** is a growing database of census returns which have been transcribed by volunteers and made freely available. A directory of other free census records is at **www.censusfinder.com**. If you find what you want, then you win: if you do not, do not make any assumptions about what has or has not been indexed, and seek what you want in the pay-to-view sites.

QUICK REFERENCE

See main sources in Useful Addresses, page 306

HOW TO SEARCH

Don't run before you can walk, as the plethora of information available can be very confusing. If you have not used General Registration properly to trace back records to 1901, then focus on doing so: only when you have found the birth or marriage closest to 1901 is it time to start using censuses. Once you know exactly who was who at that time it is time to start using these exciting records. First, look for the family in the 1901 census. Even if you are not yet computer-literate, the ease with which people can now be found in online versions makes it worth your while learning how to use the search facility when trying this method, or prevailing on someone else to do it for you. The sites' search facilities are easy to follow: if the name is a very rare one, just look at all the entries under your surname; if it is not, you can use the 'advanced search' options to narrow the search down, but be open-minded when you do so – just because someone lived in Kent, for example, does not mean they were definitely born there, and whilst men having children around 1901 were most probably aged between 18-40, they *could* have been anything from 12 to 80-plus!

If all goes well, you will find the family in the 1901 census. Your pennies are precious, of course, but please don't stop when you see a transcription of the right entry – pay the extra and see (and print) the image of the original page. This (and not the transcription or index reference) is the original record, and you are far less likely to go wrong, or become confused, if you have this in front of you.

The people you have found in 1901 are likely to appear more or less ten years younger in the 1891 returns, so you can now seek them there, and if you are lucky you can work right back to 1841. At each stage, you will see the story of your family unfolding through the century – children growing up, leaving home, starting work, living with their young spouses and having children, and then grow older as their own children grow up and repeat the same process. Now that the returns are fully indexed you can do what we never could in the past, by finding children away at boarding school, or working in service, or people away on ships or in hotels or prisons, staying with relatives or working night-shifts in factories, and the elderly living with one of their grown-up children, or in workhouses or hospitals. In fact, since the online censuses appeared, we can learn more about 19th century families than ever before, and with a better overview of what happened to these families than, in many cases, the families knew themselves. We live in privileged times indeed!

DATES OF CENSUSES

TNA REFERENCE NUMBERS FROM 1841

10 March 1801	(no records at TNA)
27 May 1811	(no records at TNA)
28 May 1821	(no records at TNA)
30 May 1831	HO 71
6 June 1841	HO 107
30 March 1851	HO 107
7 April 1861	RG 9
2 April 1871	RG 10
3 April 1881	RG 11
5 April 1891	RG 12
31 March 1901	RG 13
2 April 1911	RG 14

Do not ever base your research solely on censuses. Right back to 1837, birth and marriage certificates can be found, and you should always seek these for your direct ancestors, *regardless of how complete you feel the census returns are*. They will help you avoid making errors, and will tell you more detail than will be found in censuses. They compliment each other, and the details from both are very precious.

OVERCOMING PROBLEMS

In many cases, your research will not go smoothly and you will not be able to find the right people straight away. A chief reason for this is that the indexes are full of mistakes, made by the indexers either through carelessness, or failure to understand the records (some of the 1901 census returns were indexed by prisoners), or because the handwriting in the originals can be very hard to read. So, if you think you know where the family lived but cannot find them using the indexes, search the originals (see page 74). The other main problem with using the indexes is that your ancestors were not recorded originally in the way you would expect. You might expect your ancestor to appear as 'James Dinnie' age 24, born in Kirkintilloch, but he might actually have been recorded as Jim Dinny, 23, born in neighbouring Lenzie. You may therefore need to try and second-guess how someone might have been misrecorded at the time, before successfully finding them in the indexes. If you do find someone whose details are slightly different to what you expected, as in the foregoing example, you will of course need to make sure the other co-ordinates match up and that you have found the right person. You can see, for example, if the father's name matches that given on James's marriage certificate.

Almost all records used in family history are likely to be inaccurate, but censuses are amongst the worst. This is because if you ask people fairly intrusive questions, they are likely to be rather evasive in their answers. People were, and continue to be, highly suspicious of the Government's reasons for wanting to know about them. In the 19th century, many poorer people were (not always unjustly) afraid that, if they owned up to having come from somewhere else, they would be ordered to return thence. Therefore, the most common answer enumerators received to the question 'where were you born?', was therefore a blunt 'here!'.

Places of birth could be wrong for other reasons too. Someone who was born in Oxford but grew up from an early age in Cambridge might very well think that the latter was their birth place. People also tended to generalise. If someone was born in the tiny village of Sturry near Canterbury and then moved away, they would probably tell everyone they were from Canterbury, and this is what might then be recorded on a census form (and hence in the census indexes).

Information about the family was usually supplied by only one person, but not necessarily the head of the household. A child might supply information about their parents and siblings, and there are cases when the task seems to have been delegated to servants or even the lodger: no wonder details were sometimes inaccurate. Ages could also be wrong when people did not want to admit to being as old or as young as they really were. In 1876 it became compulsory for children under 13 to go to school. However, many hard-up parents still sent their children out to work and lied to the enumerators, saying their children were 'scholars', the standard term for a child at school, when they were in fact out at work every day and receiving no education at all.

Greater inaccuracies arose when institutions were enumerated. In some cases, prison governors simply noted down the inmates' initials.

Relationships to the head of the household were sometimes given inaccurately or falsely. The illegitimate son of the head of the household's daughter might end up being enumerated as the head's youngest son, for instance.

Addresses can cause problems, not least because streets could be renamed. House numbering was virtually unknown in rural areas and, when used in towns, it would change as extra houses were built in streets. Therefore, if your ancestors are not at the house number you expected, check the rest of the street, and if they are not there look around the area or examine maps and contemporary street directories (see page 82) for guidance. Related problems arise when houses had doors on two different streets, thus giving the house two potential addresses. This is another area in which studying a map can suggest different solutions to the problem of not finding your ancestors where you expected them to be.

When using the censuses to ascertain where someone was born before 1837, bear in mind that their place of birth might not be the

LIFETIMES: EVEN OFFICIALS MAKE MISTAKES

CHARLES TOWNER was listed in 3 April 1881 census returns for Hastings Union Workhouse as a 50-year-old basketmaker born in Lydd. The census form would have been filled in by an official, so you would expect it to have been accurate. And you would expect the same of a death certificate filled in by John Pearce, master of the Union Workhouse, two days later. It related to the death in the workhouse, on 5 April, of Charles Towner, a 51-year-old cooper of Hastings! It just shows – discrepancies occurred and ultimately (and most unfortunately), the officials may not have cared less.

CENSUS RETURNS OUTSIDE ENGLAND & WALES

An extraordinary guide to census returns around the world is published in the somewhat unlikely guise of G. Johnson's *Census Records for Scottish Families at Home and Abroad* (Aberdeen and North East Scotland FHS, 1997).

SCOTLAND

The foregoing applies to Scotland as well as England and Wales. The records are kept by the **Registrar General of Scotland** and are covered by the same £16 search fee as for General Registration records. The returns are almost identical, except that, from 1861 onwards, they state the number of rooms with one or more windows, whether people were employers and, if so, how many people they employed. The Scottish censuses are indexed online for 1841–1901 **www.scotlandspeople.gov.uk**. This site also includes downloadable images.

IRELAND

Censuses were taken every decade from 1821, but 1861–91 were destroyed by the Government and most of 1821–51 burned when the Four Courts were bombed in 1922. The surviving sections, which list all occupants, are at the National Archives of Ireland as explained in *Collins Tracing Your Irish Family History* (Collins, 2007).

The 1901 and 1911 returns, which were filled in by the householders (or enumerators on their behalf), have survived and are on open access, arranged by Poor Law Union and then by district, parish and townland, which are indexed. They list names, age, gender, religious denomination, marital status and relationship to the head of the household, but the place of birth is no more precise than the county or city, or country if born outside Ireland. The 1911 returns state how long women had been married and how many surviving children they had.

The 1901 and 1911 censuses have started to appear online at **www.census.nationalarchives.ie**. Otherwise, if you know a general location, you can check the heads-of-households lists, which accompany the census forms, for a townland or street name. The other approach is to seek an address from a **GRO** certificate first. Some **heritage centres** have their own indexes, which can be searched for a fee.

You can also check applications for old age pensions made between 1908 and 1921 where, as proof of age, extracts from the later-destroyed census returns could be submitted. The applications are indexed: copies are at **TNA**, **PRONI** and the **SoG** and **www.pensear.org**.

▷ A census enumerator collects a completed census form.

QUICK REFERENCE

See also main sources in Useful Addresses, page 306

REGISTRAR GENERAL OF SCOTLAND
New Register House
Charlotte Square
Edinburgh EH1 3YT
Scotland
☎ 0131 334 0380
www.gro-scotland.gov.uk

For the Channel Islands and Isle of Man addresses, see page 311

NORTHERN IRELAND

As Ireland. Copies of the relevant section of the Irish census are at the **PRONI**. An index to the 1901 census of Fermanagh is L. K. Kuchenbach Meehan's *1901 Irish Census Index, Vol. 1, County Fermanagh* (Largy Books, 1992).

CHANNEL ISLANDS

As England and Wales. Copies of the returns for Guernsey are held by **Her Majesty's Greffier** at the General Register Office, and for Jersey at the St Helier Public Library and **Société Jersiaise**: all returns for 1841–91 have been indexed by Jersey Library. There are also (indexed) censuses for 1806 and 1815, called 'General Don's muster rolls'. Those for 1806 list some 4000 heads of households with the numbers of people in their families, whilst those for 1816 list all men aged 17–80, with the numbers of women, boys and girls in their households.

ISLE OF MAN

As England and Wales. Copies of returns for the island are at the **Manx Museum**. The 1851, 1881, 1891 and 1901 returns are fully indexed.

EXAMPLES OF CENSUS RETURNS IN OTHER COUNTRIES

AUSTRALIA

Although musters were kept of men in Australia from 1788, proper Australian censuses kicked off with the 1828 census of New South Wales and Tasmania, giving ages, occupations, where people lived, and whether they were born in Australia or, if not, when they landed. There is a surname index at the SoG and a microfilm copy at **TNA** in class HO 10. The first national census was made in 1881, but few returns have survived.

CARIBBEAN

A guide to censuses in **TNA** is in G. Grannum's *Tracing your West Indian Ancestors; Sources at the PRO* (PRO Publications, 1995). Most early ones focus on the white population. There are returns of Maroons of Mooretown, Charlestown, Scot's Hall and Accompanying, giving name, age, colour and some notes on the father's name, and slaves belonging to Maroons. Jamaica's own censuses are at the Department of Statistics.

INDIA AND PAKISTAN

The first all-India census was taken in 1871–2 and have been taken regularly every ten years from 1881. However, these record nothing of any help to genealogists. Equally, although Pakistan has taken census decennially since 1951, including names and relationships, only the other two categories, ages and occupations, are available to the public, making them virtually useless for our purposes.

KENYA

Censuses were taken in 1911, 1921, 1926 and 1931, but these did not include Africans. The first complete census was in 1948 followed by one in 1969. These are at the **Central Bureau of Statistics**.

NEW ZEALAND

The few preserved census records for this country are at the **New Zealand National Archives**.

SIERRA LEONE

TNA have a Sierra Leone census for 30 June 1831 in class CO 267/111, which includes the whole population with ages and occupation of the head of household. There is also an 1833 census in CO 267/127.

SOUTH AFRICA

Censuses date back to 1865 for the Cape, and 1904 for the rest of the country, but they were later destroyed.

QUICK REFERENCE

See also main sources in Useful Addresses, page 306

CENTRAL BUREAU OF STATISTICS
PO Box 30266
Nairobi
Kenya

NEW ZEALAND NATIONAL ARCHIVES
10 Mulgrave Street
Thorndon
Wellington

➤ **www.curiousfox.com**. Message boards arranged by place for Britain and Ireland, enabling you to contact other people researching families from your ancestral homes – a very good idea!

➤ **www.familyrelatives.com**. The quarterly General Registration indexes (which, uniquely, are fully indexed for the years 1866-1920), with the added facility of being able to leave a message against entries relating to your ancestors, so as to facilitate contact with other researchers with the same forbears. They also have some datasets drawn from army records and parish registers.

➤ **www.findmypast.org**. Has the quarterly General Registration indexes and all the subsidiary ones, such as consular and army births, marriages and deaths, the censuses 1841–1891, death duty registers 1796–1903 and a growing number of other useful datasets, such as various published military records and passport applications 1851–1903. It also includes the many indexes of the FFHS member family history societies, some compiled decades ago, formerly at **www.familyhistoryonline.net**.

➤ **www.genesreunited.co.uk**. The foremost British-based genealogical contact website. See page 31.

➤ **http://genforum.genealogy.com**. Message boards offering a question-and-answer facility for most surnames and many genealogical topics.

➤ **www.nationalarchives.gov.uk/documentsonline/**. Documents online-indexes and makes available images of documents at TNA. At the time of writing, the main ones include: First World War Campaign Medals, Second World War Seamen's Medals, Prerogative Court of Canterbury wills; Death Duty registers; Victorian Prisoners Photograph Albums; Registers of Seamen's Services; Women's Army Auxiliary Corps; First World War Prisoners of War Interviews; Royal Naval Division (1914–1919); Victoria Cross Registers; Recommendations for Honours and Awards (Army); Ancient Petitions, Henry III – James I; Poor Law Union Correspondence; Aliens Registration Cards; Domesday Book.

➤ **www.origins.net**. The origins network is divided into Britain, Ireland and Scotland and contains pay-to-view access to many sets of data, particularly will indexes, apprentice records, Boyd's Marriage Index, Trinity House petitions, militia attestations and Boyd's Inhabitants of London. The 'British' section is drawn mainly from the Society of Genealogists' collections, which are referred to elsewhere in this book.

➤ **www.rootsweb.com**. Run by Ancestry, consists mainly of mailing lists, message boards and many personal family history websites.

➤ **www.thegenealogist.co.uk** and **www.ukbmdindex.co.uk**. These addresses point to the same site that contains images of the quarterly General Registration indexes, and various other datasets, including the Protestant Nonconformist registers in GR 4 (see page 263).

COUSINSHIP

Sites such as **www.genesreunited.co.uk** and Ancestry's Ancestry World Tree will enable you to discover distant relatives all over the world. But working out the terminology for distant relatives is confusing because of its slightly eccentric terminology. Your grandchild's child is your great grandchild, and their child in turn is your great great grandchild, and you are the latter's great great grandparent. These are often abbreviated to 'gg grandchild/parent' or '2 x great grandparent' and so on. Your nephew or niece's children, however, are not your grandnephews/nieces, as you might expect, but great nephews/nieces, and their offspring your great great nephews/nieces (and you are the latter's great great uncle/aunt).

Cousinship is best worked out using a chart like the one at the very front of this book, with the common ancestor at the top, and each generation arranged on its own line. The first generation down from the common ancestor are siblings – brothers and sisters. The descendants on the next generation down, the children of siblings, are first cousins. Their children in turn are each other's second cousins. The next generation down still, the gg grandchildren of the common ancestor, are third cousins, and so on. Cousinship extends as far out as you can trace it. Myself and Madonna's husband Guy Ritchie, for example are direct 10th cousins, through our common descent from our mutual gggggggggg (or 9 x) grandfather Benjamin Fairfax (1592-1676).

Where things become complicated is when two cousins do not appear on the same level. A generation difference up or down the family tree is described as 'once removed', two generations as 'twice removed', and so on. Terminology does not account for which direction the removal goes, so 'once removed' might indicate someone in the generation above or below the direct cousin being referred to. Guy's father, Captain John Ritchie, is my 10th cousin once removed, and so is Guy's son Rocco. Relationships are thus stated from the point of view of the person concerned. Captain John Ritchie is my 10th cousin once removed, but I am not his. From his point of view, looking across the family tree, he is 9th cousin of my father, so I am John's 9th cousin once removed. This applies, incidentally, even when parts of the family tree are blank: I have no children, yet my non-existent offspring would be Rocco's 11th cousins, making me Rocco's 11th cousin once removed. At the present moment, Guy and I are keeping our fingers crossed that our mutual 10th cousin once removed, Kate Middleton, marries Prince William. If so, and they have a child who becomes king or queen, that monarch will be our 10th cousin twice removed!

CHAPTER EIGHT
DIRECTORIES & ALMANACS

Directories are published lists of peoples' addresses and occupations, which in the 18th, 19th and early–mid-20th centuries fulfilled broadly the same role as telephone directories do today. They are useful for gaining a snapshot of the communities in which ancestors lived. By searching a series of directories, they can give an idea of when our forbears lived and died. Their main genealogical use, however, is to learn where ancestors lived so as to facilitate census searches.

DIRECTORIES

With the exception of a merchant's directory for London published in 1677, directories started to appear in the 18th century. Those for London were published annually from 1734; Dublin's first appeared in the mid-18th century; Birmingham's earliest directory appeared in 1763; Edinburgh's in 1773 and Glasgow's in 1783. The earliest known English county directory was for Hampshire and was published in 1784. There were some national directories, such as the Universal British Directory 1793–98, although its coverage of people was limited to the most important residents and businessmen.

Directories started to appear in much more significant numbers for town and county alike in the early 19th century. They were produced by competing firms so some counties may have several directories for one year, but equally there may be gaps in coverage with some years not covered at all. Directories generally listed tradesmen, craftsmen, merchants, professionals, farmers, clergy, gentry and nobility, but as the 19th century progressed, the number of people listed increased as directories included many private residents, rich and poor alike.

DIRECTORY

The 1677 London Merchant's directory can be found online at http://freepages.history. rootsweb.com/~frpayments/ LM1677

A BIRD'S EYE VIEW

Directories provided short descriptions of the parishes, towns and cities they covered, combining practical details of population and geography; soil types and the main forms of agriculture and industry; schools and hospitals, with more antiquarian information on local history. These descriptions provide marvellous detail of the world our forbears inhabited. You may even find an advertisement placed by your ancestor to promote his business.

Directories can also help explain your family history. If an ancestor became a coal miner, a directory might tell you that a mine had been opened in his home parish about the same time. If he came from a poor background yet became highly literate, you might learn from a directory that a free school had been opened in their village.

Directories stated which poor law unions and thus which workhouses covered the place concerned. As poor law unions equated to General Registration districts, you can use directories to establish the parameters for General Registration index searching (see page 57). They also indicate which manors covered the parish, and where the local burial grounds and non-conformist chapels were.

Furthermore, directories provided details of roads, canals and railways and the whereabouts of local markets. When trying to work out where an ancestor came from, it is helpful to know the lines of communication on which their place of residence lay. Many couples met at the local market, so if you know where one ancestor came from and want to work out the origins of their spouse, find out which the local market town was and then work out which other villages were in its catchment area.

WHAT DIRECTORIES CONTAIN

From the mid-19th century onwards, directories tended to be divided into the following sections:

➤**Commercial:** traders, professionals, farmers and suchlike, in an alphabetical list.

➤**Trades:** individual alphabetical lists of the foregoing arranged under each trade or profession.

➤**Streets:** lists of tradesmen and private residents listed house by house, street by street.

➤**Court:** originally these were the heads of wealthier households, but this rapidly became simply an alphabetical listing of the heads of all families save the poor.

By following your ancestors forward through a series of directories, you may be able to watch their careers developing – opening a new shop, expanding an existing one, changing occupations and finally handing over to their children. Finding out when an ancestor disappears from directories can provide a clue to when they might have died.

Directories may also introduce you to other relatives you had not encountered before. If you cannot find your ancestor listed, but there were other people with the same surname in the area, look them up in census returns as you may find your ancestor was living with them.

WHERE TO SEARCH

DIRECTORIES

⊟ Substantial collections of directories covering the British Isles are held by the **SoG** at the **Guildhall Library** and a smaller collection by the **IHGS**. **County record offices** and many **libraries**, especially local studies libraries and museums, hold collections for the area.

⊟ Original directories are sold in antiquarian bookshops and even car boot sales, and some have been reproduced on microfiche, such as much of the 1830 Pigot county series, available from the **SoG**.

⊟ There is no comprehensive guide to all directories, but G. Shaw & A Tipper's *British Directories: A Bibliography and Guide to Directories Published in England & Wales (1850–1950) and Scotland (1773–1950)* (Leicester University Press, 1997) is useful.

⊟ Leicester University has a national collection of directories online at **www.historicaldirectories.org**. Many are also available on CD, and online at sites such as **www.archivecdbooks. org** and **www.genealogysupplies.com** as advertised in the family history magazines. Electronic versions of directories have the advantage of being easily searched.

⊟ Many other countries have directories. For example, **www. rootsweb.com/~ttowgw/research/ almanacs.htm** provides a catalogue of Trinidad directories held in Britain. Many Jamaican almanacs, listing mainly white inhabitants from 1811 onwards are on **www.jamaicafamilysearch.com.**

QUICK REFERENCE
See also main sources in Useful Addresses, page 306

GUILDHALL LIBRARY
Aldermanbury
London EC2P 2EJ
☎ 020 7332 1868
www.cityoflondon.gov.uk

WHERE TO SEARCH

TELEPHONE DIRECTORIES

▭ Telephone directories are available in **local libraries** and **county record offices**, with a national collection viewable by appointment at **British Telecom Archives**.

▭ They are also available for many countries on the internet with services such as **www.192.com** and **www.infobel.com**, which have telephone directories for Britain, much of Europe, USA, Canada and others.

QUICK REFERENCE

BRITISH TELECOM ARCHIVES
3rd Floor, Holborn Telephone Exchange
268–270 High Holborn
London WC1V 7EE
☎ **020 7492 8792**
www.btplc.com/archives

OVERCOMING PROBLEMS

➤**Directories were commercial ventures,** usually compiled in the year prior to publication but not always fully updated between editions. It is best, therefore, to think of an entry for an ancestor in an 1874 directory as an indication of what their state of play may have been in 1873.

➤**The information provided was so scant** – name, address and/or trade – that numerous possibilities exist for confusing people with the same name, so be very careful before making the assumption that you have definitely found the right person. The descriptions may be inaccurate; for example, a man with several occupations, such as farmer and butcher, may be listed under only one. Continuity of name and trade, such as listings each year for John Smith, butcher, may mask the death of John Smith senior and the succession of John Smith junior to the business.

➤**Directories did not list the majority of the poor,** and were never intended to be in any sense complete, so if an ancestor is not listed where you expect them to be, this is no indication that they were not there. Obviously, however, if it is feasible, it is worth seeking them elsewhere, in other years or in neighbouring towns or counties.

➤**When searching in London,** do not forget that the city grew so big that from 1799 separate directories were published for the suburbs.

TELEPHONE DIRECTORIES

Telephone directories date from the 1880s and eventually took over from trade and street directories after the Second World War. They can fulfil a similar role to that of the older directories but bear in mind for research purposes that they may be out of date as soon as they are published.

Be aware, too, that telephone directories are very incomplete in their coverage; only about 70% of households have telephones and the directories usually only list the main householder. They exclude all those who wish to be ex-directory (about 70% in London) or who have opted for mobile phones rather than landlines.

Because of data protection, directory enquiries are very limited in the information they will supply.

SIXTH EDITION.

THE UNITED TELEPHONE COMPANY, LIMITED.

Head Offices:
OXFORD COURT, CANNON STREET, LONDON E.C.

BOARD OF DIRECTORS.

Chairman:
JAMES BRAND, Esq.

Vice-Chairman:
JAMES STAATS FORBES, Esq.
DILLWYN PARISH, Esq.
W. CUTHBERT QUILTER, Esq.
JOHN W. BATTEN, Esq.

Managing Director:
JOSEPH B. MORGAN, Esq.

Secretary:
THOMAS BLAIKIE, Esq.

LIST OF SUBSCRIBERS TO THE EXCHANGE SYSTEM.
UNDER LICENSE FROM THE POSTMASTER-GENERAL.
CLASSIFIED INTO
PROFESSIONS & TRADES.

Subscribers are requested to notify any mistake in their Names, Addresses, Classifications, or Exchange Numbers; and it is most particularly desired that gratuities be not, under any circumstances, offered to the Servants of the Company.
All Communications to be addressed to the Secretary.

September, 1886.

LIFETIMES: ALL AROUND THE HOUSES

DIRECTORIES proved both informative and useful in solving the mystery of the origins of George John Stewart. I knew that his son was supposed to have been born in St George's, Southwark in about 1827, and that when the son married in 1856 he described his father as a coffeehouse keeper, but all further searches for him failed, so I decided to seek the father in directories.

I was delighted to find a listing for a George Stewart in the commercial section of an 1856 directory as coffeehouse keeper, 183 Union Street, Borough, which was in St George's, Southwark. I was fairly sure this was the right entry, so I followed him forwards, checking each year until he disappeared after 1861. However, in 1860 and 1867 there were also entries for a George Stewart owning coffee rooms, 44 High Street, Bow.

This provided addresses for searching in the 1851 and 1861 censuses, but sadly he was not at either address. However, by searching the census returns for the streets around Bow High Street, I located George John R. Stewart, a married 53-year-old listed as a house proprietor, born in Bromley. So here was George with his correct middle name, John, and it seems that he had indeed had a coffeehouse in Southwark, and then opened coffee rooms in Bow, and finally ended up living there.

▽ Mixed company patronise a popular London coffee shop near the 'Olympic' theatre, Wych Street, Strand by Robert & George Cruikshank from *Life in London*, 1820.

CHAPTER NINE
LIVES LESS ORDINARY

If all your family were born within wedlock, married once and stayed happily and faithfully married, you are likely to find tracing your ancestry quite easy – and probably quite boring. Events such as illegitimacy cause great problems to genealogists, but can also prove the most interesting overall.

△ *Forgiven* by Thomas Faed (1826–1900).

FOUNDLINGS

MANY SINGLE or destitute mothers abandoned babies in places where they could be found and cared for. These children often received the Christian name of the parish's patron saint, or the location where they were found, such as Church and Porch. Parish registers may identify foundling children as such. Sadly, you will have little hope of tracing their parentage, but at least you will know you have reached the beginning of the line.

ILLEGITIMACY

People think of illegitimacy as a modern phenomenon, but between 1837 and 1965, some 5–7% of all children born in England and Wales were born out of wedlock and the situation was little different over the preceding centuries. But while illegitimacy no longer carries a social stigma, and we can celebrate the diverse lives of our forbears, it does pose problems for genealogists. If the mother subsequently married, her illegitimate child would often informally adopt the surname of the new husband, whether or not this was its father. This can place you in a Catch-22 situation, looking for the birth of a child whose original surname was that of its mother before her marriage, but you can't find the marriage record because you may not know what the mother's original name was! The solution: to seek other co-ordinates on the family from some of the other sources suggested in this book.

Another problem is that illegitimate children either make up or do not state at all their father's name when asked later in life, such as on General Registration marriage certificates. If the father's name is left blank, you are almost certainly dealing with an illegitimate child. In many cases, however, the illegitimate person did not wish to admit to this fact, and would give inaccurate information. Sometimes they would give the name of a man with the same surname as their own but say the man was dead, or an accountant, lawyer or auctioneer – popular occupations, it seems, for our ancestors' fictitious fathers. Alternatively, they might state the true forename and occupation of the father, but give the man their own surname. These cases offer researchers a ray of hope as other sources can then be searched for men with the right forename and occupation, and then evidence sought to prove they were the true father.

DISCOVERING ILLEGITIMACY

Most illegitimacies come to light from birth certificates, where the father's name is left blank, and the mother is recorded with just her

△ *The Consequences of the Seduction*
by Antoine Beranger (1785–1867).

maiden surname and without a married name. This may mean that the natural father's identity will never be known, but there is always hope. For one reason or another, registrars (and before them, clergymen) would often ask the mother who the real father was, and then suggest (or insist on) giving the baby its father's surname as a middle name. Thus, Herbert Schofield Langan, illegitimate son of Emma Langan, was almost certainly the son of a Mr Schofield, and probably of a man called Herbert Schofield.

Parish clerks were often better able to record the truth than registrars and were more likely to record that a child was illegitimate, 'baseborn' or a 'bastard', sometimes even noting the father's name.

Parish chests (see page 166) may contain bastardy bonds whereby men indemnified the parish against the expense of supporting their illegitimate offspring. From 1576, Justices of the Peace could root out illegitimate children's fathers and issue bastardy orders, which will be in the Quarter Session records (see page 232), requiring them to marry the mother or pay for her child, and if he refused, they could issue maintenance orders to force him to reach into his pocket. Sometimes arguments ensued, with women (or their enraged fathers) pointing the finger, and men – guilty or not – flatly denying any responsibility. These records provide essential information on ancestors' paternity and, in many cases, colourful episodes of family history.

RECTIFYING ILLEGITIMACY

IN THE INSULAR COMMUNITY of manor and parish, direct action was often taken to rectify illegitimacy. Mothers might be locked up or whipped, and fathers forced to marry their pregnant lovers or pay money to the overseers (and this would be recorded in the overseers' accounts) towards the support of their offspring.

LIFETIMES: ORDERS

ROBERT JEFFERIES was baptised on 7 June 1829 at Wroughton, Wiltshire, the illegitimate son of Mary Ann Jefferies. But who was his father? Fortunately for us, the Wroughton churchwardens and overseers of the poor brought the culprit to book at the Quarter Sessions, and the following bastardy order was made:

Mary Ann Jefferies: On the 7th day of March now last past, was delivered of a male bastard child, in the said parish of Wroughton in the county of Wilts, and that the said bastard child is now living the said parish of Wroughton and further that Robert Cook of Roundway in the said county yeoman did beget the said bastard child on the body of her the said Mary Ann Jefferies. And whereas the said Robert Cook hath appeared before us in pursuance of our summons for that purpose, but have not showed any sufficient cause why he should not be the reputed father of the said bastard child, we therefore upon examination of the cause and circumstances of the premises as well as upon the oath of the said Mary Ann Jefferies as otherwise, do hereby adjudge him the said Robert Cook to be the reputed father of the said bastard child.

Cook was ordered to pay the Wroughton vestry £2-16s-00d for Mary Ann's upkeep, and a further 2s a week for the child. But Mary Ann's future was not all roses – she had to pay the vestry a shilling a week for her child's maintenance as well!

A typical bastardy order providing information on a child's paternity.

ADOPTION AND FOSTERING

In most cases, a desire to find one's biological family in no way implies disloyalty towards the adoptive or foster one. Likewise, tracing the ancestry of one's adoptive or foster family is meaningful too. Genetics aside, we inherit many things, such as our accent, social attitudes, mannerisms and so on, from the parents who brought us up and thus from their ancestors, whether or not a blood relationship existed. But for all this, biological ancestors matter to many people as well.

BEFORE 1926

Before the 1926 Adoption Act, which came into effect in January 1927, children were adopted or fostered, often out of workhouses and later foster homes, on an informal basis. Sometimes, if formality was required, a conveyance would be drawn up by a solicitor. They were usually given new surnames under equally informal circumstances, and so their origins can be very hard to trace. Many arrangements were handled by Dr Barnardo's. Dr Barnardo founded his first home for orphaned and destitute children in 1865 and this grew into an organisation which dealt with over 300,000 cases, especially assisting child emigration around the British Empire, until the last home closed in 1981. Records of fostered children appear in poor law and workhouse records and the records of foundling hospitals, such as Thomas Coram's Hospital, whose records are at the London Metropolitan Archives. Information is confidential for 100 years at Barnardo's After-Care Department except to the adopted people concerned. Unfortunately, Barnardo's records are filed under the original birth surname only. If you approach them with the adopted or foster surname and ask for the original one, they will not be able to help you.

To this day, some children are fostered rather than adopted. Records are kept by the local Social Services Department. Those from 1970 onwards all survive. Records of fostering between 1930 and 1969 vary in their survival rate. Theoretically, none survive before 1930. In all cases, however, ask the local Social Services for help. If you are trying to contact someone who was fostered they may be willing to forward a letter from you.

AFTER 1926

From 1927 onwards, adoption was sanctioned by a court order, resulting in the original birth entry at the GRO being annotated with the word 'adopted', and a new birth certificate being issued to the child under their new name(s). The procedure was repeated for re-adoption.

FINDING OUT MORE

Some people are content once they have found their birth certificate. But for many, this is just the start of the quest to find out more about family origins, or even to locate living parents or relatives. Before starting, bear in mind the process may be costly and even unsuccessful. Equally, you might trace biological parents who may not want to know you. They might now have their own partners and even other children, who probably will not know you exist. Your natural parents will probably know that, since 1974, adopted children have had the right to know their biological parents' names, but your re-appearance in their lives may still be a shock, so a sensitive approach is important.

SEEKING AN ADOPTED PERSON

Until 30 December 2005 there was no mechanism for birth mothers or other blood relatives to trace a person who had been adopted out of their family. Now, however, if you are in this situation you can apply to an Intermediary Agency via your local social services. This agency will try to trace and contact the adopted person and, if they agree to be

FAMILY HISTORY

QUITE OFTEN, people who are not particularly interested in tracing family trees ask why anybody should be bothered with such a pastime. In reply, I often cite the cases of adopted or fostered children who want to find out the first generation of their family tree: their biological parents. By understanding this, and then extending the principal backwards in time, it becomes easier to understand how important family trees can be to people.

LIFETIMES: AMOS FOSTER

AMOS FOSTER was 20 when he married in Portsea, Hampshire in 1871. Censuses indicated a birth in Portsmouth, but no birth record could be found. However, a search of the 1851 census revealed an eight-month-old child called Amos Foster in the household of William Cooper. His relationship to the head was described as that of foster child and that, we infer, is exactly how he got his surname.

TRACING NATURAL PARENTS

IF YOU WERE ADOPTED, The first step in tracing natural parents or relations is to obtain a copy of your original birth certificate. Unlike the one you were given when you were adopted, this will provide information about your natural parents. If you have been told your original name, you can seek the certificate through the normal means as described on page 47. If you do not, contact the Registrar General's office at the Office for National Statistics, who will issue you with an application form.

If you were adopted before 12 November 1975, you will need to attend a birth records counselling interview. Ironically, if you were adopted after that date, you will not, though these sessions can be useful in preparing you for the possible traumas of finding unpleasant information and advising you how to proceed should you wish to trace your birth family. Counselling can be obtained locally to where you live and British social services also make it available abroad for those living overseas.

WHAT HAPPENS NEXT

The counsellor will give you a form (CAS 5/6) with which to apply for your original birth certificate and also tell you which court authorised your adoption order as well as giving you a form enabling you to ask the court to tell you which adoption agency or local authority handled your case. Sadly, many court records before 1946 have been thrown away. The court should also have a special report on your adoption, called a *Guardian ad Litem* report. If the court proves unwilling to release this, your counsellor may be able to persuade them to do so by contacting the Lord Chancellor's department.

A number of organisations may have been involved in your case: an adoption society, a local education officer (up to 1948), a children's department (1948–71) or a social services department (1971–84), or even a private individual (up to but not beyond February 1982). Although many adoption societies (and the Mother and Baby Homes which usually referred cases to them) have closed or merged, the records can be traced through G. Stafford's *Where to find Adoption Records*, copies of which are held by NORCAP (see page 93).

Be sure to ask the counsellor if she has any further personal information about your origins or whether any members of your natural family have enquired about you. If your adoption was arranged by the agency from whom you receive the counselling, they should have your complete file (although some were lost in the Second World War). If not, ask the counsellor to contact the organisation that arranged your adoption and ask for your file to be made available to you. If you do not specifically ask for this information, the counsellor may not volunteer it.

The file will be important because it should give you extra clues about your origins, such as your mother's date of birth and normal occupation. If you are lucky, the file will also contain letters and photographs from your birth relatives (ask whether these can be photocopied for the file so you can take away the originals). Remember that you might not learn anything useful from the file or that, if the circumstances leading to your adoption were very traumatic, the counsellor might decide you would be better off not seeing the file at all.

NEW DEVELOPMENTS

An increasing number of adopted children and parents who gave their children up for adoption are being reunited through **www.genesreunited.co.uk**.

contacted, will put you in touch. Even if the adopted person does not want to be contacted, you can still do so under some circumstances. TNA holds the Adopted Children Register, to which access is open, and birth certificates can be bought by any who choose. The register states that the child's adopted name but not the original name. It does, however, state the date of birth, the names and address of the adoptive parents, the date of the adoption order and the name of the court that issued it. Therefore, if you are trying to find out what happened to a child who was adopted, and know their date of birth, you can pay to have every possible entry for the appropriate gender checked for a child with the right birth date. This could cost you a great deal of money but, hopefully, you will only find one, or perhaps a small number of possibilities, to follow up on. A considerable amount of detective work would then be required to determine which, if any, really is the right person – and frankly anybody wanting to do this should think very long and hard about the distress it would very likely cause to the adopted persons and their adoptive families – but that, at any rate, is the method. (See also Where to Search, overleaf.)

MISSING PEOPLE

Attempting to trace a missing person is almost impossible without knowing their name. If this is not known, searches in the General Registration indexes may help or, alternatively, if you are adopted, follow the procedure described overleaf. It also helps to have some idea of how old they were. This section applies equally to seeking birth parents if you are adopted, a distant relation, or an old friend.

CHANGE OF NAME

Except during the Second World War, British subjects have always been able to call themselves anything they want, and change their names as often as their socks, provided there is no intent to commit fraud. However, most people who change their name need proof they have done so and create a deed poll, enrolled in the High Court of Justice and recorded in class J 18 at TNA. Those made before 1903 are in the Close Rolls at TNA. From 1914 it was obligatory to publish deed polls in the *London Gazette*. Many notices were published in newspapers, particularly *The Times* (see page 144). It is also worth consulting W. P. Phillimore and E. A. Fry's *An Index to Changes of Name under Authority of Act of Parliament or Royal Licence and Including Irregular Changes from 1760 to 1901* (GPC, 1968).

YOUR BIRTH CERTIFICATE

AS A TOOL for starting research your birth certificate on its own might be relatively unhelpful. It will give your original name and date and place or birth, and it should also provide your mother's name, address and occupation. Be aware, though, that in many cases the reason for adoption was illegitimacy, and women giving birth to illegitimate children often purposely went somewhere where they were not known in order to give birth, so the place of birth and mother's address might very well bear no relation to her normal home. Also, do not be too surprised if no details of your father are given on the certificate. Since 1875, mothers were not allowed to register the name of their natural child's father without his consent. Equally, little if any information about the father may appear in your adoption file. There are many cases, after all, such as rapes or one-night-stands, when mothers would not even know the forename of the men who made them pregnant. Equally, however, the absence of the father's name from a birth certificate is often because a mother might not have had the name of the father recorded unless she was married to him, or he was present in person to give his consent.

Church baptism records can be an excellent solution – just because the father's name is not on a birth certificate does not mean it will not be on a baptism certificate.

SEEKING A BIRTH RELATIVE

⊡ The first step to take is an easy one and may result in immediate success. Since 1991, the Registrar General has maintained an **Adoption Contact Register** for England and Wales. For a fee of £15, adopted people can register their wish to be put in touch with a birth relative, and birth relatives can register for a fee of £30. If two such people match, the adopted person will be given the name and address (or post box address) of the birth relative.

⊡ A subsidiary register, which has been running for a longer period, is run by the charity **NORCAP**.

⊡ Also contact the other places where birth relatives may already have tried to obtain information about you – the **adoption society** or **local authority** that arranged your adoption and the address given on your original birth certificate (check the electoral roll to see who is now living there before visiting or telephoning).

⊡ Armed with the name of your mother and perhaps of your father too, you are now ready to start searching in earnest (see Missing People, right). If your original birth certificate has been annotated with a Statutory Declaration, this will usually indicate that the husband named on the certificate was not the baby's father, in which case, seek a divorce record.

SCOTLAND

⊡ Adoption records from 1930 are with the **Registrar General of Scotland**.

IRELAND

⊡ The records from 1953 are held at the **General Register Office** and the **Adoption Board**.

For Eire only non-identifying information will be released and original birth certificates are not released. The **Federation of Services for Unmarried Parents and their Children** maintains an unofficial Adoption Contact Register.

NORTHERN IRELAND

⊡ Adoption records from 1931 are on the **Adoption Contact Register** at the General Register Office.

CHANNEL ISLANDS

⊡ The Jersey **Superintendent Registrar** keeps an adoption contact register and will release the original birth certificate after counselling by the Children's Service, who can be contacted via Social Services. For Guernsey, apply for your original birth certificate from **Her Majesty's Greffier** at the General Register Office, which also keeps an Adoption Contact Register.

ISLE OF MAN

⊡ Adoption records are with the **Chief Registrar**.

SEEKING AN ADOPTED PERSON

⊡ Birth relatives can register with the **Adoption Contact Register** and make themselves known to the other organisations listed above.

⊡ The Children's Society will give birth mothers selected information provided it does not enable the children to be traced. They can be contacted at the **Children's Society**'s Post Adoption and Care Project. There is also a society called the **Natural Parents' Network**.

⊡ Other useful organisations are **British Agencies for Adoption & Fostering (BAAF)** and the **Salvation Army**.

MISSING PEOPLE

⊡ The most direct way is to seek missing people in telephone directories and electoral registers (see pages 82 and 164). If you are seeking a woman who might have married, you may be able to guess the year of the wedding by her disappearance from the registers or, if she stayed at the same address, to be sure about the year of her marriage by her change of name.

⊡ If you do not find what you want, then by working back from the present (or forward from the past) you should be able to establish when the person or family you are seeking left. If they only moved a short distance away, a search through the electoral registers may establish a current or more recent address. Note the names of any long-term neighbours; they might be able to tell you what happened to the family you are seeking. If the streets you are searching turn out to be council houses, the local council might allow you access to their re-housing records.

⊡ Try typing the missing persons' name into an internet search engine. The finding tools on page 165 such as **www.eroll.co.uk** and **www.192.com** will often come up with a good list of possibilities.

⊡ General Registration records of birth, marriage and death (see pages 44) can be a valuable tool. There are limits, of course, the most important being that if the person you are tracing was born outside the country, and has neither married or died, they will not appear in them. Equally, they only cover set areas, and if someone decided, say, to get married on holiday abroad, they will not appear in the indexes. However, they can usually be used very effectively.

The most obvious searches to undertake for a missing person are to see if they married (see page 49), or whether they have died (see page 52). Sometimes such searches end in failure. The person you want may have changed their name, or emigrated. You may not be able to find the person you want, but there is no reason why you should not try to find someone else who already knows.

If you know when the person was born, or can make a guess, look through the birth indexes (see page 46). You may find the right entry, or at least a couple of possibilities. These will give you the names of the person's parents, and an address where they lived at the time. They may be alive and still living at the same address.

If not, you could seek their death records and contact the informants, or seek the records of the birth of other children born to the same couple and work forward, seeking their whereabouts. Indeed, the very reason why someone is missing in the first place suggests they may have been restless, or otherwise keen to move or change their lives, whereas their siblings could very well have been the stay-at-home type.

The **GRO**'s 'Alive or Dead' service, free to adopted people or available for a fee at **www.traceline.co.uk**, will help you find out if someone is still alive.

For those who have gone abroad, the Passport Office may hold a forwarding address and foreign embassies hold electoral registers of whose who have emigrated, which can occasionally be useful.

QUICK REFERENCE

ADOPTION CONTACT REGISTER
(England and Wales)
Smedley Hydro
Trafalgar Road
Southport
Merseyside PR8 2HH
☎ 0151 471 4830
www.statistics.gov.uk/registration

NORCAP
112 Church Road
Wheatley
Oxford OX33 1LU
☎ 01865 875000
www.norcap.org.uk

REGISTRAR GENERAL OF SCOTLAND
New Register House
Charlotte Square
Edinburgh EH1 3YT
☎ 0131 334 0380
www.gro-scotland.gov.uk

IRISH GENERAL REGISTER OFFICE
Joyce House
8–11 Lombard Street East
Dublin 2
Eire
☎ 00 353 1 635 4000
www.groireland.ie

ADOPTION BOARD
Shelbourne House
Shelbourne Road
Ballsbridge
Dublin 4
Eire
☎ 00 353 1 667 1392
www.adoptionboard.ie

FEDERATION OF SERVICES FOR UNMARRIED PARENTS AND THEIR CHILDREN
The Adopted Peoples Association
27 Templeview Green
Clare Hall
Dublin 13
Eire
☎ 00 353 1 868 3020
www.adoptionireland.com

ADOPTION CONTACT REGISTER
(Northern Ireland)
General Register Office
Oxford House
49–55 Chichester Street
Belfast BT1 4HL
Northern Ireland
☎ 028 9025 2000
www.groni.gov.uk

For Channel Islands and Isle of Man addresses, see page 311

CHILDREN'S SOCIETY
Post Adoption and Care Project
91–93 Queen's Road
Peckham
London SE15 2EZ
☎ 020 7732 9089
www.the-childrens-society.org.uk

NATURAL PARENTS' NETWORK
Garden Suburb
Oldham
Lancashire OL8 3AY
☎ 01273 307597
www.n-p-n.fsnet.co.uk

BRITISH AGENCIES FOR ADOPTION & FOSTERING (BAAF)
Skyline House
200 Union Street
London SE1 0LY
☎ 020 7593 2000
www.baaf.org.uk

SALVATION ARMY
Social Work Department
101 Newington Causeway
London SE1 6BN
☎ 0845 634 0101
www.salvationarmy.org.uk

G. I. Trace helps children of the American G. I's who came to Britain in the Second World War.
www.gitrace.org

LIFETIMES: REVEALING ALL

IT WAS KNOWN that Peter Critchley left his wife and children in Warrington, Lancashire, and emigrated to America. He was at last located in www.ancestry.com's index of the 1920 census of Manhattan, which shows Peter Crotzly, engineer, 69, married, who immigrated in 1878 and was naturalised in 1890: both he and his parents were born in England. This entry corresponds with an entry in the 1900 census for Manhattan for Peter Critchley, engineer, 50, who immigrated in 1879. Meanwhile, his abandoned wife Eunice remarried, in 1883 – saying she was a widow!

DIVORCE ...

Until 1858, divorce could only be obtained by a private act of Parliament. Records of the 318 successful cases prior to 1858 are at the House of Lords Record Office and TNA. The process was way beyond most people, but quarrelling couples could go to church courts to seek annulment on the grounds that one party was a bigamist or (from 1754) had married below 21 years of age without parental consent. They could also grant a decree of separation *a mensa et thoro*, which released a spouse from the obligation to live with a violent or adulterous partner. Usually, a couple wishing to separate simply did so unofficially, and if one of them wished to remarry, they went elsewhere and hoped their bigamous union would not be found out. In 1858 divorces became much more easily obtainable, through the Court for Divorce and Matrimonial Causes, but it was not until 1923 that women were accorded equal rights with men.

Wife selling, whereby a cuckolded husband sold his wife to her lover at the local market, was without legal basis, but because it was done so publicly it had the effect of protecting the first husband from his wife's debts, and the new 'husband' from any further action from the original one. There are only a few hundred recorded cases but newspapers can provide a useful source for many such shenanigans.

In Scotland, church courts could dissolve marriages as in England and Wales, but divorces were much easier to obtain, on grounds of adultery or desertion, through the Commissary Court of Edinburgh from 1536 to 1830 and thereafter from the Court of Sessions.

... AND BIGAMY

It is impossible to tell how widespread bigamy, the illegal marriage of a person while their spouse is still alive, ever was. It is, however, something that may crop up from time to time in your research. When discovered, bigamy was punished in ecclesiastical (see page 231) and, latterly, civil courts (see page 226), and may appear in local newspapers (see page 144).

EVACUEES

During the Second World War, evacuated children were placed with families on an entirely informal basis. When they got off the train they were just farmed out willy-nilly, without any formal records being kept.

QUICK REFERENCE

See also main sources in Useful Addresses, page 306

PRINCIPAL REGISTRY OF THE FAMILY DIVISION
First Avenue House
42–49 High Holborn
London WC1V 6NP
☎ 020 7947 6980
www.courtservice.gov.uk

LAMBETH PALACE LIBRARY
Lambeth Palace Road
London SE1 7JU
☎ 020 7898 1400
www.lambethpalacelibrary.org

DIVORCE

⊟ The only divorces available before 1858 were by private Act of Parliament. These (and all Acts of Parliament) are searchable on **www.a2a.org.uk**).

⊟ Records for 1858–1943 are at **TNA** (class J 77), and searchable through **www.catalogue.nationalarchives. gov.uk**, although few for 1937–43 survive. Those after 1943 are held by the **Principal Registry of the Family Division**, who will search them for a fee: see L. Stone's *Road to Divorce – England 1530–1987* (OUP, 1990). Access to the files themselves is closed for the last 75 years except to either party concerned. You can apply for a form or turn up in person and have the search done immediately.

⊟ The Court of Arches, whose records are at **Lambeth Palace Library** (and indexed in J. Houston's *Cases in the Court of Arches 1660–1913* (BRS 85, 1972)), contains 1400 cases of marital squabbling, which may include your ancestor.

⊟ Divorce records for 1858–1903 are indexed at **www.findmypast.com**.

SCOTLAND

⊟ Scottish divorce records from 1560 are with the **National Archives of Scotland**.

IRELAND

⊟ In Ireland, separations were granted through the church courts until 1870, then responsibility passed to the Irish High Court. Divorce proper still had to be sought though Act of Parliament until 1939, when British divorce law was first applied to Northern Ireland. Civil divorce was forbidden in Southern Ireland until 1995: records are only available to the parties themselves.

PERHAPS THE MOST EXTRAORDINARY CASE of tracing a missing person with which I have been involved was a request that came to me from a private detective, who phoned me at lunchtime on 20 March 1996. A Catholic knight had been legally married to an English Catholic divorcee for many long and happy years, but now she was dying. A friend of his, a very high-ranking Catholic clergyman, reminded him that unless the couple were married in a Catholic church they would not be regarded as husband and wife in the eyes of the Almighty. The only way to do this was if the woman's first husband was dead, making her (in Catholic eyes) a widow. The trouble was, they had no idea what had happened to the first husband: he could have gone anywhere in the world in the last 50 years.

The woman's first marriage record gave the age of her first husband and his father's name . A search for his birth certificate in England and Wales failed to reveal it, so we looked in Scotland and there it was. Now we knew his date of birth and parents' names, we could proceed with confidence to seek his death certificate, in Scotland. We started in the year of the divorce, and worked forwards, on and on, until we came so close to the present we were beginning to think he was probably alive and that the hopes of the elderly Catholic couple would be dashed. But then, when hope had almost faded to nothing, we found a reference and obtained a certificate that included details of the parents' names, which corresponded exactly with what we had already found about the first husband. And then I noticed the date and time of death – lunchtime on 20 March 1996.

CHAPTER TEN
PARISH RECORDS

The first generally useful census was taken in 1841 and General Registration began in 1837. To trace information from before these years, family historians rely on different sorts of records, mostly based around the church and many kept by parishes and manors.

In the early Middles Ages, manorial lords would keep a priest in their household, and usually ended up building a separate chapel for them to say Mass. Out of the lord's manorial landholdings grew the parishes, and from the private chapels developed parish churches.

Many parish registers were kept during the Middle Ages, but sadly none survive outside the Vatican Archives, whence many were sent by anxious priests during the Reformation. Very few of these registers are identified by place and access to them is not allowed.

Before 1830 there were some 11,000 parishes in England and Wales. Since then, many new parishes have been created out of older, larger ones, with former 'chapels of ease' (built to save parishioners' lengthy journeys to the parish church) becoming parish churches in their own right. The parish was run by a clergyman, or incumbent, either a vicar, rector or parson. When clergymen had more than one parish, they either neglected their duties in one or paid a curate to undertake the work on their behalf. The clergyman or curate's work of baptising, marrying and burying resulted in one of the most important genealogical tools, parish registers (PRs).

Below the clergyman was a council called the vestry and also a staff of parish officials, who performed many of the functions that had been performed before the Reformation by manorial officials. They generated a wealth of records relating to our ancestors, known by their traditional place of storage, the parish chest (see page 166).

PARISH REGISTERS

Parish registers to which access is permitted date from 1538 and consist of baptisms, marriages and burials. We normally turn to PRs once we have gone as far back as we can through General Registration records and census returns, and indeed the latter will indicate in which parish you will need to search. Baptism records provide parents' names, which lead back to searches for marriages. Marriage records do not provide ages or parents' names, so we use the ages usually

▽ *The Christening* by Francis Wheatley (1747–1801).

△ *Thomas Cromwell, Earl of Essex* by Hans Holbein (1497/8–1543). Cromwell was the creator of the parish register and thus a posthumous hero of family historians.

recorded in burial registers to ascertain when our ancestors would have been baptised. By working back step by step, it is sometimes possible to trace back to the 16th century unaided by any other categories of records. But because PRs are not always very informative, genealogists end up seeking further co-ordinates on their ancestors from sources such as manorial records, wills and so on.

According to Steve Thomas, the registers of Tipton, Staffordshire, date from 1513 and Altham, Lancashire, from 1518, with some 18 more just predating 1538. In that year Thomas Cromwell, Vicar-General to Henry VIII, inadvertently laid the foundations of modern English genealogy by issuing orders to all parish clergy to keep registers of baptisms, marriages and burials. Unfortunately, most were kept on paper and have been lost to damp, rats, fire or flood, so only a small proportion of registers date from 1538. In 1558, orders were issued for registers to be kept on parchment, and the survival rate increases rapidly, though in general terms relatively few have survived from before 1600.

While the Anglican church was a religious institution, it was also a branch of the state and if anyone, except Quakers and Jews, wanted

WHERE TO SEARCH

PARISH REGISTERS

⊟ The location of the registers of all parishes that existed up to 1832 is given in *The Phillimore Atlas and Index of Parish Registers* (Phillimore, 2003) together with details of their coverage (or lack of it) by indexes, including the **IGI** (see page 110). Most are in **county record offices**, but some are still at the **parish churches** to which they relate, so you will need to write to the incumbent and ask for a search, or make an appointment to do so yourself. Much more detailed coverage is given in the county record offices' own catalogues, now available on **www.A2A.org.uk**.

⊟ The alternative is to use bishops' transcripts (see page 114) instead. Most registers are now in county or city record offices, which will also hold many of the records described in the rest of this book. Before visiting a record office, telephone or check its website, as in most cases it is necessary to book, sometimes well in advance.

⊟ It can, however, be easier and cheaper to pay a record searcher to examine a **PR** instead of visiting the record office yourself.

⊟ Many new parishes were created by dividing up old ones after 1832, five years before General Registration began. The **SoG**'s *National Index of Parish Registers* series provides in-depth details of all PRs, including the post-1832 parishes.

⊟ Many **PR**s have been indexed in the **IGI**, available on the internet at **www.familysearch.org** (see page 110) or studied on microfilm or fiche at a Mormon Family History Centre.

⊟ Many **PR**s have been transcribed. Brief details of coverage are in the *Phillimore Atlas* (Phillimore, 2003) with more detail in the *National Index of Parish Registers*: collections for each county will be in the relevant **county record offices**. Many transcriptions have the advantage of an index. Remember that these are finding aids, not primary sources and are subject to the same shortcomings as any non-original document – transcriber and indexer-error.

⊟ **http://freereg.rootsweb.com/** is a growing free database of parish register entries 1538–1837 and some are now appearing on commercial sites.

QUICK REFERENCE
See main sources in Useful Addresses, page 306

PLEASE REMEMBER that baptisms are not the same as births (nor are burials), deaths and you should record them as such in family trees, i.e.:

'John Smith, bpt. [or chr.] 2 April 1790, Dawlish, Devon'.

If you see a family tree showing people born before 1837, be aware that it could have been compiled by someone with very little knowledge of the subject.

BAPTISMS

See Where to Search: Parish registers, page 97

legal proof of their marriages and their children's ages and legitimacy, they had no choice but to have Anglican marriages and baptisms. Equally, until relatively recently, there were very few places to bury a body except for the ancient, consecrated ground of parish churches, so most people, Anglican, atheist, agnostic and non-conformist alike, lie buried in parish church yards. It is often helpful, therefore, to think of PRs not so much as religious records, but as civil ones.

BAPTISMS

These provide the date of baptism, name of the child and the father's full name. In the 16th and early 17th centuries, parents' names were sometimes not recorded, reducing genealogical research to a guessing-game, although hopefully other sources such as manorial records (see page 118) will have survived to provide further co-ordinates. Mothers' Christian names usually appear from the 17th century. Between 1780 and 1812, mothers' maiden names appear fairly often and, as the 18th century progressed, it became more usual to record the child's date of birth as well. Fathers' occupations and places of residence within the parish were often recorded.

In 1812, Rose's Act introduced printed registers with spaces requiring:

➤ **Date of baptism**
➤ **Name of child**

▽ An original baptism certificate issued by the incumbent of St Mary, Newington. Such documents sometimes turn up in family papers.

When Baptized.	Child's Christian Name.	Parents' Name.		Abode.	Quality, Trade, or Profession.	By whom the Ceremony was performed.
		istian	Surname.			
1787 Nov. 26, Born Oct. 25. 1787	William S. of	Richard & Margaret	Goodwin			

The above is a true Copy of the Baptism Register of the Parish aforesaid, extracted this *13* Day of *July* in the Year One Thousand Eight Hundred and *Twenty five*

> **Name, residence and occupation of father and Christian name of mother,** all of which are excellent for genealogy, but removed most of the optional extra information, which many clergymen had been recording.

If the child was too ill to be bought to church, it might be privately baptised at home. The register entry may record this as 'P' or 'Priv', and when the child was finally brought to church for a public ceremony, the register entry might be annotated 'rec'd' or 'received into the church'.

MARRIAGES

Marriages before 1754 gave the date of marriage and the Christian and surnames of both parties. Additional information was sometimes given, such as groom's occupation, bride's father's name and whether the marriage was by banns or licence. Marriages usually took place in the bride's parish, but those by licence might take place in the town where the licence was issued.

On 25 March 1754, Hardwicke's Marriage Act came into force and remained so until 1837. Marriages had now to take place (with certain exceptions) in the bride or groom's parish by an Anglican clergyman, either after banns had been read in both parties' home parishes for three Sundays running, or on production of a marriage licence. Jews and Quakers were not obliged to comply, but everyone else had to, regardless of denomination. Boys could still marry at 14 and girls at 12, but parental consent was required for all under 21. Marriages were now to be recorded in a separate register (until then they were usually listed with the baptisms and burials, sometimes neatly separated, other times jumbled up together), with a form requiring:
> **Date**
> **Names of both parties**
> **Whether they had been married before** ('bach[elor]', 'spin[ster]', 'wid[ow/er]').
> **Whether married by banns or licence**
> **Parish of residence** ('otp' means 'of this parish', 'soj[ourner]' meant someone who had only recently settled there).
> **Signatures or marks of both parties**
> **Names and signatures of two witnesses,** who would usually be siblings of the bride and groom.

Generally, the printed forms prevented any extra comments which clergy might have been tempted to make – but some still did: the registers of St Mary, Lewisham, around 1803, for example, contain many marriages of people not from that parish. To satisfy the law they had

SOME CLERGYMEN made their own rules, such as Rev. Thomas Patten, Vicar of Seasalter, Kent, from Cote, Somerset, who served as Vicar of Seasalter and Curate of Whitstable from 1712 until his death on 9 October 1764. When Edward Tried and Mary Aeres married at Seasalter on 12 November 1737(?) we learn that:

'a Bowl of Punch was made almost as big as the Caspian.'

Another of his gems was:

'Little Osiah Oakham and Sarah Slater, both of Seasalter, were married by License, September 27 1744. Sarah was his first wife's sister... and now very pregnant.'

△ An original marriage certificate showing the wedding of my 4 x great-grandparents William Hammond and Emma Ayres, on 10 June 1815, only eight days before the Battle of Waterloo.

been resident there for three weeks – or so they claimed – and were officially 'of this parish'. But next to their signatures or marks the incumbent wrote their real parishes of residence – from as far afield as Sussex and Birmingham. As someone who hates filling in forms, I say hurrah for the incumbent of Lewisham!

Ancestors also appear in marriage registers as witnesses. If they do, there is a good chance they may be related to one of the two parties, indicating wider family connections than you suspected. Such references may also provide useful evidence that an ancestor was alive on that date. Be aware, though, that some people were regular witnesses – if you see them witnessing several marriages on the same day, they probably were not related to either party at all.

From July 1837, civil registration marriage certificates were used both in and outside of parish churches.

Marriage licences, allegations and bonds

Marriage licences, which originated in the 14th century, enabled marriages to take place immediately – especially if the girl was pregnant – but were more usually obtained as status symbols for those who thought it above their dignity to have banns read out in front of the hoi polloi.

Apart from some issued by the Archbishop of Canterbury, which allowed the marriage to take place anywhere, marriage licences would specify one of two places, theoretically the parties' home parishes. But in practice at least one was often the parish in which the couple were staying at the time for a minimum of four weeks (after 1753) or 15 days (after 1823).

Licences may be found in family papers but were more often handed in to the officiating priest. What survive in record offices are more usually the associated bonds (until 1823) and allegations. An allegation was a statement made by the prospective groom swearing that both parties were free to marry, usually stating names, ages, places of residence, marital status, groom's occupation, where the couple intended to get married and name of consenting parent of either party under 21. Be aware that, between September 1822 and March 1823 only, both couples had to produce evidence of baptism or an equivalent certificate proving their age: these will be found with the allegation and are well worth seeking.

A bond was made stating a sum of money to be forfeited should the information on the allegation (especially regarding the parties' freedom to marry) be found to be incorrect. There were two bondsmen, one of

BANNS OF MARRIAGE

THE READING or 'calling' of banns was a means of preventing bigamous or clandestine marriages, dating back to 1215. They were either recorded in the same register or in a separate banns book. These may state the parishes of residence of both parties, so they can lead you from the groom's parish to the one in which he married, or from the parish of marriage back to the groom's original parish.

MARRIAGES

See also Where to Search: Parish registers, page 97.

Licences were issued by broadly the same ecclesiastical authorities that proved wills (see page 124) and are generally found in **county record offices**. Their whereabouts are outlined in detail in J. Gibson's *Bishops' Transcripts and Marriage Licences, Bonds and Allegations: A Guide to their Location and Indexes* (FFHS, 1997). This also lists the many indexes and calendars available

If the bride and groom lived in different dioceses within the same archdiocese, licences were issued by the relevant Vicar-General. Those for York are at the **Borthwick Institute** and those for Canterbury are at **Lambeth Palace Library** and indexed (surnames only) 1694–1850 on **www.englishorigins.com**, along with Faculty Office licences 1701–1850.

York Faculty Office marriage allegations from 1567, the originals of which have been lost, were copied by Paver, published by the Yorkshire Archaeological Society and are included in Boyd's marriage index (see page 114).

If the two parties lived in different dioceses they were issued by the Archbishop of Canterbury's Faculty Office. These are especially useful because of the wide range of people and places they cover, and are partially covered by published indexes. None for the Isle of Man.

Most licences have been thrown away, but some collections of original licences survive, notably those collected by Frederick Crisp from some 20,000 London parish churches and held at the **IHGS** and some at the **SoG**.

www.englishorigins.net has an index to marriage licence allegations 1694–1850 containing some 670,000 names.

Although many Irish marriage licences were blown up in 1922, **TNA** in Kew hold indexes made before that date, which provide names and dates of bonds for most of Ireland except for Derry, and it also holds abstracts of licences collected together after the bombing.

Marriage licences that concern landed families are often found in family papers, record offices and there are also many in the manuscripts section of the **British Library**, and more still collected and abstracted by Frederick Crisp in *Fragmenta Genealogica, Vol. 11*. They are sometimes referred to and abstracted in family wills ('whereas by a deed of settlement dated ...').

Many irregular marriages were not recorded at all, and many that were have been lost. For those London ones that have survived, see T. Benton's *Irregular Marriages in London before 1754* (SoG, 1993). Many (for London and elsewhere) will be recorded perfectly normally in PRs but, unlike the angry parents or guardians of the parties concerned, you have access to marriage indexes which in many cases will reveal the unexpected location of the event.

The location of elopement records is detailed in *Family Tree Magazine*, December 1981, updated in March 1994, since when the **IHGS** acquired four registers from Lang's house at Springfield near Gretna Green.

QUICK REFERENCE
See also main sources in Useful Addresses, page 306

BORTHWICK INSTITUTE FOR ARCHIVES
University of York
Heslington
York YO10 5DD
☎ 01904 321166
www.york.ac.uk/inst/bihr

LAMBETH PALACE LIBRARY
Lambeth Palace Road
London SE1 7JU
☎ 020 7898 1400
www.lambethpalacelibrary.org

WHERE TO SEARCH

them usually the groom, the other often a relative (perhaps the bride's father) or a good friend, and provided similar information to the allegation.

Remember that licences were issued to facilitate marriages but are not evidence that a marriage took place: the couple may have had a last-minute change of heart, or one or both may have dropped dead.

LIFETIMES: A RARE FIND

ACCORDING TO the parish registers of Kildale, North Riding of Yorkshire, George Lincoln of Kildale, farmer, married Elizabeth Smith of Kildale, by licence, on 19 February 1765. The corresponding marriage bond, dated 18 February 1765, issued by the Archbishop of York, states that George was 37 and Elizabeth 29. To find the ages of a couple marrying at this time is very rare and was a great help in finding their origins.

Marriage settlements

These were deeds signed before weddings arranging for the future ownership of property. Parents might settle property or income on one of the two parties marrying (often as a dowry); grooms (or their families) would guarantee property or income for their brides. They provide excellent details not only of who was getting married and when, but also names of relatives on both sides, family friends and the location and nature of lands held.

Irregular and clandestine marriages

Before Hardwicke's Marriage Act (1753), and despite the Anglican church's disapproval, unions between two parties were regarded as legal under Common Law provided both parties consented and exchanged vows, regardless of whether witnesses, priests or anybody else were present. Sadly, these generated no records for genealogists.

Before 1754 there were also clandestine or irregular marriages. Irregular marriages took place by banns or licence, but away from one of the spouses' home parishes, or in private houses, or at times of the year when marriages were not supposed to take place, such as Lent.

Clandestine marriages were those conducted in secret, away from the parties' home parishes. This happened for many reasons, such as an apprentice wishing to marry without waiting until his seven-year term of apprenticeship had expired; an heir or heiress desirous of marrying without their guardian's consent; widows wishing to receive income from their deceased husband's estate yet have a new husband into the bargain; couples in a very great hurry to have sex – and, of course, aspiring bigamists. Both would be conducted by priests on receipt of a backhander, often on production of a corruptly obtained marriage licence.

These practises were brought to a halt by Hardwicke's Marriage Act. However, the Act did not apply to Scotland and the Channel Islands, whither many of the English couples who might have tried the Fleet Prison (see box, opposite) now eloped. Scotland's Gretna Green was the most popular, although this was only one of many such marriage houses. An Act of 1856, declaring such run-away marriages illegal unless the couple had resided in Scotland for at least three weeks, led to a great decline in the popularity of Gretna Green and its neighbours.

△ **Many couples opted for less conventional forms of marriage as depicted in *The Elopement* by George Morland (1763–1804).**

IN LONDON, many clandestine marriages took place around the Fleet Prison; St James, Dukes Place; Holy Trinity, Minories; St Pancras; St Botolph, Aldgate; St Katherine by the Tower; St Dunstan, Stepney and May Fair Chapel. In the decades leading up to 1754, increasing numbers of marriages were taking place in and around the Fleet Prison, a debtors' prison which claimed to be exempt from ecclesiastical law, and which numbered many corrupt priests among its inmates and visitors.

The marriages were recorded in numerous registers and notebooks, one of which is at the Bodleian Library, Oxford, with the others at TNA in class RG 7. They have been partly transcribed, indexed and published in M. Herber's *Clandestine Marriages in the Chapel and Rules of the Fleet Prison 1680–1754* (Francis Boutle Publishers). These often-neglected sources should always be borne in mind, for families from London and all over the country. Be aware that some of the entries may be partial forgeries indicating, for example, that a marriage took place before it really did, or even a complete fabrication paid for by fortune-seekers wishing to claim they were married to heiresses they had never even met.

BURIALS

Burial entries can help in seeking wills, but their main use is in providing ages, which in turn indicate a year of birth and thus an indication of when a baptism might have taken place. The records provide the names of the deceased and date of burial. As the 17th century progressed, it became more usual than before to add extra details, such as age, place of residence and occupation. Married women were often described as 'wife of X' and widows were described as such, with or without the deceased husband's name. The father's name was usually provided in cases of deceased children. 'P' denoted a pauper.

From 1666 we have burials in wool. To revive the flagging English wool industry, Charles II ordered that all corpses be wrapped in woollen shrouds, hence the notes 'buried in wool', 'P' – paupers were exempt – or 'aff[idavit]' next to burial entries, the latter denoting an affidavit sworn before a JP that a woollen shroud had indeed been used. Some survive, usually providing a close relative's name. There was a £5 fine for disobedience and it became a status symbol to pay the fine and use a

WHERE TO SEARCH

BURIALS

See Where to Search: Parish registers, page 97

LIFETIMES: QUACKS AND TRAMMELLERS

BESIDES OR INSTEAD OF what they were supposed to record, parish clergy and clerks sometimes made comments of their own. These can be wonderful finds, and remind us too how essential it is to check original register entries of events found through indexes.

Leek, Staffordshire, marriage 10 February 1707/8
  'Thomas Bowler of Ashbourne, Quack Pharmachopolar to Ellin Thorpe of Leek a widow.'
This a man who made drugs, the term coming from the book he used, a pharmacopoeia.

Manuden, Essex, 31 December 1847
  'John Bush farmer of Manuden aged 48 hung himself on Friday Dec 24th.'
A sad story for Christmas.

Eglingham, Northumberland
  'John Morpeth, W[est] Lilburn, South Sheds, Baptised 26 August 1803, born 15 August 2nd but 1st in Wedlock of John & Eleanor Morpeth Farmers there under N. Collingwood Esq. Her maiden name was Ormston.'
The detailed northeastern entries for this period can be highly informative.

  'John Housdon, widower, a young gape-mouth'd lazy fellow and Hannah Matthews, Hotupont, an old toothless wriggling Hagg, both of Faversham, were trammel'd by licence at the cathedral of Seasalter, June 6th, 1744.'
NB: It was not a cathedral: the incumbent was delightfully short of his marbles.

These entries from the Walloon or Stranger's church in Canterbury clearly map the migration of Gervais Despagne from Lisle to Canterbury after the birth of Andre and before the birth of Marie:
  'Août 14 1603 Andre Despagne, filz de fue Geruois, natif de Lisle, et Marie Pancouq, fille de fue Noel, natifue de Ypres' and *'Jan 10 1607/8 Michel le Clerc, vefu, natif de Ham, et Marie d,Espanne, fille de fue Geruoys, natifue de Canturbery,'*

silk shroud instead. The Act was generally ignored after the 1770s. Rose's Act of 1812 provided forms requiring:
➢ Date
➢ Name
➢ Residence
➢ Age
This is all useful information, but again we lose the odd extra notes, which could bring colour to earlier entries.

PR TRANSCRIPTS

Transcripts of PRs, made at any time from the last century to the present day (but more so before the advent of the internet), can be found in county record offices. They are often a compilation of the original register and the bishops' transcripts, so what the transcript says might not be a verbatim quote from either of the original sources, and of course, like anything else, errors and omissions can creep in. An advantage of the PR transcripts is that they are often indexed, enabling speedy searches.

PARISH RECORDS OUTSIDE ENGLAND AND WALES

SCOTLAND

The vast majority of Scottish PRs are at New Register House and available on **www.scotlandspeople.gov.uk**, with a few others and copies of many local ones at the regional register offices. Maps showing the location of the approximately 900 Scottish PRs are included in the *Phillimore Atlas and Index* (Phillimore, 2003).

One of the great problems of Scottish research is that registers tend to start more recently than English ones and, even when they survive, they are easily as incomplete as their counterparts south of the border. A few survive from the 16th century but most have only survived from the very late 17th century or early–mid-18th century, and one down-side of having no bishops was that there are no bishops' transcripts (see page 114).

A plus is that the registers are usually slightly more detailed. Women did not automatically change their names on marriage, so their maiden names tend to appear in the registers. Births were often recorded instead of baptisms, but where baptisms appear, you may well find godparents recorded too.

In Scotland, married women kept their maiden names by law. Until the 20th century, most marriages took place at the bride's house or the local manse, after the proclamation of banns. It is the proclamations, rather than the marriage itself, that you will often find recorded in the registers of *both* parties' parishes. If the marriage did not then take place, the forfeit of the cautionary bond may appear in the Kirk Sessions.

IRELAND

Ireland originally consisted of the four provinces of Connaught, Leinster, Munster and Ulster. These were divided into 32 counties, 325 baronies,

---

LIFETIMES: INTERESTING INTERMENTS

THE PARISH REGISTERS of Rushbrooke, Suffolk, include the burial of one of the most influential, yet little-known, statesmen of the 17th century, the probable secret second husband of Queen Henrietta Maria and maybe even the real father of Charles II. The entry reads:

'The Right Honorble Henry Jermyn Earle of St Alban was Buried in the South side of the Chancel Janry 10 1683. because he was Buried in Linnen contrary to an Act for Burying in woolen only therefore by Order of A warrant from a Justice of the Peace fifty shillings as Paid to the Informer and fifty shillings to the Poor of the Parish upon the Sunday next following.'

Our loopy friend Rev. Patten of Seasalter (see page 99) couldn't resist a few comments in his burial register. One is of an old man who: *'Lived 40 years in a little cottage near the sea-side. He was 78 years old. And, when he was happy, always sung.'* And another is about Martha Chamber, *'the most accomplish'd woman that ever liv'd in a Country Hole'*. That was the last time he bothered to record a burial – thereafter he simply noted the death of the odd aristocrat from the newspapers.

GENERALLY, AN ENTRY from an original entry will be as follows:

DAVID BEECHAM

Male	Death:
Event(s):	Burial:
Birth:	Parents:
Christening: 27 MAR 1842	Father: THOMAS BEECHAM
Kirton In Holland, Lincoln,	Mother: ANN
England	

Messages: Extracted birth or christening record for locality listed in the record. The source records are usually arranged chronologically by the birth or christening date.

These will probably be derived from original sources but remember that they may be inaccurate and will almost certainly not contain all the information (occupations, previous marital status and so on) in the original register. In contrast to the foregoing are entries from private submitters, which should always set alarm bells ringing, such as:

SILVESTER SALISBURY

Male	Christening:
Event(s):	Death: About 1690
Birth: About 1629, England	Burial:

Messages: Record submitted after 1991 by a member of the LDS Church. No additional information is available. Ancestral File may list the same family and the submitter. 'About' is generally a euphemism for 'I don't know', and the idea that someone thought Sylvester (the spelling of his Christian name varies, as we can see) was probably born around 1629 in England is scarcely going to help you. But that's not the only entry for him in the IGI. Here is another:

SYLVESTER SALISBURY

Male	
Event(s):	Christening:
Birth: 1629 Albany, Albany,	Death: About 1680
New York	Burial:

Messages: Record submitted after 1991 by a member of the LDS Church. No additional information is available. Ancestral File may list the same family and the submitter.

Equally unimpressive and, as we shall see, a complete shot in the dark. Here is yet another entry:

SILVESTER SALISBURY

Male	Death:
Event(s):	Burial:
Birth:	Parents:
Christening: 07 SEP 1631	Father: ROBERT SALISBURY
Swepstone, Leicester,	Family
England	Mother: MARY

Messages: Record submitted after 1991 by a member of the LDS Church. No additional information is available. Ancestral File may list the same family and the submitter. That looks much more reliable, doesn't it? But beware, it is still a private submission and it turns out that it is actually an entry for what the submitter thought the original register ought to say. In fact, Sylvester is clearly stated in the original register to be 'the supposed and reputed sonn of Robert Burgeland and Mary Salisbury'.

So, the IGI helped by directing us to Swepstone, but it would have been a disaster if the entry had been accepted without checking the original.

However, do not dismiss the false entries entirely. Through the website you may be able to order copies of the original submission or contact the submitter: in some cases the information may turn out to be highly accurate and derived from a rare source, such as original family papers. Even if the information turns out to be wrong, though, you may still end up contacting a long-lost (if a little misguided) cousin as a result!

➤ **The IGI** has various criteria for searching. You can seek all references to a surname in a certain country (Great Britain and the whole of Ireland can be searched in one go) but, if the surname is a very popular one, you can 'filter' your search on the CD version to cover only one county, although bear in mind that if an event took place just over a county border, you will miss it.

theoretically covered by the IGI or not. If you base any decisions or any aspects of your family tree solely on the presence or absence of entries in the IGI, you are almost certainly to come a cropper.

➤**The IGI is helpful in grouping variant spellings of surnames together,** but be aware that the groupings are ultimately random and the variant under which your ancestor was recorded might not have been picked up by the indexers, so will appear on its own under its own individual spelling. Be creative when entering possible variants: scribble the name down and then think of ways it could be misread, or mumble it to someone and ask them to say what they thought you said. The surname Coldbreath, for example, exists in Sussex, and puzzled me for ages, so I started going around mumbling it to people in various different accents and then asking them what they thought I had said. Finally, someone said 'Galbraith?'. I looked up the Scottish surname Galbraith and, to my delight, found that Coldbreath was indeed listed as a recognised variant.

➤**As with all indexes, the entries are only as good as the people who copied them,** and there are many omissions and mistranscriptions (such as John Thomas baptised at Hexham being indexed as John Thomas Hexham, and so on). To make matters worse, in a somewhat misguided move in 1992, the Mormons allowed private researchers to submit their own information, some based on accurate sources, such as family bibles, and some derived from pure fantasy (see box, opposite).

➤**Until recently, Wales was like many Scandinavian, Eastern European and non-European countries for its continued use of patronymics that changed with each generation** (see page 285). The IGI on CD enables you to search a region and time frame for the birth of anyone with a particular forename. Say your Welsh ancestor was Evan Jones, born about 1850. His father might have been called Jones as well, or Evan could literally have been 'son of John', so his father would have had a different patronymic surname, according to his father's name, such as John Thomas, resulting in Evan's baptism being entered as 'Evan son of John Thomas'. Without knowing in advance who John's father was, you would not know that you had to look under Thomas, not Jones. With the IGI's help, though, you can see a list of possible baptisms for boys called Evan, which you can then explore in the original records.

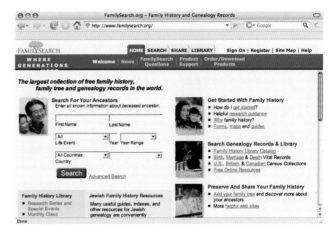

△ The familysearch website home page: www.familysearch.org.

YOU CAN FIND all the IGI entries for a surname from a particular parish using the website
http://tinyurl.com/8dkr
Click on the county; find the parish you want; select the batch you want, and click on it. Then enter the surname you want in the top right-hand box and press 'submit query'. All the entries will appear. Fantastic!

A NEW TRICK

NIEUW AMSTERDAM OFTE NUE NIEUW IORX OPT T.EYLA...

CAPTAIN SYLVESTER SALISBURY was a 17th-century soldier who went to America in 1664 to help capture New Amsterdam from the Dutch and turn it into New York. Sylvester settled nearby at Albany, leaving a son, Francis, who subsequently produced many descendants, still living there today.

But who was he? American descendants enthusiastically tried to turn him into a younger son of Cadwalladr Salisbury of Llyweni, the scion of an extraordinary and very well-documented family claiming descent from Adam de Salzberg, grandson of Eberhard, the deposed duke of Eastern Bavaria, who came to England with William the Conqueror. However, no amount of searching among the wills and muniments of the Salisburys of Llyweni

△ New Amsterdam, now New York, destination of the intrepid Sylvester.

produced even the slightest mention of him – and no wonder. His baptism, albeit inaccurately entered, finally turned up in a routine search of the IGI (see page 111) and the original register entry told us that he was baptised on 7 September 1631 at Swepstone, Leicestershire, 'the supposed and reputed sonn of Robert Burgeland and Mary Salisbury'. Mary was herself baptised there on 9 March 1602. Mary later married John Robinson on 16 July 1634.

SYLVESTER'S SIRES

Mary may have been promiscuous, but she was not from an un-privileged background. Her parents were William Salisbury of Newton and Cornelia, daughter and heiress of John Benrye of Bocheston. In fact, the family were gentry and appear on a pedigree in Jonathan Nichols' *History and Antiquities of Leicestershire*, which then was taken from the Heralds' visitation pedigrees of 1619 and 1682 (see page 302). It turns out that Mary was the fourth of five daughters (perhaps significantly her marriage to John Robinson is not shown) and had seven brothers too, including a brother Richard who married another member of the Burgoland family.

The pedigree traces back to Mary's great-great-grandfather Richard Salisbury of Newton Burgoland. It does not go any further back, but it is significant that no less a herald and antiquary than William Camden allowed the family to continue using its coat of arms, which were exactly the same as those of the Salisburys of Llyweni. In other words, they believed the Salisburys of Newton were a younger branch of the Welsh Salisburys, meaning Sylvester was descended from Duke Eberhard after all.

IF THE FACE FITS

Why had the American researchers plumped for Cadwalladr? The simple truth is that undertaking research in America before the advent of the internet meant many researchers were confined to libraries of printed sources. If they found a printed pedigree – in this case that of the Welsh Salisburys – they might tend to forget or not even realise that there could be other families of the same name. Add an illustrious noble descent and the temptation was often too great: 'Sylvester must have been a younger son of, hmm let's see, which generation would fit best …?'

When a tenant died, the heir would appear at the next Court Baron and state their right to inherit the tenancy. They would then have their right acknowledged, thus being 'admitted' to the tenancy, and paying a forfeit to do so. The forfeit was traditionally a 'heriot', the tenant's best beast, but after the Restoration (1660) a money payment was made instead.

COPYHOLD TENANCIES

Copyhold tenancies were hereditary and could not technically be sold. Of course, in reality they were, all the time, both to neighbours and incomers. This involved a little pantomime, by which the vendor would attend the Court Baron and surrender their holdings to the lord, who would then admit the purchaser, while cash changed hands behind the scenes.

Copyhold land fell into two categories, heritable copyhold and copyhold for lives. Heritable copyhold passed to the holder's heir, according to the custom of the manor. The heir was usually the eldest son, but manors in some areas practised 'gavelkind' (dividing the land between all sons, with the hearth – the family home – going to the youngest) or 'borough English' (which allowed the youngest son to inherit). Copyholders sometimes managed to overcome these strict rules by attending the manorial court to surrender the holding 'to the use of his will', and then bequeathing the land to whomever they wanted. Copyhold 'for lives' allowed the holding to remain in the family during the lives of a set number of people, usually three – holder, wife and son – and when all three had died the land reverted to the lord, though the custom of 'free bench' allowed the widow of the last 'life' to keep her deceased husband's holding for life. Copyhold for lives often altered over time to become straightforward leasehold land.

OTHER RECORDS

Manors generated other sorts of records too, such as:
➤ **Surveys** (also called extents) of the lord's holdings, which can include the tenants' names and obligations of rents.
➤ **Custumals** setting out the manor's customs and sometimes naming tenants.
➤ **Relief rolls** recording freeholders paying what was usually the equivalent of a year's rent to inherit freehold land within the manor.
➤ **Rent rolls,** which came in as paying of rent started to replace performance of services.

When you examine these records, you may notice that, for his own ease of searching, the steward had written the names of those concerned in the margin.

▷ *Landscape with Harvesters Returning Home* by Henry Peacham (c.1576–1643).

MANORIAL ROLLS (or, later, books) can survive from the 13th century. Before 1732 (except for the Commonwealth period, 1653–60) they were often compiled in Latin. Most of the records are formulaic and therefore relatively easy to decipher. Good guides are P. Palgrave-Moore's *How to Locate and use Manorial Records* (Elvery Dowers, 1985), which contains examples of these formulae and D. Stuart's *Manorial Records: An Introduction to their Transcription and Translation* (Phillimore, 1992), which explains many of the terms you may encounter. On a basic level, you only need to know that John was son of Tom, and if you discover a record that definitely relates to your ancestor and appears to contain some interesting text, you can always pay a translator, and many translators charge very reasonable rates.

A TYPICAL COURT BARON WILL PROVIDE NAMES OF POTENTIAL ANCESTORS IN SEVERAL CATEGORIES:

➤ **Names of the lord and steward.** Lords of manors are usually well documented in heraldic records and wills and it is unusual to need to track them down through manorial records, unless you are studying their lives in depth. Stewards tended to be quite well-off but you may not even realise an ancestor was one until you encounter him holding a series of Court Barons for his master. Their jobs were often unofficially hereditary.

➤ **Amercements and misericorda.** These are fines for tenants without a good excuse for non-attendance – useful evidence that an ancestor was alive at a particular date. These were sometimes recorded in separate estreat rolls.

➤ **Essoins.** Fines for those with a good excuse for being absent.

➤ **Swearing in of jurors.** Jurors were normal tenants and their job was to arbitrate disputes and make sure that everyone who appeared was telling the truth.

➤ **Proceedings before the jury.** Here we have the business of the court, in which your ancestor might appear for breaking the rules of the manor, not paying his rent, disputing a boundary with a neighbour or a host of other interesting things, which will add colour to your family tree. Most importantly, you should find the inheritance or transfer of copyhold or, if you are really lucky, a jolly good row over which of several members of the family were to inherit a holding. Argumentative families are usually much better documented than compliant ones. Those inheriting or otherwise acquiring a landholding paid a fine called a heriot, payment of which was sometimes recorded separately in estreat rolls.

MANORIAL RECORDS

⊡ Many manorial records have been deposited in their relevant **county record offices**. However, many manors were owned by people and institutions from other counties – the Oxford and Cambridge colleges, for example, owned manors all over England – and are now deposited in the archive or record office most local to the owner's residence.

⊡ A large number of manorial records are in the hands of private owners in Britain and abroad. A vast number of documents was thrown out and burned after the abolition of the manorial system in 1922, and yet more have been sold to document collectors, especially in America, and cut up, framed, misused or lost.

⊡ Finding the surviving records' is usually a matter of consulting the Manorial Documents Register of the **Historic Manuscripts Commission (HMC)**, now part of **TNA**. This will tell you which manors covered a particular parish, and what surviving records have been reported to the **HMC**. It is slowly being computerised – see **www.nationalarchives.gov.uk/mdr**.

⊡ If no records are listed for the manor you want, try to trace the present lord or lady of the manor and see if they have records which they have not reported to the **HMC**.

⊡ Lists of manorial lords in 1925 are in **TNA** in class HMC 5. The volumes of the *Victoria County History* series often indicate the most recent known lord, as will directories (see page 127) published up to the mid-20th century. You can then trace forwards to try to locate the present lord and write a very polite letter asking if he has any records which might help you.

⊡ Although the manorial system was abolished in the 1920s, the lordships were not. They are now a saleable commodity, sometimes conveying some

△ *Month of October: Sowing*, from 'Breviarium Grimani' (Italian School, 16th century).

practical rights (over fishing, gravel extraction and so on), but more usually valued simply for their perceived social caché. Being the lord of a manor, though, is just that: buying a manorial lordship does not make one 'Lord Bloggs'. For more information about manorial titles, contact the **Manorial Society of Great Britain**.

QUICK REFERENCE
See also main sources in Useful Addresses, page 306

MANORIAL SOCIETY OF GREAT BRITAIN
104 Kennington Road
London SE11 6RE
☎ 020 7735 6633
www.msgb.co.uk

HAVING TRACED THE ELLIOTT FAMILY back from London to the Sussex village of Tillington, I decided to examine the records of the local manor, Petworth. Here I found the earliest known Thomas, who is the second Thomas mentioned in the record:

Capital Court, 3 September 1822
DEATH OF THOMAS ELLIOTT A FREEHOLDER

Also the homage present that Thomas Elliott late of Tillington, Sussex, yeoman ... who held a freehold tenement Barn Stable Orchard and Croft and several new built tenements thereon near the Church in Tillington and formerly called the Roebuck (late copyhold and enfranchised to the Lord to the said Thomas Elliott deceased) ... died ... (no heriot, as no living beast) now at this Court comes Thomas Elliott only son and heir ... and acknowledges to hold ... by the said yearly rent of two shillings and six pence heriot Relief ffealty suit of court and other services And thereupon pays to the Lord for a Relief two shillings and six pence and doth to the Lord his ffealty.

So now I knew that Thomas's father was another Thomas. There were several other Elliott references in the records, including this one:

Capital Court, 8 September 1789
DEATH OF SARAH DAY

Also the homage presents that Sarah Day widow who held of the Lord all that Copyhold or Customary Messuage or tenement Barn Garden Orchard Land and Premises with their appurtenances frmerly called the Roebuck lying in Tillington the yearly rent of two shillings and sixpence since the last court [26 August 1788] died thereof seized (no heriot as no living beast) NOW ... comes Hannah wife of Thomas Elliott of Tillington shopkeeper ... and produces the will of Sarah Day bearing date 29 December 1788- wherein she devises said premises to her niece Hannah Elliott wife of Thomas Elliott and her Heirs for ever. She is admitted. Fine £10-00-00.

Thus, it was possible to add a new maternal aunt to the family tree, who might never have been discovered otherwise. Later, the will of Sarah, proved in 1787, was discovered, and this confirmed the manorial record:

whereas I have surrendered all my customary tenement, garden, barn, stables and orchard with croft of land of the same formerly called the Roebuck in Tillington held of the manor of Petworth to the use of my will now I devise the sd copyhold or customary premises and all the rest of my real estate to my niece Hannah Elliott the wife of Thomas Elliott and her heirs forever.

In other words, Sarah had taken the steps necessary to bequeath her copyhold land to whoever she wanted, in this case, her niece.

LIFETIMES: THE ROEBUCK REDISCOVERED

WILLS BEFORE 1858

Archdioceses were divided in very complicated ways (see page 126), so start looking for your ancestor's will or administration in the most local court. If you don't find it there, search in the calendars and indexes of each court, working up to the most senior, the **PCC** (see right).

Records of the **PCY** are at the **Borthwick Institute**. Those for the dioceses and archdeaconries will be in the **county record office** covering the location of the court concerned, and bear in mind that these do not coincide with county boundaries.

Finding out the layers of jurisdiction under which your ancestral parish lay could not be simpler. *The Phillimore Atlas and Index* (Phillimore, 2003) marks out the different areas of ecclesiastical jurisdiction in different colours, while J. Gibson and E. Churchill's *Probate Jurisdictions: Where to Look for Wills* (FFHS, 2002) will tell you exactly which record office holds wills for the parishes you want.

All pre-1858 wills for Wales are at the **National Library of Wales**. Some Welsh wills will be found in neighbouring English courts.

Some probate records have only been calendared, a form of index arranged annually but within which surnames are grouped together by initial letter rather than strict alphabetical order. Most, fortunately, have been indexed, and all indexes and other finding aids are listed in J. Gibson and E. Churchill's *Probate Jurisdictions, Where to Look for Wills* (FFHS, 2002).

Indexes may be published or they may exist as card indexes in the relevant record office. There are also privately held probate indexes, not least some record offices, such as Cheshire's and **David Wright**'s index covering the patchwork courts that covered London, complete for 1750–1800 and 1820–58.

Some will indexes are now on the internet, such as **www.originsnetwork.com**, which includes indexes to many York and London wills.

If you are lucky, you will find that the wills you want to examine have been transcribed or abstracted, and printed. Many county record societies have done this for early **PCC** wills relating to their counties. Gibson and Churchill's guide, cited above, indicates what is available, and where.

For the period 1796–1903, many wills were abstracted in estate (or death) duty registers, at **TNA** in class IR 26, indexed in IR 27, fully indexed at **www.findmypast.com** and **www.nationalarchivist.com**. The Government's aim was to tax deceased peoples' estates. Up to 1805 about 25% of wills were abstracted and details noted of who received what, and what tax was due, the figure rising to almost 100% after 1815. The indexes are not in strictly alphabetical order, but these national records can be very helpful if you are not sure where a will might have been proved. They can tell you the state of the family when the will was written and also when it was proved. They may indicate, for example,

that the testator's wife had died in the interim or that daughters had married (and thus give their married names). They can also tell you what the testator was actually worth, as opposed to what he fancied he was worth.

Similar abstracts for estates including government stocks, 1717–1845, are held in the **Bank of England Archives** and indexed in **www.originsnetwork.com**.

WILLS AT THE PCC

PCC wills, which are likely be relevant at some point to anyone with English or Welsh ancestry, are fully indexed from 1383 to 1857 at **www.documentsonline. nationalarchives.gov.uk**. Digital images of wills can be downloaded for £3. You can also search by word, e.g. an occupation or place, as well as a name, making this a very useful research tool. The indexes to 1700 are quite detailed, those from 1801 onwards less so but still give names, years of probate and counties of residence. If the person died on or beyond the seas, they are denoted 'pts' or 'parts', meaning 'foreign parts'. The printed indexes are available at **TNA** and **FRC**, many **record offices** and **libraries** such as the **SoG** and **IHGS**. Original documents are at **TNA**. Probate copies are in class PROB 11, original wills in PROB 10 and administrations in PROB 6 and 7.

PCC Administrations (class PROB 6) are fully indexed at **TNA** in PROB 12, with published indexes for the periods 1581–1660 and 1853–8.

INDEX DETAILS

Indexes generally tell you:
☑ **Full name of the deceased**
☑ **Place of residence**
☑ **Occupation**
☑ **Date of probate**
☑ **Page number** or other form of reference to lead to you the original document.
☑ **Some go into more detail** (such as the names of executors and so on).

Examining a **PCC** will from an index reference requires a little patience. The reference number after the testator's name in the index is the number of a 'quire', which was originally a bundle of 16 pages. The class lists at the **FRC** and **TNA** will tell you which **TNA** piece numbers cover the year you want, and within them which piece number covers the quire number you require, and indicates the relevant microfilm. You must then reel through that film until you find the right quire (do not be confused by the pages numbers!), within whose 16 pages you will find the will you want.

QUICK REFERENCE

See also main sources in Useful Addresses, page 306

BORTHWICK INSTITUTE
St Anthony's Hall
Peasholme Green
York YO1 7PW
☎ 01904 642315
www.york.ac.uk/inst/bihr

DAVID WRIGHT
71 Island Wall
Whitstable
Kent CT5 1EL
(enclose an SAE)

BANK OF ENGLAND ARCHIVES
Threadneedle Street
London EC2R 8AH
☎ 020 7601 5096
www.bankofengland.co.uk/archive.htm

England and Wales, and all English and Welsh subjects dying abroad, not least soldiers and sailors, fell under the jurisdiction if the Archbishop of Canterbury. Anyone who wished could take a will to the Archbishop's court, the Prerogative Court of Canterbury (PCC), which (somewhat confusingly) was at Doctor's Commons near St Paul's Cathedral, London. This was often the option of the wealthy, for whom the PCC had a certain caché. During the Cromwellian Commonwealth (1653–60) it was renamed the Court of Probate of Wills and Granting of Administrations and was the only place where these activities could take place.

The Archbishop's own archbishopric itself only extended as far north of the River Trent, beyond which probate jurisdiction fell to the Archbishop of York. If someone had property worth more than £5 in both archbishoprics, their will had to be proved at the PCC. Because government stock held at the Bank of England was deemed to be property in London, Bank of England clients from all over the country had to have their wills proved at the PCC, and after 1812 the Bank of England did not recognise any wills not proved there. However, if the person's property was only within Cheshire, Cumberland, Durham, Northumberland, Westmoreland and Yorkshire, it could be proved at the Prerogative Court of the Archbishop of York (PCY) or, before 1577, at his Exchequer Court.

OVERCOMING PROBLEMS

➤**Remember that wills are arranged by date of probate, not date of death,** so if your ancestor died in 1720 but their will was not proved until 1740, then that is the year in which the will appears in the index. Generally, the broad periods of time covered by the indexes make them easy to search and it is usually straightforward to find both the person you want and also to note others of the same name who could be relatives. It is not uncommon to search for an ancestor's will and to end up finding wills for their parents and grandparents in the same index.

➤**Indexes seldom take variant spellings into account,** and sometimes indexers may have mistranscribed a testator's name, so you must be as alert to these problems, as when conducting any other searches.

➤**If you are lucky, you will find wills and associated documentation relating to your direct ancestors.** You can then enjoy obtaining photocopies or even photographs of the records, and seeing how much they will tell you about your ancestors' lives. Do not forget, however, that much of the wording itself was usually imposed on the testator by lawyers and clerks. When the will of your farmer ancestor states, 'I devise and bequeath unto my eldest son Thomas my black coat', he probably said something much

BECAUSE ONE OF THE problems of dealing with old wills is trying to decipher difficult handwriting, it is helpful to know the sort of phrases you might expect to encounter in a will written in or around the 17th century.

In the name of God Amen,

Wills were religious documents and almost always started thus, until the 18th century when this opening was often dropped and a more secular style adopted.

I John Havers of Winfarthinge in the Countie of Norff[olk] gent[leman].

You can usually expect to find the place of residence and occupation stated. Women will usually give their 'occupation' either as widow or spinster: wives very rarely wrote in their husbands' lifetimes.

beinge sick of bodie but of sounde memorye and perfecte remembrance

Well or ill, it was important to emphasise that the testator was indeed of sound mind, so as to lessen the chance of the will being challenged later.

Make this my last will and testament in manner and forme followinge

Technically, property is divided into land and buildings, 'real estate', which is 'devised' by a testament and movable goods and money, 'personal estate', which is bequeathed by a will. However, because both were contained in the same document, these terms have come to be used interchangeably.

And my body to be buried in the churche of Winfarthinge aforesaid or in the chappell of the same Church as close as maybe to the grave of Agnes my firste wife.

People often stated where they wished to be buried and sometimes, as here, gave incidental genealogical information about the burial places of other members of the family. If the place of burial was a different parish to the parish of residence, it will almost certainly be the person's parish of origin.

I desire after the payment of my just debts and funerall expenses

This was standard and did not necessarily mean the testator was in debt.

I bequeathe to the parish church of ... and the poore of the parish of ...

When such bequests mentioned parishes other than the parish of residence they usually denoted where the testator held other property or had ancestral connections.

I will and bequeathe unto Charles Havers my eldest son xxxli vs 2d of lawful money of Englande to be paid unto him when he attain the age of twentie one yeares

Wills will often name all the children, either in age order or specifically numbered 'second son', 'third son' and so on, and give a clue as to their ages. The bequest here, made in Latin and followed by abbreviated words, is for 30 pounds (livres), 5 shillings and 2 pence (denarii).

I bequeathe my tenements, hereditaments and messuages situate within the parish of...

A tenement was any sort of property held by one person from another; an hereditament was any property which may be inherited; and a messuage was a dwelling house with the land around it including outbuildings. These phrases together, then, covered any sort of building the testator might own or be likely to own.

I bequeathe my sylver and gilte cupp in the lyttle parlour and the bedd and cupborde standeing in the great parlour

Sometimes the testator takes you on a written tour of their house.

I appointe my said wife Anne and my said son Thomas Havers.... to be executrix and executors of this my said will

Men were executors and women executrixes. Testators might appoint one or several of these, usually spouses, very close relations, trusted friends or family lawyers. Their task was to have the will proved once the testator was deceased and ensure that the instructions in the will were carried out.

And I therefore set my hande and seale

The testator's signature will appear on an original will but not on a probate copy. The seal will usually be a standard lawyer's seal, with a pattern or simple picture on it, but if the testator had a coat of arms the seal may well be from his own sealing ring and will show you his arms or crest. If a record office issues you with a probate copy but you want to see the original signature or seal, ask for this specifically.

In the presence of Henrye Abbott and Joseph Horne...

Witnesses were often friends or relations. Their names may not be immediately familiar to you but they may turn up later as you extend the family tree upwards and sideways, so always note them.

a codicil

If the testator wanted to alter a small part of their will, rather than have the whole thing drawn up again (and thus incurring lawyers' and scriveners' fees), they might add a codicil, revoking or altering a bequest. This might be done months or years after the will was written.

Testament

more like 'and I want Tommy to have this 'ere coat'. Equally, you may encounter much legal jargon, which will have little bearing on your ancestors' true lives and can often be safely ignored.

➤**Wills are excellent tools for searching for ancestors.** Your earliest known forbear might – and probably shall – be mentioned in a will written by someone else of the same surname, such as a grandfather, uncle, brother, nephew or cousin. Therefore an ancestor who died in 1760 could be mentioned in a will written before 1760 but not proved until years after, so keep on searching. Equally, a will mentioning one of your ancestor's children as a cousin can point the way back to a line of relatives and thus a common parish of origin.

➤**Think too about your ancestors' other relatives.** You are as likely to be left bequests by your mother's family as your father's. If you have found a marriage which you suspect is that of your ancestor's parents, look for wills for people with the wife's maiden name and you may come across your ancestor's maternal grandfather or uncle. If your ancestor came from a small village and you are completely stuck, look for wills of anyone else living in the same place, and before long you will probably find your ancestor mentioned as a relation, neighbour, witness or executor: this might provide the clue you need.

➤**Searching wills.** The technique when searching wills in such a speculative way is to make very brief genealogical abstracts, recording only the names, relationships and places that are mentioned. In the foregoing example, all you need note is 'son Thomas' – the fact that he was due to inherit a coat is, at this stage, irrelevant. Should the will subsequently turn out to fit into your family tree, you can always make a more detailed abstract of it later.

➤**Some counties are compiling will beneficiary indexes.** Essex Record Office has one covering all names appearing in wills written by people in the county of Essex (except those proved in the PCC) 1675–1858. Such indexes can help you accomplish the searches suggested above in a very short time.

➤**Destruction of wills for some areas during Second World War bombing.** Those for Somerset, Devon and Cornwall from before 1858, for example, were almost entirely destroyed in the bombing of Exeter in 1942. In such cases, surviving abstracts and copies that had already been made of wills have been collected together and information on manuscript or published sources for these can be obtained from the relevant record offices. Copies of all wills sent to the Estate Duty Office from 1796 have been returned to these three county record offices.

△ **Part of a 17th-century inventory.**

WHERE TO SEARCH

PAPERWORK ATTACHED TO WILLS

CHURCH COURT RECORDS

These include probate accounts, which the courts could order the executors to produce to prove they had distributed the deceased's estate correctly. P. Spufford's *Index to the Probate Accounts of England and Wales* (BRS, vols 112 and 113, 1999) covers the probate courts for various periods between the 16th and 19th centuries, depending on the survival of records.

PROBATE ACT BOOKS

These record the grant of probate, name of testator and names and residences of executors, and sometimes the renunciation by an executor of their right to deal with the estate (if they were ill, say, or simply could not be bothered) and the regranting of probate to a new executor. Those for the **PCC** are published for 1630–55.

They are indexed for administrators as well as testators so you can often pick up references to ancestors acting in such capacities in relation to the estates of relatives and friends, thus expanding your family history in often unexpected directions.

CAVEAT BOOKS AND ADMINISTRATION LETTERS AND BONDS

Act books or separate caveat books also record objections to grants of probate made by those, for example, who suspected the will being proved was not the final one. Applications for grants of letters of administration, prove details including the deceased's date of death. Administration bonds were sometimes required, detailing the amount of money that would be forfeited should the executors or administrators fail to discharge his duty.

INVENTORIES

Especially in the period 1530–1700 inventories of the deceased's moveable goods and their values often had to be compiled. They give you a fantastic insight into your ancestors' lives; what clothes they had, what furniture was in their house, what tools of the trade they possessed, how many animals they owned and so on and, of course, it is fascinating to see how much all these items were worth at the time. Inventories were often compiled by friends and relatives, possibly adding a few extra names to the family tree.

TESTAMENTARY CASES

Disputes over wills were heard in testamentary cases in church courts, usually that of the local bishop. These were generally arguments within families over unpaid legacies, or the validity of nuncupative wills, or disputes over which of several wills written by the same testator was truly their 'last will'. **PCC** cases are at **TNA**, and there is a card index to testators and plaintiffs complaining of unfair treatment 1665–1858 in PROB 25 and written evidence ('exhibits') 1722–1858 indexed in PROB 33.

Many disputes also appear in Chancery cases (page 226).

NEWSPAPERS

Be aware too that newspapers (see page 144), especially *The Times* and the *London Gazette*, carry many notices placed by executors and administrators trying to locate missing or potential beneficiaries. Many are indexed in the Andrews Index at the **IHGS**, a card index of notices from the *London Gazette*, *The Times* and other sources relating to unclaimed estates, next of kin, missing persons and the like, from 1970 back to the early 20th century, and therefore mainly relating to people born in the 19th century.

QUICK REFERENCE

See main sources in Useful Addresses, page 306

PAPERWORK ATTACHED TO WILLS

Wills and letters of administration could generate much other paperwork. In some dioceses (Chester, for example), this tended to be filed with the wills and administrations while in others it was filed separately and so much harder to access. (See Where to search, above.)

LIFETIMES: CURIOSITIES

WILLS CONTAIN ALL SORTS OF CURIOSITIES. HERE ARE SOME FAVOURITES:

Christopher Dowlinge, a husbandman of Stowey, Somerset, wrote his will in 1571, itemising his animals by name. His oxen Martin and Pike were left to his daughters Juliana and Alice respectively, while his cows Filpaile, Chirrie, Violet and Cople went to his wife and three of his daughters. Some other oxen and cows lacked names, and his sheep seem to have been anonymous too.

Benjamin Smart, a lawyer of the Middle Temple in London, had other things on his mind when he wrote his will in 1760 (which was proved in the PCC), specifying that 'in order to avoid some very ill practises in making skeletons of deceased persons

... I do most especially make it my Earnest Request not to be buried from any Undertakers or public Hal l... but from my Chambers ... and that some of my ffriends or servants may see me immediately before my coffin shall be ffastened ... and as I have Reason to think that several persons have inadvertently been buried alive I do hereby make it my earnest request that my coffin may not be fastened up till full forty-eight Hours after my decease (if it can be avoided) and if it can be kept open longer without inconvenience I desire it may be so kept open and not ffastened up till it become necessary'.

The following is from the will of Thomas Jefferies of Draycott Foliat, Wiltshire (1872): presumably Thomas senior did not like his nephew's prospective wife very much.

And in case my nephew Thomas Jefferies shall marry Elizabeth Waldron of Draycott.. in the Lifetime of his mother then I leave his share to her to dispose of as she shall think proper

WILLS OUTSIDE ENGLAND AND WALES
SCOTLAND

Until 1868, the inheritance of land was rigidly fixed, going automatically to the eldest surviving son (or his heir), or if there were no sons to the eldest surviving daughter, so technically there were no wills (which bequeath land), but only testaments, whereby people could bequeath their movable goods to whomever they liked. The equivalent of letters of administration, appointing an administrator to distribute the goods of someone who had died intestate, was known as a testament dative.

Probate matters were dealt with in church courts until 1560 when, unlike England and Wales, probate was handed over to secular commissary courts or commissariots under the overall jurisdiction of the Principal Commissariot of Edinburgh, which also dealt with Scots who had goods in Scotland but who had died elsewhere, and from 1824 by Sheriff Courts.

In Scotland there are also services to heirs (also called retours).

MANY FAMILIES HAVE STORIES that they are entitled to great wealth from a distant ancestor or relative's will, or that their forbear would have come into a great deal of money but was 'cut off with/without a shilling'. Most of these stories are mere pie-in-the-sky, excuses made by daydreamers or people embarrassed by lack of money. In many cases, it turns out that the 'cut off' ancestor received their legacy after all, and promptly spent it. In other cases, such notions arise because parents sometimes made generous provision for a particular child while they were alive, and left them a shilling in their will to preclude them or their heirs from claiming anything further.

Family stories are sometimes started by missing kin notices. In 1950, say, Mr Evans sees a missing kin notice for heirs of the late millionaire Miss Agnes Evans, and remarks fancifully that it would be a fine thing if she turned out to be a relation. In 1975, Mr Evans's son Tom recalls the remark and tells his own daughter, *'my father used to say we were related to Miss Evans, the millionairess.'* By 2000, Tom's daughter is convinced her grandfather was the heir to millions but never claimed it, and ruins the rest of her life in a wild-goose chase to try to locate what she by now regards as her rightful inheritance.

Sometimes such stories arise due to contact from a Chancery agent. Chancery agents often trace and contact 'missing' heirs and offer to reunite them with their legacies if they will sign a percentage over to them. If this happens to you, think carefully. If you have no idea where the money came from, there is no harm in signing up and rewarding the Chancery agent for their hard work. However, if you have the slightest inkling of who might have left the money, do not sign anything, because if you can find the deceased relative's will you can establish who the executors were or contact the Treasury solicitor (who has ultimate responsibility for unclaimed funds) and claim your share yourself. You may gain useful clues as to which side of the family the deceased relative was on by finding out which of your other relatives has also been contacted. If your cousin on your mother's mother's side has also been contacted, you will know that the deceased relation was someone on that side of the family, and by a process of elimination you may successfully identify who the deceased relative was.

Britain has an incredibly rich store of archives containing a vast amount of written records. This section covers the main areas, from feet of fines to freemen records, which will enable you to solve problems and add a huge amount of extra detail to your family's history.

◁ Besides newspapers, specially printed pamphlets can provide some pretty weird family history information.

SCOTTISH AND IRISH NEWSPAPERS

Scottish newspapers appeared at the same time as English ones, with the *Edinburgh Evening Courant* published thrice weekly from 1718, followed by the *Glasgow Journal* in 1741 and *Aberdeen Journal* in 1748. The first daily paper was the *Conservative*, established in 1837. The equivalent of the *Gentleman's Magazine* was the *Edinburgh Magazine*, founded in 1739 and renamed the *Scots Magazine* in 1817, which is indexed annually for births, deaths and marriages.

Irish newspapers started appearing in the 17th century, first in Dublin and Belfast (though copies for the latter apparently do not survive before 1737), and then spreading to towns and cities such as Limerick and Waterford in the early 18th century.

'The Times *indexes contain a plethora of insights into our ancestors' lives. Under the surname Angel, for example, we have Charles, bankrupt in 1843; William, tried for stealing in 1865; Charles and David, drowned while bathing in 1879, and, weirdest of all, in 1887* 'Death, Mysterious, of Rachel Angel, found poisoned by nitric acid in bed, and a man found lying under the bed, in Whitechapel'.'

LIFETIMES: MARRIAGE LINES

The following is an account of my grandfather's wedding, including all sorts of intimate details I would never have learned from other family sources – or even from him himself!

'*Considerable interest was evinced in the wedding of Mr Jerome Collingwood Rietchel, son of Mr and Mrs J. Rietchel, of 10, Culverden Grange, Tunbridge Wells, and Miss Maureen Josephine Denning, daughter of the late Mr and Mrs W. Denning, of Knockatane, South-drive, Ruislip, which took place at the Church of the Sacred Heart, Ruislip, on Wednesday. The Rev. W. P. Denning, brother of the bride, came especially from Rome to conduct the service, and he was assisted by the Rev. A. E. S. Blount, and the Rev. J. J. Curtin ... Mr W. Hyde presided at the organ ... who played at the entrance of the bride, who was given away by Mr J. B. Dore. Her beautiful dress of dull parchment satin ... The bride defied superstition, for the colour of the bridesmaids' dresses was green. The bride and bridegroom left later in the day for their honeymoon, which is being spent in the South of France.*'

WHERE TO SEARCH

NEWSPAPERS

⊡ The best place to search newspapers, national and local, for the entire British Isles, is the **British Library Newspaper Library** whose collection will be online by 2012. A good bibliography of newspapers is the *Tercentenary Handlist of English & Welsh Newspapers, Magazines & Reviews, 1620–1919* (Dawsons, 1966), and you can also consult J. Gibson's *Local Newspapers 1750–1920, England and Wales, Channel Islands and Isle of Man: A Select Location List* (FFHS, 1991). Otherwise, ask at **local libraries**, **museums** and **archives**, as many hold good collections and may also have indexes to their holdings.

⊡ *The Times* digital archive 1785–1985 is available online in some libraries. It can also be searched by two CD-Rom indexes, 1785–1905 (incorporating the earlier index compiled by Palmer) and 1906–80 (using the official *Times* index) – both are at the **Guildhall Library**. Searches can be made under names or topics. For the periods 1785–1790 and 1906–present there is the more cumbersome *Official Index to the Times*, in quarterly volumes, which can also be searched at **Guildhall Library** (which also holds microfilm copies of the newspapers themselves). These and copies of the *Official Index* may also be found at other locations, such as some **university libraries**.

⊡ *London Gazette*: Complete sets are at **TNA**, **British Library** and **Guildhall Library**, with annual indexes from 1787.

⊡ *The Gentleman's Magazine*: There are indexes covering 1731–1810 and a complete typescript index exists at the **Family History Library** at Salt Lake City (942 B2g index V.26) – it costs very little to pay a searcher there to examine the index for you. Collections of the magazine itself are at the **British Library**, **NA** and a partial set at the **SoG**. Indexes to obituaries to 1855 are in a manuscript volume at **Guildhall Library** and those for the 16th–18th centuries are included in J. G. Armitage's *Obituary, Obituary Prior to 1800 (as far as relates to England, Scotland & Ireland) compiled by Sir William Musgrave* (Harleian Society, vols 44-49, 1899–1901).

⊡ *The Scotsman* newspaper, published since 1817, is now fully online up to 1900 at **www.archive.scotsman.com** at £7.95 a day.

⊡ Good collections of newspapers for their respective areas are at the **National Libraries of Wales and Scotland** and the **India Office Library**.

⊡ For Irish newspapers there are collections at the **British Library Newspaper Library** and also at the **National Library of Ireland** and the **PRONI**. Most include birth, marriage and death announcements, making excellent substitutes for the many destroyed parish registers. *The Irish Times*, 1859–2004, is going online at **www.ireland.com**.

EXAMPLES OF NEWSPAPERS IN OTHER COUNTRIES

⊡ A detailed list of Trinidad newspapers and where they are held of them in Britain and the USA is given in **www.rootsweb.com/~ttowgw/research/newspapers.htm**.

⊡ Some Jamaican newspapers, including extracts from the *Royal Gazeteer* and the *Gleaner*, are on **www.jamaicanfamilysearch.com**.

QUICK REFERENCE

See also main sources in Useful Addresses, page 306

BRITISH LIBRARY NEWSPAPER LIBRARY
Colindale Avenue
Colindale
London NW9 5HE
☎ 020 7412 7353
www.bl.uk/collections/newspapers.html

FAMILY HISTORY LIBRARY
35 North West Temple Street
Salt Lake City
Utah 84150, USA

NATIONAL LIBRARY OF SCOTLAND
George IV Bridge
Edinburgh EH1 1EW
Scotland
☎ 0131 466 2812
www.nls.uk

INDIA OFFICE LIBRARY
British Library
96 Euston Road
London NW1 2DB
☎ 020 7412 7513
www.bl.uk/collections/orientalandindian.html

NATIONAL LIBRARY OF IRELAND
Kildare Street
Dublin 2, Eire
☎ 00 353 1 603 0200
www.nli.ie

LIFETIMES: GRAHAM EVELYN

ONE OF MY FAVOURITE *Extraordinary Ancestors* cases concerned the ancestry of Graham Evelyn, a young Bristolian descended from a mixed-race Jamaican family called Drummond.

The *Scots Magazine* for October 1754 contains a record of his ancestor: 'June 20, At Savannah la Mer, Jamaica, Dr John Drummond. He was killed in a duel, by one Donaldson, an Irishman.' It also records under deaths in 1804, 'April 14. In Westmorland, Jamaica, Dr John Drummond, who had practised 40 years in that parish with great reputation.' The second Dr John, who was son of the first, appears very briefly in the records of Edinburgh University, having come over from Jamaica for a year to attend a handful of lectures, after which he felt himself qualified to become a doctor back home. He appears in a slave owner's published diary, ministering to slaves, particularly with his home-made smallpox vaccine: 'inoculated 17 of my Negroes, on each arm between the elbow and shoulder; just raised the skin with a lancet, dipped in matter and let it dry' – a method that was apparently very successful.

JOHN DRUMMOND'S WILL

A copy of the second Dr John's will has survived in Edinburgh University library. In it he describes himself as John Drummond 'practitioner of physic and surgery, Westmorland, Jamaica', and leaves 'a free negro woman Mary Drummond [born] of slaves, an annuity of £50 current money', and also his furniture, horses and cows and the right to live at Drummond Lodge. He then left bequests to Thomas Drummond, whom he acknowledged as his son by Mary. He also left legacies to Peggy Bartlett, a free quadroon (i.e. a quarter black), and a mulatto slave, Hannah Browning, and provided for the manumission (freedom) of two other children he had had by slaves, who were currently Mary's property.

The freeing of Thomas, 'a mulatto', son of John, had, in fact, required a special Act in the Jamaican House of Assembly in 1793. In the 1840 *Jamaica Almanac* Thomas is recorded as holding a 1200-acre plantation in Westmoreland.

The returns of slaves for Westmoreland, made in 1817 to record which slaves were there and so prevent the acquisition of new ones by purchase from outside the island, show what happened next. The son Thomas Drummond, 'of colour', owned 86 slaves, while his mother Mary had 28. There was also William Drummond, also 'of colour' and probably another son of Dr John, with two slaves. Finally there was Bazillia or 'Bazzy' Drummond, a 'free black', who had two slaves in her capacity as guardian for John and Elizabeth Drummond.

This combination of records shows a clear line coming down from white Scotsmen to mixed-race Jamaicans.

◁ Illustration of a Slave Camp (French School, 18th century).

SLAVES

Many records relating to British people in the Caribbean – and including somewhat incidental information about their slaves – are in Britain. Holdings at **TNA** are described in G. Grannum's *Tracing your West Indian Ancestors: Sources at the PRO* (PRO Publications, 1995). Published sources include the *Calendar of State Papers Colonial: America and West Indies 1574–1739* (HMSO).

The **SoG**'s Smith collection of manuscript genealogies of British families in the Caribbean is worth consulting, and there are published works for many islands. The upper- and middle-class white families of Antigua, for example, are minutely recorded in V. L. Oliver's *The History of Antigua* (Mitchell and Hughes, 1899).

There were no records of lists of slaves transported to the Caribbean until the trade was abolished, and only a few after that date when ships carrying slaves illegally were captured. There are plenty of records of the Mixed Commission Courts at **TNA**, particularly that in Sierra Leone (FO 313), concerning the capture of slave ships, but the Africans usually only appear as numbers, not names. There are some records of petitions and passenger lists for freed black people travelling from Sierra Leone to Jamaica in the 1840s in CO 267.

Besides the sources (civil registration, census, parish registers and so on) listed in this book, slave ancestry can also sometimes be studied through slave registers 1812–34 in class T 71 in **TNA** and online at **www.ancestry.co.uk/s31356/t10197/rd.ashx**. These recorded the slaves on each plantation (arranged alphabetically) to prevent the illegal import of more Africans. They name the slaves (though often only by a single name), with details of colour (i.e. black, mulatto, etc.) and their 'increase' (birth) and 'decrease' (death). However, after first registration in 1812, many islands just give numbers, not names. Others, though, retained the initial high level of detail, even giving mothers' names in some cases. Those for St Lucia are arranged by family with siblings and cousins, though fathers are rarely recorded.

The records of the Slave Compensation Commission at **TNA** in class T 71 give statistical details of slaves to be freed when slavery was abolished in 1833, but little about the people themselves is recorded. Among other sources for slave ancestry are newspapers, which include rewards offered for slaves who had escaped.

WHERE TO SEARCH

△ Engraving of a slave ship (American school, 18th century), showing just how closely packed was its unfortunate human cargo.

Most black Jamaicans therefore can trace their lines of ancestry back to Arawak Indians, African slaves, maybe some East Indians and Chinese, and very often to white slave owners. Indeed, because many slave owners had aristocratic connections, many modern Jamaicans are probably more closely related to British nobility than the majority of white Britons. One mixed race Jamaican immigrant to Oldham whom I researched turned out to be a direct cousin of the Queen herself.

CHAPTER SEVENTEEN
MAPS & LOCAL HISTORIES

When you research your family tree, you will discover not just who your ancestors were, but also where they lived. Places affected every aspect of our ancestors' lives, dictating what sort of jobs they did, how they fared and whom they met and married.

ORDNANCE SURVEY MAPS

THE FIRST SURVEYS started in 1784 in order to provide the army with effective maps to use in case of French invasion. The first maps were produced between 1817 and 1839, and included contour lines from 1847. The maps were reprinted up to 1870, with railways overlaid. Thus, the maps show things that may never have been exactly so, such as a village as it was in 1790 with a railway built in 1850 running past it. A second survey was started in 1840, with subsequent editions updated in the 20th century.

The more you find out about where your ancestors lived, the more fulfilling your research will be, and the easier it will become to work out the answer to that all-important question – 'Where did they come from?'

MAPS

The function of maps in genealogy is two-fold. Most records are arranged geographically, so it is important to know where your ancestors lived and what villages and towns were nearby. They are also a fabulous way of bringing your family history to life, helping you to get a feel for what the places where your ancestors lived were like at the time.

By examining a series of historical maps of the county in which your ancestors lived, you can trace forward and see how the towns grew, roads, canals, railways and bridges were built, estates were enclosed and forests diminished with the progress of the Industrial Revolution.

County maps, so familiar from the walls of many a pub and hotel, can date from the 16th century, especially those made by Christopher Saxton in the 1570s to benefit Lord Burghley's intelligence service.

Many maps were produced from the 17th century to show proposed routes of railways, turnpike roads or canals. Some of these show routes that were never built, and other maps can be misleading too: Burdell's map of Cheshire from the 1770s shows woods and roads accurately but, as far as can be told, the salt mines depicted were simply strewn about for general effect.

◁ Old Ordnance Survey map from 1913 of Camberwell and Stockwell in London.

△ The county of Norfolk, engraved by Jodocus Hondius (1563–1612).

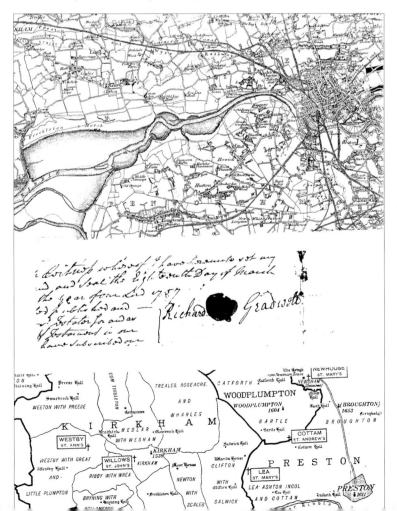

LIFETIMES: JAMES SIMPSON DINNIE

A PERSONAL FAVOURITE topographical dictionary entry is the one I found in Lewis's *Topographical Dictionary of Scotland* (see page 163) when I was researching the Dinnie family for the pilot of *Antiques Ghostshow*.

James Simpson Dinnie's birth was located at Ayr in 1892, with parents Agnes Smith Dinnie, née Wilson, and James Simpson Dinnie, a warder. In the 1891 census, the then unmarried James was found listed as a 22-year-old asylum attendant, born in Glenbervie, Kinkardineshire and indeed there he was in the 1881 census of Glenbervie, working as a 12-year-old farm servant. Lewis's dictionary devotes half a page to the parish, telling me that Glenbervie contained '1296 inhabitants, of whom 397 are in the village of Drumlithie'. It then went on to say: 'This parish, which obviously derives its name from the situation of its church in a small glen on the north-eastern bank of the river Bervie, is totally unconnected with any event of historical importance.' No wonder James went elsewhere to establish a new life for himself!

◁ Two maps of Preston, Lancashire, illustrate the different landscapes in which Catholic yeoman Richard Gradwell lived. One is physical and the other shows the location of Catholic chapels where he and his extended family could worship.

MAPS

Many 17th-century maps are in the **House of Lords Record Office**, while each **county record office** will hold collections relevant to their area.

The county maps from J. Bell's *A New and Comprehensive Gazeteer of England and Wales*, dated 1834, are reproduced in the *Phillimore Atlas and Index* (Phillimore, 2003) along with the maps showing the borders of parishes and ecclesiastical jurisdictions. They are tremendously useful, but they carry with them the danger of creating the mind-set that counties existed as self-contained islands. When searching for ancestors in parish registers, don't just blindly search every register for the county where the family ended up living, especially if they lived near the border of another county. They were as likely to have come across a nearby county border as they were to have come from the farthest reaches of the county they ended up in.

The original Ordnance Survey maps for the British Isles are fascinating to examine at local **libraries**, **museums** or **county record offices**. Full sets are held at the **British Library**, **IHGS** and so on, while replica copies are sold by David & Charles. The Ordnance Survey's excellent **www.getamap.ordnancesurvey.co.uk** includes the option 'search for', allowing you to type in the name of the place you want. You can see the relevant modern map on-screen, zoom in and out of it, and also compare it with the 1878 version.

www.maps.google.co.uk is excellent, as is **www.mapseeker.co.uk**.

On a more local level, libraries and **county record offices** hold collections of town plans, sometimes dating back to the Tudor period, and Ordnance Survey town maps, both of which can be essential when seeking ancestors in census returns or understanding which church or chapel they were most likely to have attended.

There are 18th- and 19th-century fire insurance plans, covering many towns, held at the **British Library** and **Guildhall Library**. These include details of the materials used for the house, number of storeys and sometimes even names of the householders. Sun Insurance Company records 1816–24 are indexed on **www.A2A.org.uk** (the original records are at the Guildhall Library).

Parochial assessment maps at **TNA** date from the 18th and 19th centuries, and many were made following the Parochial Assessments Act of 1836, to enable the accurate levying of rates.

Old large-scale maps often depicted the houses standing in streets. I remember researching a family in 16th-century London and finding their very house, next to the old Bedlam Hospital in Aldgate, depicted in the Agas map, copies of which are in **Guildhall Library** and **TNA** and published in A. Prockter and R. Taylor's *The A–Z of Elizabethan London* (Harry Margary in association with the Guildhall Library, 1979)). Don't expect these drawings to be accurate, however.

For the county parishes there are tithe apportionment maps. These covered roughly three-quarters of the English and Welsh parishes, and were made between 1838 and 1854. Their purpose was to regularise the payment of tithes, and they show and number each field and building. The numbers refer to corresponding tithe schedule books, which describe the land and its rentable value and supply names of owners and occupiers – providing you with a fine written and graphic description of where your ancestors were living. Copies are at **county record offices** and also at **TNA** in classes IR 29 (schedules) and IR 30 (maps).

Enclosure maps were produced when landowners wished to do away with the medieval open field system with its associated smallholdings and commons, and reallocate the land as hedged fields, often making space too for elegant deer parks or landscaped gardens. Dating from the 17th century onwards, the maps and associated enclosure awards, detailing which landowners were allocated what, can be found at **county record offices** and TNA, while those carried out by Act of Parliament are at the **House of Lords Record Office**.

QUICK REFERENCE

See also main sources in Useful Addresses, page 306

HOUSE OF LORDS RECORD OFFICE
Palace of Westminster
London SW1A 0PW
☎ 020 7219 3074
www.parliament.uk

BOOKS

There are usually several antiquarian county histories for each county, many of which are beautifully illustrated with prints, especially of churches and mansions. G. Ormerod's *The History of the County Palatine of Chester* (George Routledge & Sons, 1882), for example, contains so many prints of old Chester that it is not difficult to imagine walking round the city in the 17th or 18th centuries. Much emphasis is given to landowning families, and very detailed and usually excellently researched pedigrees are a common feature, but they do not by any means exclude normal inhabitants. One of their virtues is that the authors had intimate knowledge of the areas they were writing about and had access to many records that may now have been lost.

ONLINE GAZETEERS

THERE ARE SEVERAL online gazetteers for locating places:

⊠ www.ordnancesurvey.co.uk/ oswebsite/freefun/didyouknow

⊠ www.gazeteer.co.uk

⊠ www.digitaldocuments.co.uk/ archi/placenames.htm

Also useful are:

⊠ www.genuki.org.uk is a portal to maps and gazetteers, amongst much else.

⊠ www.visionofbritain.org.uk. Contains historic maps, historic gazetteers, population figures, travellers' accounts and details of boundary changes.

⊠ www.scotlandsfamily.com includes many Scottish maps, as well as much more help for people researching Scottish ancestry.

WHERE TO SEARCH

BOOKS

⊟ Among the topographical dictionaries that are so useful for familyhistory purposes is S. Lewis's *A Topographical Dictionary of England ... and the Islands of Guernsey, Jersey and Man* (S. Lewis & Co., 1831), with similarly titled volumes for Wales (1838), Scotland (1847) and Ireland (1837). They provide excellent snapshot descriptions of the parishes, including details of institutions, churches, agriculture and historical events.

⊟ Many local histories have been published over the last century, and many are still being written. Most are well illustrated with old photographs, so besides finding surprising references to your family, you may even see pictures of them. Wherever your ancestors came from, it is worth studying these books, which can be found through local **libraries** and **museums**, **county record offices** and (for Britain) the British Library's online catalogue: www.blpc.bl.uk.

⊟ The *Victoria History of the Counties of England*, normally called *Victoria County Histories*, are a series of books still being written, with over 200 volumes already in print, detailing the general history and geography of the English counties, followed by histories of the individual parishes, with particular attention to the manorial histories. They are excellent for identifying old records relevant to each parish (which may in turn mention your forbears) and for providing a solid background to the lives of your family, especially in places that have been urbanised or have changed a great deal in other respects.

⊟ Much local printed material can also be identified through Stuart Raymond's county bibliographies (see page 34).

CHAPTER NINETEEN
THE PARISH CHEST

Besides registers, the parishes generated a great deal of other records. Because they were kept with the parish registers in the iron-bound parish chest, these records are often called 'parish chest' material. Survival of records varies greatly from parish to parish.

THE RECORDS

The type of record you might expect to find in a parish chest varies enormously. Outlined here are the main records, starting with vestry minutes and moving on to removal orders and information about parish apprentices, each of which may add colour to your family tree.

VESTRY MINUTES

From the 14th century until they were superseded in 1834 by the Poor Law Guardians and then replaced by parish councils in 1894, parishes were administered by the vestry, a council usually chaired by the resident clergyman. Disputes within the vestry were often resolved by the Justices of the Peace, whose records usually contain much information about parish life.

Vestry minutes can tell you about the administration and maintenance of the parish schools and almshouses, the church, water supply and the care (or otherwise) of the poor.

PARISH RATES

During the 16th and 17th centuries, vestries took over many of the roles previously exercised by manorial courts, and were granted the right to raise rates for looking after bridges (1531), building prisons (1532), caring for the poor (1598) and maintaining roads (1654). These were generally combined with the 'poor rate' from the 18th century. The rate books provide an annual 'census' of heads of household who were not exempt by being paupers, and can be used to determine the spans of their adult lives and observe families' arrivals in and departures from the parish.

SETTLEMENT RECORDS

Probably the most important parish chest material for genealogists are those that record the comings and goings of the poor. From 1601,

LONDON PATENT ATTORNEY Simon Mountenay wanted to trace his ancestry and learn whether he was entitled to use the ancient coat of arms of the de Mounteneys. Many people think there is simply a coat of arms for each family name, but Simon was aware that a coat of arms is granted to a specific individual, and only male-line descendants of the original grantee are entitled, subject to the College of Arms' permission, to use the arms.

In contrast to his own prosperity, Simon's 19th-century ancestors were not at all well-to-do and included some general labourers. I traced the line back to Thomas Mounteney of Southwell, Nottinghamshire, who was baptised in the neighbouring parish of Bleasby in 1785, son of Benjamin and Anne Mounteney. Benjamin and Anne had married there in 1781, but his origins simply could not be found in the registers of Bleasby, or any of the nearby parishes.

The Bleasby parish chest, however, came up trumps. A settlement certificate had survived, dated 24 November 1783, concerning Benjamin Mountney, a tailor, and his wife, Anne, and stating that Benjamin had the right of settlement in Keyworth, Nottinghamshire. He was allowed to stay, the Bleasby vestry having reassured itself that, should Benjamin or his family need financial assistance in the future, it was the Keyworth vestry that would have to come up with the cash.

DELVING BACK YET FURTHER

Keyworth is 14 miles from Bleasby and it would have been impossible to prove his origins there, because his baptism in fact took place close by in Quorndon, over the country border in Leicestershire. He was baptised in 1751, the son of an earlier Benjamin, who was baptised there in 1711, son of an earlier Benjamin still. This earliest Benjamin was not baptised in Quorndon, but again settlement records came to our aid – Benjamin and his wife and family had handed in a settlement certificate stating their legal place of settlement was Atherstone in Warwickshire.

Atherstone was a hamlet in the parish of Mancetter, whose registers show Benjamin's baptism on 10 September 1680, the fifth son of Thomas Mounteney. And after several generations of poor weavers and 'ag. labs' (agricultural labourers) moving from parish to parish, presumably looking for work, we had a great surprise, because Thomas appears in John Nichols' *History and Antiquities of Leicestershire* (vol. 4, pt 2, p. 848) as the third son of George Mountney Esquire, of Newbold Verdon, Leicestershire, whose father's coat of arms was recorded when the Heralds visited Leicestershire in 1619. Benjamin may have been a landed gentleman's grandson, but he was the fifth son of the third son, and clearly there had not been enough money to go around.

Simon discovered his right to bear the ancient arms of de Mountenay, and I gained a splendid example of how some families of labourers really do have blue blood in their veins after all.

anyone who had lived in a parish for a month was entitled to claim poor relief. As this money came out of the pockets of the other inhabitants, newcomers were not generally welcomed with open arms. In 1662, the Settlement Act limited the right to claim poor relief to include wives of men settled in the parish, office holders and rate payers, illegitimate children who were born in the parish (until 1744) and anyone who had been in the parish over 40 days having previously informed the parish that they were going to do so.

SETTLEMENT EXAMINATIONS

Both the vestry or Justices of the Peace could and often did examine newcomers to determine where they were legally settled – in other words, who was responsible for their upkeep should they fall ill. The records, sometimes kept in special settlement examination books, provide marvellous detail of newcomers' places of birth, where they had been apprenticed, worked and lived, to whom they were married and who their children were.

REMOVAL ORDERS

Nothing makes people so nervous as the prospect of having to give money to others. If incomers to the parish were or seemed likely to be in need of upkeep then the settlement examination was usually followed by a removal order, issued by the Justice of the Peace at the request of the parish. Armed with the removal order, the parish constable would march the offending family to the parish border, where, if they were unlucky, the neighbouring constable would be present to hurry them across the parish to the next boundary and so on until they got back to their place of legal settlement. Supporting the unfortunate travellers with food or shelter on the journey was entirely discretionary.

Single, pregnant mothers were viewed with the greatest horror by overseers – if the baby was born in their parish, they would be lumbered with paying for its upkeep until it was at least seven. Pregnant women were therefore hustled mercilessly from parish to parish, until the practice was forbidden by an act of 1723, followed by another in 1744 stating that the illegitimate child's parish of settlement would be the same as its mother, thus taking the pressure off the parish within which the birth occurred.

After 1795, people could only be removed to their parish of settlement if they were actually in need of relief and not too sick to travel: otherwise, they were to be left alone. After 1834, paupers were

△ Settlement examination of Ann Nursey, single woman, in 1767. Ann states here that she was born in Fressingfield but later moved with her parents to Stradbrooke.

FARM SERVANTS

AGRICULTURAL LABOURERS were often taken on for a year at annual hiring fairs, often held at Michaelmas (25 September). Thus, if they always attended the same fair, they could move about each year, but only within the radius of parishes that the fair covered.

LIFETIMES: A CARING NIECE

THE RECORDS OF THE OVERSEERS of the poor may list your ancestors as recipients of outdoor relief, either because they were needy or because they were caring for someone who was. Reasons for the payments were recorded – illness, injury, birth of illegitimate children and a host of other circumstances – which all cast a sharp light on the parish life of our forbears.

Richard Wildish, who was baptised at Wartling, Sussex, in 1706, arrived in St Thomas at Cliffe, Kent, in the early 1730s, probably looking for work. He met and married Rebecca Oldfield (as 'Richard Whildish & Rebeckah Owldfild') in August 1736 and had five children. He appears in the assessment made by the overseers and churchwardens for the relief of the poor in February 1763. His yearly rent was £1, he had no stock, and the column for how much he was to pay was left blank, probably because he was too poor to do so. Indeed, by 1766, we find the St Thomas's vestry deciding to pay three years' rent for him. His burial appears in the registers in 1781. His sister Mary had either accompanied him to St Thomas's or had joined him there later. She never married, and in later life we know that she lived with Richard's daughter Ann, wife of William Vinal, because the St Thomas's vestry records tell us:

May 25 1772, Agreed that Ann Vinal should be allowed 2/6 per wk for providing & taking proper care of Mary Wildish during her illness.

Mary died in 1772, and her brother a decade later.

removed not to their parish of settlement, but to the workhouse (see page 172) of the Poor Law Union in which they had settlement.

If you find someone having children in a parish but who was not himself born there, you might find a removal order stating where they originated (and, by implication, where they ended up too).

SETTLEMENT CERTIFICATES

Clearly, during the 17th century, life for the able bodied who wished to travel around looking for work was becoming farcically complicated, so in 1697 the government passed another Settlement Act creating settlement certificates. If someone wanted to leave their parish and avoid being forcibly repatriated, they obtained a certificate from their overseers of the poor stating that their home parish was responsible for their upkeep should they fall on hard times. Once the overseers of the poor had received such a certificate from an incomer, they could sleep soundly in the knowledge they had been indemnified against any future expense. For genealogists, there is nothing more useful than a settlement certficate, stating clearly where a migrant ancestor had originated.

CHAPTER TWENTY
HOSPITALS & WORKHOUSES

We are used to ancestors living at home, but many spent time away, in hospital or the dreaded workhouse. These institutions kept records that can provide stark details about our forbears.

HOSPITALS

Many hospitals maintained by monasteries were closed at the Reformation (1534), but they were rapidly substituted by ones founded by the charitable donations of the wealthy or later by the parish (usually in the same building as the workhouse). In the 18th century, lying-in hospitals, where women could give birth, were established in some towns and cities.

▽ *Bird's-eye View of Guy's Hospital, Southwark, with Figures in the Foreground* (English School, 18th century).

M^r. Guy's Hospital for Incurables, in the Borough of Southwark

WORKHOUSES

In the 17th and 18th centuries, the most common system of poor relief was 'outdoor' relief, whereby overseers of the poor gave paupers – those who were sick, infirm or otherwise unable to work – money, food and clothing at home, while the unemployed were out to work within the parish. 'Indoor' relief was administered via the dreaded workhouses, which originated in the 17th century as relatively benign refuges and hospitals for people who were too young, old or ill to look after themselves. Either built by a parish for its own needs or (from 1723) by a group of co-operating parishes, workhouses were sometimes made as unpleasant as possible as a means of deterring what were known as the 'idle poor' – those who were seen as able but too lazy to work – from seeking relief. From 1782, with the passing of Gilbert's Act, parishes could form unions to maintain a workhouse and pay guardians to staff them.

So unpopular and expensive was the workhouse system and its prohibition of outdoor relief that some hundreds of parishes succeeded in disincorporating themselves and returning their poor to parish care. The 1834 Poor Law Amendment Act overhauled the system completely, but in quite the opposite direction. The parishes were united into unions responsible for funding the workhouses, which were placed under the direct control of a board of guardians responsible to commissioners at Somerset House. Besides the parish overseers of the poor continuing to collect the poor rates, the vestries ceased to be involved.

WHERE TO SEARCH

HOSPITALS

- Those records of patients and burials that have survived are either in the **hospital's own archives** or at the **county record offices**.

- A database of hospital records, mainly those now deposited elsewhere, is on **www.nationalarchives.gov.uk/hospitalrecords**.

- Records of lunatic asylums, which could be established by Justices of the Peace from 1828, are in Quarter Session records in the relevant **county record office** (see page 232) until 1888, when county councils assumed control.

LIFETIMES: UNLUCKY LUCY

THE BIRTH CERTIFICATE of James Lucy showed that he was born on 14 October 1862 at Princes Street Workhouse, St George in the East, London. He was the illegitimate son of Catherine Lucy, who signed her name with a cross, indicating that she was illiterate.

Many records have survived for the workhouse, including the register of births (1854–65). Here was confirmation that Catherine Lucy gave birth to an illegitimate son, James Lucy, on 14 October: most of the workhouse births were for illegitimate children. The admissions and discharge register showed that Catherine had been admitted on Friday, 22 August that year, classed as an able-bodied woman but needing help due to 'destitution'. I wonder whether she may have been thrown out of where ever she was living or working because of her pregnancy.

There was also an entry for the 'admission' of James Lucy on Tuesday, 14 October – his 'cause of seeking relief' was simply this: 'born'.

The discharge record lists Catherine Lucy who, it usefully tells us, was born in 1841, leaving the workhouse by her 'own desire' on Wednesday, 28 January 1863. Little James was discharged too, 'with mother', and off they went into the wide world.

While the elderly, sick or widows with young children could still receive outdoor relief, the choice for the able-bodied poor in need of assistance was stark: enter the workhouse, or starve. The Act centralised the system, moving it a step closer to direct state intervention in the lives of individuals and the transfer of responsibility for the poor from the gentry to the government. The introduction of old age pensions in 1908 and unemployment benefits in 1911 was effectively a return to 'outdoor relief', but the workhouses remained until the Poor Law was abolished in 1948. Many ex-workhouses still function as NHS hospitals to this day.

▽ Inside a workhouse: *The Westminster School of Industry, Old Pye Street*, printed by Leighton Brothers (19th century).

WORKHOUSES

⊡ Many of our ancestors spent time in workhouses other than when they were born, married or died and consequently you may not find out about this aspect of their lives unless you find them there in an indexed census, such as those for 1901 or 1881 (see pages 66–72), or specifically look for them. Directories will tell you which Poor Law Union covered their parish of residence.

⊡ The post-1834 records of the board of guardians will be at the relevant **county record office**. Of most use are the admission and discharge registers, which will tell you:
  ➲ Name
  ➲ Age
  ➲ Occupation
  ➲ Marital status
  ➲ Parish of settlement
  ➲ Denomination
  ➲ Sometimes a physical description
  ➲ Why the person needed help

⊡ Indoor relief lists were made twice a year and can be much easier to search. There were also:
  ➲ Registers of births, baptisms, deaths and burials of inmates, which contain many events omitted from General Registration.
  ➲ Records of those receiving outdoor relief.
  ➲ Binding of apprentices.
  ➲ Registers of offences and punishment of inmates and payments to prevent poor families from costing any further expense by assisting them to emigrate!

⊡ Records of workhouse staff are in class MH 9 at **TNA**. Much correspondence between the guardians and commissioners concerning inmates is in **TNA** class MH 15, but there are no indexes to names or places.

⊡ Workhouse records also include records of smallpox vaccination. This was compulsory from 1853 until 1948, and workhouses that administered the system kept registers from 1862, noting children's names, ages and birthplaces. Most records are in the relevant **county record office**. A detailed guide to the whereabouts of all post-1834 records is provided by J. Gibson, C. Rogers and C. Webb's *Poor Law Union Records* (FFHS, 1993/97). A guide to workshouse records is at **www.workhouses.org.uk**.

IRELAND

⊡ Irish workhouse records survive (from 1838) in great quantities and are particularly useful in view of the relative lack of parochial records. The records are at **local** and **national archives** and can best be traced through J. G. Ryan's *Irish Records – Sources for Family and Local History* (Ancestry, 1997).

△ *Applicants for Admission to a Casual Ward* by Luke Fildes (1874). How little things have changed!

QUICK REFERENCE

See main sources in Useful Addresses, page 306

WHERE TO SEARCH

CHAPTER TWENTY-ONE
WHAT PEOPLE DID

Occupational records can often provide a very useful way of overcoming genealogical problems. They may provide details of age, birthplace, parents', spouse's or children's names, but their use is more often in gaining further co-ordinates about when people were alive and where they lived, and suggesting connections with others of the same name.

WHERE TO SEARCH

OCCUPATIONS IN GENERAL

⊟ S. A. Raymond's *Londoners' Occupations: A Genealogical Guide* (FFHS, 1994) is a very useful guide to old occupations.

⊟ For Scotland, look at D. R. Torrance's *Scottish Trades and Professions: A Selected Bibliography* (SAFHS, 1991).

⊟ There are many books and indexes relating to people who followed different trades and occupations. It is always worth checking in J. Gibson and E. Hampson's *Specialist Indexes for Family Historians* (FFHS, 1998), which includes a section on indexes relating to people in various occupations.

OCCUPATIONAL RECORDS

The jobs we do have a massive impact on our lives, and so occupational records are one of the best ways of finding out more about forbears, beyond mere names and dates. For people such as soldiers or policemen, records may tell you what they did in their careers, and sometimes even tell you about their characters and physical appearance.

Our ancestors would be perplexed by terms such as 'data processor' or 'mobile phone technician' and, equally, many of theirs are unfamiliar to us. The *Oxford English Dictionary* provides many definitions, but my favourite book for finding out what many occupations really entailed is R. Campbell's *The London Tradesman* (1747, reissued by David & Charles). Here are a few lines from the section on apothecaries:

> *This is the mere Apothecary; a Creature that requires very little Brains; he wants only a strong Memory, to retain such a Number of cramp Words as he is daily conversant to: There is no Branch of Business, in which a Man requires less Money to set him up … Ten or twenty Pounds, judiciously applied, will buy Gallipots and Counters, and as many Drugs to fill them as might poison the whole Island.*

▷ *Fish Fags* by Thomas Rowlandson (1756–1827). A reminder that, even though the fact was seldom recorded, most women worked just as hard as men.

LIFETIMES: LOOK TO THE FAMILY

IN THE PAST, sons were much more likely than now to do the same work as their fathers. If your ancestor made saddle trees – the wooden moulds used by saddle makers – his father was probably one as well. Equally, people tended to marry within their own 'caste', so apprentice saddle-tree makers often married their masters' daughters, or became friends with other saddle-tree makers and ended up marrying their sisters. Thus, it is worth seeing who else was doing the same thing in your ancestor's community and see if they were indeed part of your wider family history. It is also worth considering how people who did want a change often took sideways steps, such as saddle tree makers becoming last makers.

Take, for example, Lorna Barbour's family. In 1911, her great-great uncle Henry Alexander drove a Model T Ford up Ben Nevis. The journey took him five days and 18 hours.

His father, James Robert Alexander, was closely involved with transport. He was listed in the 1900 Edinburgh Post Office Directory as a cycle manufacturer and agent at 7 Clerk Street, Newington, also running Alexander & Co., cycle agents and Alexander & Co., wholesale boot manufacturers at different addresses. By 1915, he had taken the next logical step and opened a motor agency and garage – and it's no surprise to know from family sources that it was a Ford dealership! By 1941 this had grown so large that the sales and service branch and agricultural departments were at different addresses. He died in 1941 in Edinburgh, described on his death certificate as a motor agent.

FROM SADDLE-TREE MAKER TO BOOT MANUFACTURER

James's death, marriage and birth certificates all name his father as an earlier James Robert Alexander. He was a last maker and this is clearly why the family had moved into shoemaking. James senior was in turn the son of Nicol Alexander, a saddle-tree maker, born in 1793 and buried in 1835 at South Leith. He was described in the burial record as a freeman of Calton, as was his father, an earlier Nicol Alexander, a saddle-tree maker buried at Calton in 1799.

◁ *A Village Scene with a Cobbler* by Jan Victors (1620–76).

WHERE TO SEARCH

SELECTED OCCUPATIONS

Almost all occupations operated records, now covered by indexes, books and so on. Here are some examples.

ACTORS

Actors are problematical as there were very few formal records, especially before the foundation of Equity in 1930. However, the **Theatre Museum** has a vast collection of playbills and programmes. For actors since 1912 you can consult *Who's Who in the Theatre*, which includes some dates of birth and parents' names (and, of course, the parents could themselves have been on the stage).

There were a number of 19th-century journals, starting with *The Era* (founded in 1838), which can also be searched at the **Theatre Museum**.

ARCHITECTS

There are several biographical dictionaries of architects, especially H. A. Colvin's *A Biographical Dictionary of British Architects 1600–1840* (Yale University Press, 1995) and A. Felstead, J. Franklin and L. Pinfield's *Dictionary of British Architects 1834–1900* (Mansel Publishing, 1993).

ARTISTS AND SCULPTORS

There are many biographical dictionaries of artists, mainly focusing on what they exhibited rather than providing much of genealogical use, save (often) places of residence and a date of death, which can lead you to a will. **Westminster Central Reference Library** is one of the best places to research an artist's career. See also my article 'Artists' in *Family History Monthly*, April 2003, no. 91.

CIVIL SERVANTS

Most documentation for civil servants is at **TNA**, in the records of their department. Pension records 1855–1924 are in class PMG 28 and examination records 1876–1962 are in CSC 10. Prior to the 19th century, you may find civil servants mentioned in the records of government such as the State Papers Domestic. Many civil service appointments were announced in the *London Gazette* (see page 144) and appear in the *Civil Service Year Book*, the Foreign Office list and almanacs such as the *Royal Kalendar*.

Records of British civil servants in India to 1947 are at the **India Office Library** as are the records of the East India College, where they were trained. The records include many petitions for employment, accompanied by baptism or birth certificates, pension records, and published lists of civil servants for each of the Indian presidencies.

CLERGYMEN

The following remarks concern clergymen in the Churches of England, Wales, Ireland or the Episcopal Church of Scotland. For others, see page 256.

Until the establishment of theological colleges in the mid-19th century, it was highly unusual for anyone to become a clergyman without having a university degree, so details of most clergymen, including fathers' names, can usually be found in the printed lists of university students (see page 239). Most English and Welsh clergy were therefore graduates of either Oxford or Cambridge, although some had, of course, come from universities further afield.

△ **Rev. Perry Nursey (1799–1867), an alumnus of Sidney College, Cambridge (1819–23) who became an Anglican clergyman.**

Equally, until 1858, the wills of many clergymen were proved at the Prerogative Court of Canterbury (see page 129).

Further information can be found in the *Clerical Guide*, published from 1817, the Clergy List (from 1841) and Crockford's *Clerical Directory* (OUP, since 1858), which will tell you the clergyman's position and parish, previous appointments and details of where he was educated. To supplement this there is J. Foster's *Index Ecclesiasticus* (Parker & Co, 1840 (sic)), covering many clergymen, 1800–40.

Potted biographies of higher-ranking clergy from 1066 to 1854, arranged by diocese, are listed in T.

D. Hardy's *Fasti Ecclesia Anglicanae, or A Calendar of the Principal Ecclesiastical Dignitaries in England & Wales ... From the Earliest Time to the Year 1715* (OUP, 1854), which has since been expanded in a series of volumes, *John Le Neve Fasti Ecclesia Anglicanae* (Institute of Historical Research); online at **www.british-history.ac.uk**.

⌗ The Fawcett card index to many clergymen is at the **SoG**.

⌗ Information about a clergyman's daily work can be found by studying the records of the parish or parishes where he worked. Bear in mind that the writing in the register could be that of the parish clerk.

⌗ In Scotland, details of established church clergymen up to 1638 are in D. E. R. Watt's *Fasti Ecclesiae Scoticanae Medii Aevi ad Annum 1638* (St Andrews & Scottish Record Society, 1969) and from the Reformation onwards in the *Fasti Ecclesiae Scoticanae* series (Oliver & Boyd).

⌗ In Ireland, Church of Ireland clergy are listed in the Almanack and Registry (from 1836), and the Irish Church Directory (from 1862). Irish Catholic priests can be traced through the **Catholic Directory** (from 1837). You can look, too, in bishops' transcripts (see page 114).

COASTGUARDS, CUSTOMS OFFICERS AND EXCISEMEN
⌗ Coastguards' records are in **TNA** class ADM, dating from 1822, and described in information leaflet 8. **Mrs E. R. Stage** has an index to over 70,000 coastguards.

⌗ Customs officers were supposed to collect import duties and catch smugglers, while excisemen made

sure duty was paid where due on domestic goods. Until their union in 1909, they were governed by two separate boards. The records are in **TNA** class CUST, detailed in leaflet 106 and described in J. Cox and T. Padfield's *Tracing your Ancestors at the PRO* (PRO Publications, 1999).

⌗ **Mrs J. Underwood** has an index to customs officers' superannuation allowances 1831–81. Postings of excisemen start to be recorded from 1695: the entry papers in CUST 116 cover the period 1820–70 and give age, place of birth, marital status and character.

⌗ Scotland had separate customs and excise boards from 1707 to 1829, whose records – including those of the most famous Scottish exciseman of all, Robert Burns – are at the **NAS**.

⌗ Irish customs officers' records from the 17th century to 1922 are at **TNA** in classes CUST 20 and 39.

FIREMEN
⌗ A good source of information is the **London Fire Brigade Museum**.

GYPSIES
⌗ Those with gypsy ancestry should also consult S. Floate's *My Ancestors were Gypsies* (SoG, 1999) and join the **Romany and Traveller FHS**, whose library is at **Reading University**.

INVENTORS
⌗ Did your ancestor patent an invention? Have a look in B. Woodcroft's *Alphabetical Index of Patentees of Inventions 1617–1852* (Adams & Mackay, 1969). Fuller details, and also details of patents after 1852, are in the **British Library**, printed in annual volumes, though many of these are now indexed on CD-Rom.

QUICK REFERENCE

See also main sources in Useful Addresses, page 306

THEATRE MUSEUM
1E Tavistock Street
London WC2E 7PR
☎ 020 7943 4700
www.theatremuseum.org

WESTMINSTER CENTRAL REFERENCE LIBRARY
35 St Martin's Street
London WC2H 7HP
☎ 020 7641 4636
www.westminster.gov.uk/libraries/westref

INDIA OFFICE LIBRARY
British Library
96 Euston Road
London NW1 2DB
☎ 020 7412 7513
www.bl.uk/collections/orientalandindian.html

MRS E. R. STAGE
150 Fulwell Park Avenue
Twickenham
Middlesex TW2 5HB

MRS J. UNDERWOOD
174A Wendover Road
Weston Turville
Buckinghamshire HP22 5TG

LONDON FIRE BRIGADE MUSEUM
Winchester House
94A Southwark Bridge Road
London SE9 OEG
☎ 020 7587 2894
www.london-fire.gov.uk

ROMANY AND TRAVELLER FHS
c/o Mrs J. Keet-Black
6 St James Wak
South Chailey
East Sussex
BN8 4BU

△ *The Doctor* by Arthur Miles (c.1860).

WHERE TO SEARCH

LAWYERS

The best place to start seeking a lawyer is the Law Lists, which have been published annually since 1775 and can be examined at specialist law or genealogical libraries. The **Law Society Library** holds many useful records and, for a fee, can help you trace the career of a solicitor or attorney ancestor. **Brian Brooks** keeps an index of solicitors, attorneys, notaries public, proctors and conveyancers.

Solicitors specialised in civil cases. From 1728, solicitors had to qualify by becoming articled clerks. They can be traced through the indexed registers of due execution of clerkship (i.e. successful completion of training) in **TNA** class KB 170, which cover 1749–1877 (see leaflet 112). These often state fathers' names. Most articled clerks between 1728 and 1774 appear in the **SoG's** Apprentices index (1710–74).

Lawyers in church courts and the Court of Admiralty were either proctors (similar to barristers) or advocates (solicitors). Records of admissions and appointments 1727–1841 are in **TNA** class HCA 30. An index to 658 proctors is kept by **John Titford**. Advocates were also doctors of law and belonged to the College of Advocates in Doctors' Commons, whose records are at **Lambeth Palace Library**.

Barristers were lawyers called to practise at the bar through one of the Inns of Court. Many of the admission registers have been printed and will provide a date of admission and name and residence of the father. The four surviving inns – Lincoln's Inn, Gray's Inn, Middle Temple and Inner Temple – have excellent archives for further

research, not least, in some cases, registers of baptisms, marriages and burials of lawyers and their families in their own chapels. The exact location of records is given in D. S. Bland's *A Bibliography of the Inns of Court and Chancery* (Selden Society, 1965).

Some barristers became judges. They are easily traced through E. Foss's *A Biographical Dictionary of the Judges of England, 1066–1870* (John Murray, 1870).

Justices of the Peace, who presided at the Quarter Sessions (see page 232) were seldom trained lawyers. Records of their appointments are indexed in **TNA** class C 202 and announcements of their appointment are also in the *London Gazette* (see page 144).

Scottish solicitors were called writers and can be traced through the Scottish Law List (Law Society of Scotland, from 1848). Scottish barristers were called advocates and their details, including in many cases birth, marriage and death details, are in F. J. Grant's *The Faculty of Advocates in Scotland,*

1532–1943, with Genealogical Notes (Scottish Record Society, 1944).

MEDICS

From 1511 until 1775, licences to practise medicine can be found in the records of the bishop's court that issued them, but will tell you little more than names and home parishes. From 1845 medics appeared in the *Medical Directory* and from 1859 in the *Medical Register* – there are good sets at the SoG, giving the date the medics qualified and from which institution, which should itself hold further records.

Excellent secondary sources for many doctors, dentists and midwives is P. J. and R. V. Wallis's *Eighteenth-century Medics (Subscriptions, Licences, Apprenticeships)* (Project for Historical Geography Research Series, 1994) and C. H. Talbot and E. A. Hammond's *The Medical Practitioners in Medieval England; A Biographical Register* (Wellcome Historical Medical Library, 1965).

Apothecaries made medicines and those in London were often members of the Grocers' Company. After 1815,

LIFETIMES: TRACED THROUGH A LICENCE

THOMAS ROBINSON appears in White's Suffolk directory in 1844, listed as a surgeon in Haverhill. The 1855 directory does not list him, however, and indeed the Bury and Norwich Post (1 February 1854) confirms that 'On the 24th Inst, aged 49 years, Mr Thos. Robinson, for many years surgeon at Haverhill', died. Unfortunately, he was not in Haverhill for the 1851 census, so his origins proved something of a mystery, until his apothecary's licence was discovered at the Guildhall Library. The alphabetical register of Licentiates (8421/B1) listed five Thomas Robinsons, of which the following was clearly correct.

On Valentine's day, 14 February 1833, Mr Thomas Robinson of full age (i.e. 21 or over), a candidate for a certificate to practise as an apothecary, was examined to see if he was suitable for a licence. The record states that John Bridge provided a testimonial to Thomas's moral character and Thomas himself produced evidence that he had been born on 11 June 1804. He had been apprenticed to Mr Adam Douglas of Kilenaul, Co. Tipperary, for seven years. He had attended anatomical demonstrations and courses in chemistry, 'materia medica', botany, anatomy, physiology and the principles and practice of medicine at Trinity College, Dublin, in 1826. He then spent 12 months at the Richmond Hospital, taking courses in midwifery and clinical medicine. Only one Thomas Robinson who attended Dublin University was of the right age to fit this person:

ROBINSON, THOMAS, Pen. (Mr Martin), Nov. 1, 1819, aged 15, s. of Thomas, generosus [gentleman], b. Waterford.

The registers of Christ Church, Waterford, included:

1804, June 25, Thomas, the son of Capt. Thomas Robinson of the South Cork Regt. of Militia and Mary his wife, born 11th inst.

Problem solved!

all apothecaries and many physicians and surgeons who wished to practise in England and Wales had to be licensed by the Society of Apothecaries, whose records are kept at the **Guildhall Library**, indexed 1815–40 in *A List of Persons who have Obtained Certificates of their Fitness to Practise as Apothecaries from August 1, 1815 to July 31, 1840* (SoG, 1990).

▱ Dentistry was originally undertaken by surgeons. Dentists were registered from 1878 and appear in the Dentists' Register at the **SoG**, while licentiates in dental surgery also appear in the back of some medical directories.

▱ Nurses appear in the records of nursing training schools, attached to many hospitals, from the mid-19th

QUICK REFERENCE

See also main sources in Useful Addresses, page 306

LAW SOCIETY LIBRARY
113 Chancery Lane
London WC2A 1PL
☎ 0870 606 2511
www.library.lawsociety.org.uk

BRIAN BROOKS
Cambria House
37 Pembroke Avenue
Hove
East Sussex BN3 5DB

JOHN TITFORD
Yew Tree Farm
Hallfieldgate
Higham
Derbyshire DE55 6AG

LAMBETH PALACE LIBRARY
Lambeth Palace Road
London SE1 7JU
☎ 020 7898 1400
www.lambethpalacelibrary.org

PALESTINE POLICE

This force included many British men who policed what is now Palestine and Israel between 1922 and 1948. The best records to start searching are at:
The British Empire and Commonwealth Museum
The Clock Tower Yard
Temple Meads
Bristol, BS1 6QH
0117 925 4980
www.empiremuseum.co.uk

See my articles 'Law and Order: the history and records of the Palestine Police' parts 1 and 2 in *Practical Family History*, (January and February, 2006), no.9, pp.24-7 and no.98, pp. 18-21, respectively.

century. Twentieth-century nurses up to 1973 are indexed in the register of nurses in class DT 11 at **TNA**.

Midwives had to obtain licences to practise from their local bishop's court (see page 231) until the mid-18th century.

Physicians diagnosed and treated ailments. They usually had medical degrees, especially from one of the Scottish universities, though many more attended on an ad hoc basis. the **Royal College of Physicians** holds records of many London and provincial physicians from 1518, and also a number of biographical dictionaries, which may include your ancestor and provide an age and father's name. A useful study of some 17th-century physicians is John H. Raach's *A Dictionary of English Country Physicians 1603–1643* (Dawsons of Pall Mall, 1962), compiled from various sources such as **PCC** wills.

Surgeons undertook operations. Many used to combine their trade with barbering, and in London they belonged to the Barber-Surgeons' Company, whose records, including freedom admissions from 1522, can be examined at **Guildhall Library**. the **Royal College of Surgeons** was founded in 1800 and holds records of members.

MUSICIANS

These are best studied through *Grove's Dictionary of Music and Musicians* (various eds from 1878).

POLICEMEN

The Metropolitan Police was not formed until 1829. Its records up to the 1930s are in **TNA** in class MEPO, described in leaflet 53. See also **Metropolitan Police Historical Museum** and **www.policeorders. co.uk**.

County police forces started to be formed in 1835 and became compulsory in England, Wales and Scotland by 1857. Records for the county constabularies are held variously by the constabularies or local record offices as detailed in L. A. Waters' *Notes for Family Historians* (Police History Society, 1987). You also can contact the **Police History Society**.

The Irish Constabulary was formed in 1836, added 'Royal' to its name in 1867 and was abolished in 1922. Its service records, giving name, age, denomination, previous trade, country of birth and dates of service are at **TNA** in class HO 184, with indexes there and at the **National Archives of Ireland**. Pension records are in **TNA** class PMG 48.

△ *The Postman* by William Pyne (1769–1843).

POLITICIANS

The **House of Lords Record Office** holds registers of all who attended Parliament. Careers of peers are given in G. E. Cockayne's *Complete Peerage* (see page 295) and careers of members of the House of Commons are being researched in an on-going project by the History of Parliament, currently covering MPs 1386–1832 and lords 1660–1832.

POSTMEN

Records of high-ranking post office officials date back to 1672 at the **Post Office Archives**, and from 1831 onwards there are appointment books recording all employees. Pension records survive for all staff for the 19th and 20th centuries (indexed to 1921), and these include dates of birth.

Scottish post office records from 1803 to 1910 are at the **NAS**.

TRAIN DRIVERS

Train drivers and other railway workers survive among the records of the 1000 or so railway companies that existed before 1923. That year, most merged into the London & North Eastern, Southern, London, Midland & Scottish and Great Western Railways, and these were nationalised as British Rail in 1948. Most surviving records, including some for Ireland (others for Ireland are at the **PRONI**), are at **TNA** in class RAIL: some records are in **local record offices**.

The best guide to the records, including other sources such as trades union records and staff magazines, is T. Richards' *Was your Grandfather a Railwayman? A Directory of Railway Archive*

LIFETIMES: POLICE RECORDS

IMAGINE A 5′ 8″ TALL MAN with a florid complexion, dark brown hair and brown eyes, born in 1821 in Whitechapel, London. This was the description given in the Surrey police records of one of its earliest members, Samuel Baxter.

These records also tell us that this colourful cockney, who originally worked as a groom, joined the Metropolitan Police as a constable in 1844 and served for nine years. After a couple of weeks' respite, he joined the two-year-old Surrey constabulary in 1853, starting at Merrow near Guildford as a 4th class constable, rising rapidly to 3rd and then 2nd class. Within a year of joining, he was posted to nearby Great Bookham, near Leatherhead, but on 21 December 1854 he failed to attend a meeting (too much Christmas cheer?), was demoted to 3rd class and packed off to Abinger. Here he regained his composure and won back 2nd class status the following December. May Day 1856 – another public holiday, significantly – he was re-demoted for neglect of duty and transferred, at his own expense, to Thorpe. He won back 2nd class status in November 1856 and, after three and a half years' sustained effort, reached 1st class in June 1860.

In January 1861 he moved to Addlestone, where the census shows him at Crouch Oak Lane with his wife and daughter, and a lodger. December that year saw a move to York Town, Frimley, where, in 1865, after almost a decade of keeping out of trouble, he was demoted to 2nd class for neglecting to visit a pub when ordered. Here he remained, PC (2nd class) Baxter, until he resigned in 1867 with a £50 gratuity out of the superannuation fund. He went back to London, becoming as grocer at 1 Cottage Place, Tottenam Hale, where he remained for the rest of his life.

If Samuel had been just a groom or grocer, little or no such comparable detail would have been recorded about him.

Sources for Family Historians (FFHS, 1995). An index to some railway employees is kept by **J. F. Engert**.

⊟ Searching can be complicated if you do not know the company for which your ancestor worked, because conurbations like Manchester were serviced by hundreds of separate companies. It is therefore worth seeing if the company is named alongside the job description in the **GRO** of the man's marriage or births of his children. If you persist, however, you may find detailed records including the date of birth – it is certainly worth having a go.

QUICK REFERENCE

See also main sources in Useful Addresses, page 306

ROYAL COLLEGE OF PHYSICIANS
Library and Information Services
11 St Andrews Place
London NW1 4LE
☎ 020 7935 1174 x 312
www.rcplondon.ac.uk/college/library

ROYAL COLLEGE OF SURGEONS
35–43 Lincoln's Inn Fields
London WC2A 3PE
☎ 020 7869 6520
www.rcseng.ac.uk

METROPOLITAN POLICE HISTORICAL MUSEUM
Unit 7 Meridian Estate
Bugsby Way
Charlton
London SE7 7SJ
☎ 020 8305 2824
www.met.police.uk/history

POLICE HISTORY SOCIETY
Secretary: Steve Bridge
(no mailing address given)
Email steve@bridge100.fsnet.co.uk
www.policehistorysociety.co.uk

HOUSE OF LORDS RECORD OFFICE
Palace of Westminster
London SW1A 0PW
☎ 020 7219 3074
www.parliament.uk

POST OFFICE ARCHIVES
Freeling House
Phoenix Place
Farringdon Road
London WC1X 0DL
☎ 020 7239 2570
www.royalmail.com

J. F. ENGERT
'Lundy'
31 Tennyson Road
Eastleigh
Hampshire SO50 9FS

LIFETIMES: THE CARPUES

SOMETIMES, APPRENTICESHIP RECORDS can be enough to prove a family tree. In the case of the Carpues of London, who were Catholic and therefore very hard to trace through conventional parish registers, they were essential. Edward Carpue of Serle Street, Lincoln's Inn, was a cordwainer (a superior sort of shoemaker, so-called for the use of fine-quality Cordoban leather) who married Mary Hodgson in 1779 and died in 1792. He was a Catholic so records of a baptism could not be found and his parentage could not be proved. However, the SoG's Apprentices Index showed him being apprenticed to his uncle Joseph Carpue, cordwainer, in 1755. In his will, which was found in the indexes to the Prerogative Court of Canterbury (see page 129), Joseph made his nephew Edward an executor and left £200:

> 'towards apprenticing or putting out [to trade] such children … to such respectable and honest trade and employment as [his executors] … shall think most deserving objects of such authority'.

Joseph recognised the value of apprenticeship doubly, for that was how he had started his career. The Apprentices Index reveals him being apprenticed in 1721 to his elder brother Charles Carpue of St Clement Danes, shoemaker. And Charles is there right at the beginning of the records, apprenticed in 1711 to Robert Mothersall of St Clement's, described as son of Charles Carpue of Missenden, Buckinghamshire, thus identifying Edward's grandfather and revealing the family's rural origins before they became London tradesmen.

▽ A typical apprentice indenture, this time for Henry Keogh, who, with the consent of his guardian Benjamin Humphrey Smart, was apprenticed to Thomas Spooner to become, of all things, a 'table decorator and manufacturer of desert and other ornaments'.

APPRENTICE, MASTER AND FREEMAN

Besides records of people doing jobs, there are also copious records of them being trained – or apprenticed – in trades and occupations. These are often linked to the records of boroughs and cities. They provide a lot of extra detail about people's lives and they often supply those all-important fathers' names as well.

APPRENTICESHIP

What we usually now term as 'vocational training' was in the past covered by apprenticeship, an agreement whereby a child was 'bound' to serve a master who would in turn teach him to follow his trade or profession. Apprenticeship usually started at ten years (or seven years for the navy) and seldom after 18, and lasted seven years or until the age of 21 years. The apprentice was then free, but if he submitted a test-piece, called a 'masterpiece', which passed muster, he qualified to become a master craftsman. It is not uncommon to find yourself descended from both apprentice and master, because a favoured apprentice would often be encouraged to marry his master's daughter, and less scrupulous boys endeavoured to fast-track their careers by marrying the boss's daughter in any case!

FREEMEN OF GUILDS

Many peoples' ancestors were freemen of guilds. In many cases there will be surviving records detailing what they did and who their fathers were. You could become a freeman by one of four ways:
➤ **Apprenticeship or servitude**
➤ **Honour:** honorary freedoms were occasionally bestowed on men of great distinction.
➤ **Patrimony:** being the son of a freeman.
➤ **Redemption:** buying your way in, a system abolished in 1835 in everywhere but London.

Guilds mostly flourished in towns and cities. Medieval guilds came in three varieties, religious, merchant and craft. The first were abolished at the Reformation, and the third tended to be absorbed by craft guilds, although in small towns there might be only one craft guild, to which all craftsmen belonged, regardless of their trade. Guilds had many functions, including regulating quality of produced goods, and acting as friendly societies, caring for elderly members and their widows and orphans.

WOMEN'S WORK

MOST PEOPLE THINK THAT, in the past, men went out to work and women stayed at home producing babies. While this was sometimes true, many women did work. At the surface of coalmines were miners' wives and daughters whose job was to clean and sort the newly mined coal, and quaysides reverberated with the songs of fishwives, whose role in life was to sort and clean their husbands' catches. Many working-class women worked in service until they got married (most had to leave once they had husbands) and it is true that many babies born to them resulted from liaisons, voluntary or not, with their employers' families. Once married, women worked as cleaners or took in sewing or laundry, or did more specialised work, such as embroidery or mantua (skirt) making.

Many more acted as unpaid staff in their husbands' businesses, tending the family shop or working alongside the men as potters, framework knitters, bakers and so on. And there were those who defied the odds and, when their husbands died or became incapacitated, took over the business or ran businesses themselves. Dr Sheila Sweetinburgh's work on medieval Hythe has turned up several examples, such as Katherine Peccyng who paid dues to town on the salt fish and shellfish she was selling in 1417, or Alice Heniper who left her fishing nets to her husband.

THE ARMY

GENERAL RECORDS

⊟ There are many detailed guides to using army records, particularly S. Fowler's *Army Records for Family Historians* (PRO Publications, 1998, revised by W. Spencer); M. J. and C. Watts' *My Ancestor was in the British Army: How Can I Find out More About Him?* (SoG, 1995); S. Fowler's *Tracing your First World War Ancestor* (Countryside Books, 2003) and S. Fowler's *Tracing your Second World War Ancestor* (Countryside Books, 2005).

MILITIA RECORDS

⊟ The earliest records of men at arms are the militia records. In times of emergency, able-bodied men were summoned to serve in the local militias. The whereabouts of muster rolls of all those liable for service, together with details either of their income or what arms they were supposed to provide, is given in given in W. Spencer's *Records of the Militia and Volunteer Forces* (PRO Publications, 1997). The earliest survive from the 16th century, particularly for the years 1522, 1539, 1542, 1569 and 1624, in **TNA** and **county record offices**.

⊟ **TNA** also holds records of militia men in WO 13 (1780–1878) and WO 68 (1859–1925) and there are a few birth and baptism records of serving militia men's children in WO 32 and WO 68. The latter also contains some marriage records and other information on militia men's physical appearance, places of birth, casualties, courts martials and so on. Pensions 1817–1927 are in PMG 13.

⊟ Most Welsh musters are at the National Library of Wales and are covered by a series of books *The History of the Welsh Militia and Volunteer Corps* (Palace Books).

⊟ Scottish records are at the **NAS**, both for before the Act of Union (1707) and after the re-creation of the Scottish militia in 1797.

⊟ Most Irish militia lists (1793–1876) are at **TNA** in class WO 13.

⊟ Most Channel Island militia lists are held on their respective islands although lists for Jersey and Guernsey 1843–52 are at **TNA** in class WO 13.

⊟ On the Isle of Man, the lists of the Manx Fencibles are at the **Manx Museum**.

⊟ The fear of French invasion, which lasted from the French Revolution to the fall of Napoleon (1793–1815), generated further militia-style forces. Posse Comitatus lists, covering able-bodied men aged 15–60 who were not already in the militia, were made in 1798 and a similar *Levée en Masse* list of able-bodied men aged 17–55 was

WHERE TO SEARCH

MILITIA MEN

FROM 1758 TO 1831, lists were made of all men aged 18–50 (or 18–45 after 1762). Militia men were then chosen from the lists by ballot. They had to attend a military camp for a week a year for three years, but during times of war they could be in service for the full three years, stationed anywhere in the British Isles (but not abroad). It is worth bearing this in mind if an ancestor crops up a long way from home. Those who did not want to serve could pay for someone else to be trained instead. Men with disabilities were also noted. From 1802 the number of children each man had was recorded and, from 1806, the mens' ages as well.

made in 1803. Some survive and have been printed, particularly I. F. W. Beckett's *The Buckinghamshire Posse Comitatus 1798* (Bucks Record Society, 1985).

Other militia-style forces from this period were the fencible infantry, fencible cavalry and yeomanry cavalry. Yeomanry regiments continued to be raised to deal with civil unrest during the 19th century, becoming the Territorial Army in 1921. Most records are at **TNA** and **county record offices** and are also detailed in J. Gibson and M. Medlycott's *Militia Lists and Musters 1757–1876: A Directory of Holdings in the British Isles* (FFHS, 1994).

PUBLISHED LISTS OF SOLDIERS

Some records of those who fought in famous conflicts have been published. For 1066 and all that, see A. J. Camp's *My Ancestor came over with the Conqueror: Those who Did, and Some of Those who Probably Did Not* (SoG, 1988).

Later, we have A. Livingstone, C. Aikman and B. Hart's *Muster Roll of Prince Charles Edward Stuart's Army 1745–6* (Aberdeen University Press, 1984), which attempts to trace the fate of each man, and *The Waterloo Roll Call* (Arms and Armour Press, 1978), which covers commissioned and non-commissioned officers.

THE CIVIL WAR

The officers and some soldiers on both sides of the Civil War appear in paylists and musters in **TNA** class E 315, but the best resources are published. Sir C. Firth and G. Davies' *The Regimental History of Cromwell's Army* (Clarendon Press, 1940) and E. Peacock's *The Army Lists of the Roundheads and Cavaliers* (Chatto & Windus, 1874) cover both sides well. There is also the 1663 list of Indigent Officers, detailing the claims made by former Royalist officers to the £60,000 bounty, which Charles II made available for their relief. This has been published and indexed, with some supplementary information from the Royalist news sheet ***Mercurius Aulicus***, the State Papers and other sources, in S. Reid's *Officers and Regiments of the Royalist Army* (Partizan Press, no date). Those whom Cromwell's Parliament fined for having fought for Charles I are well documented in Green's *Calendar of the Proceedings of the Committee for Advance of Money, 1642–1656* and *Calendar of the Proceedings of the Committee for Compounding, 1643–1660* (HMSO, 1888–92). Many, officers and men, appear in the printed calendars to the Domestic, Thurloe and Clarendon State Papers, which you can find in major **libraries**.

◁ **18th-century soldiers on parade outside St James's Palace. Note the multi-racial mix even then, with black bandsmen and white soldiers.**

QUICK REFERENCE

See main sources in Useful Addresses, page 306

For Channel Islands and the Isle of Man, see page 311

WHERE TO SEARCH

THE ARMY'S REGIMENTS

THE ARMY has its roots in the troops Charles II employed full-time after his Restoration (1660), whose numbers were dramatically expanded by James II (1685-8). Officers aside, though, few records exist until the 18th century. The army comprised regiments of foot soldiers (regiments of infantry-men and footguards) and mounted cavalry (regiments of hussars, dragoons, dragoon guards, lancers, lifeguards and royal horseguards), supple-mented by special regiments such as the Royal Artillery, Royal Horse Artillery and Royal Engineers. In 1881 the infantry was reorganised and most regiments were linked to a county. An online guide to regimental histories and engagements is at **www.army. mod.uk/unitsandorgs**.

THE STANDING ARMY

⊡ C. Dalton's *English Army Lists and Commission Registers 1661–1714* (Francis Edwards, 1960) and *George the First's Army 1714–1727* (Eyre & Spottiswoode, 1910–12) outline officers' careers, after which you can turn to Army Lists (see page 196).

⊡ For publications concerning the First World War, see page 198.

MUSEUMS

⊡ Many regiments have published regimental histories and maintain regimental museums. Even if they do not have specific records to do with your ancestors, they can provide a wealth of information on what your soldier ancestors wore, wielded and worried about. **The Army Museum Ogilby Trust** can put you in touch.

⊡ The **Imperial War Museum**, which is concerned with events since 1914, and the **National Army Museum** both hold splendid collections. Most useful records are kept at **TNA** in class WO (War Office), and are mainly arranged by regiment.

MEDALS

⊡ The Battle of Waterloo (1815) was the first campaign for which soldiers were awarded special medals, recorded in medal rolls. Those up to 1919 are in **TNA** (WO 100). Many have been published and can be studied at **TNA** or **SoG**. For example, Waterloo recipients are in **TNA** class MINT 16/112, published in *The Waterloo Medal Roll*, compiled from the Muster Rolls (Naval & Military Press, 1992)

⊡ Medals awarded for gallantry, such as the Victoria Cross, Military Cross and so on, with citations, were printed in the *London Gazette* (see page 144), and **TNA** has indexes to gazetted awards of certain medals

⊡ Medal rolls for the First World War are referred to on page 198. For medal awards after 1919, write to the **Army Medals Office**.

⊡ The more prestigious the medal, the more information is likely to have been recorded about an ancestor. The Victoria Cross has a splendid website, **www.chapter-one.com/vc** giving biographical details.

△ **The Victoria Cross awards for the army, 1857.**

QUICK REFERENCE

See also main sources in Useful Addresses, page 306

ARMY MUSEUM OGILBY TRUST
58 The Close
Salisbury SP1 2EX
☎ 01722 332188
www.armymuseums.org.uk

IMPERIAL WAR MUSEUM
Lambeth Road
London SE1 6HZ
☎ 020 7416 5320
www.iwm.org.uk

NATIONAL ARMY MUSEUM
Royal Hospital Road
Chelsea
London SW3 4HT
☎ 020 7730 0717
www.national-army-museum.ac.uk

ARMY MEDALS OFFICE
Government Office Buildings
Worcester Road, Droitwich
Worcestershire WR9 8AU
☎ 01905 772323
www.army.mod.uk

LIFETIMES: WILLIAM ALLEN

△ *The Battle of Isandhlwana* during the Zulu War by Charles Edwin Fripp (1854–1906).

FOR *ANTIQUES GHOSTSHOW* I visited the regimental museum of the Welsh Borderers, in Brecon, to learn about William Allen (1844–90), one of the men who was awarded the Victoria Cross for his bravery at Rourke's Drift, when a Zulu army attacked a weakly garrisoned hospital station on 22–3 January 1879. His citation (in TNA – WO 32/7390) stated that he and his friend Frederick Hitch,

'must also be mentioned. It was chiefly due to their courageous conduct that communication with the Hospital was kept up at all – holding together at all costs a most dangerous post, raked in reverse by the enemy's fire from the hill, they were both severaly wounded, but their determined conduct enabled patients to be withdrawn from the Hospital, & when incapacitated by their wounds from fighting themselves, they continued, as soon as their wounds had been contained, to serve out ammunition to their comrades during the night.'

The museum was a delight, including vivid models of the battle, showing the red-coated British soldiers battling it out with the almost completely skinned but viciously armed Zulu warriors. I was shown Allen's pocket watch, a pin cushion he had made from scraps of material found after the battle, and a picture of him having the VC pinned to his chest by the Queen herself. I was allowed to hold the very medal, which is worth about £200,000, and that of his commanding officer, Lieutenant Bromhead – the one who Michael Caine played in the film *Zulu* – worth a cool quarter of a million!

The museum gave me four pages of notes on Allen, and showed me the notice of his military funeral, published in the local paper. It transpired that although he was a hero under pressure, Allen was in fact a teacher, who spent many years teaching basic writing and arithmetic to his fellow soldiers and, after returning to Wales from South Africa, taught musketry. We know from his descendants that the events of that terrible night traumatised him deeply. I left, therefore, with a much fuller picture of the man behind the medal than I could possibly have got elsewhere.

OFFICERS

- Until the 20th century, officers were almost exclusively drawn from the middle and upper classes. The main ranks were general, colonel, lieutenant colonel, major, captain and lieutenant.

- The **Royal Military College**, originally the Royal Military Academy at Woolwich, founded in 1741, holds records of cadets, often including baptism certificates, from 1790.

- Officers' regiments can be discovered easily from Army Lists, which have been published from 1740 and are usually well indexed. Besides identifying the regiment, they will also tell you a bit about the officer, such as which medals he had been awarded, where he had fought, dates of promotion and whether he had been mentioned in the *London Gazette* (see page 144). Most good genealogical libraries have collections, and **TNA** also has manuscript lists from 1702 (WO 64–5). There are also published lists as outlined below.

- The main **TNA** holdings are services of officers on the active list (WO 25 and 76, partially indexed), dating back to 1829 and in some cases to 1764.

- In the **TNA**, WO 25 also includes various returns of officers made in 1809/10, 1829 and 1870–2, and retired officers 1828 and 1847. Once you have found the date of the officer's commission, you can seek the officer's letters applying to buy or sell it in the commander-in-chiefs' memoranda (1793–1870) in class WO 31. Announcements of promotion or retirement are in the *London Gazette*.

- Before pensions were introduced in 1871, retiring officers received 'half-pay', recorded from 1730 at **TNA** in WO 23–5 and in the Paymaster General's records (PMG 3–14), which should provide a date of death, and details of where the retired officer subsequently lived. Pensions for wounded officers are in WO 23 and pension applications by widows of officers killed in active service, 1760–1818, are in WO 25, and 1815–92 in WO 23, with further widows' pension applications, sometimes including details of birth, baptism, marriage and death, in 'miscellaneous certificates', in WO 2.

OTHER RANKS

- Until the 20th century, these were almost exclusively lower-class men. The minimum age to sign up was 18, though many boys lied about their ages to get in earlier. They would join for life, but in reality they usually served for 21 years (12 years from 1871).

- Soldiers are well recorded, but up to 1873 almost everything is arranged by regiment. **TNA** catalogue indexes soldiers 1760–1854, giving regiments. Soldiers after then may be identified by uniforms shown in pictures, or medals. Alternatively, you may find the regiment recorded on a birth or marriage certificate, in wills, parish registers or elsewhere. In frustrating cases, the occupation will simply say 'soldier' (or, if he had retired, 'pensioner'), in which case you will have to keep searching further records.

- If you find a record, such as a census, showing that a soldier had a child born somewhere unexpected, in Britain or abroad, you can find

out which regiments were stationed there from the monthly returns of regiments in **TNA** classes WO 17 and 73 or the *United Service Journal & Naval and Military Magazine*, later called *Colburn's United Service Magazine* (which also details officers' promotions).

- You may also find soldier ancestors in the Registrar General's Indexes to Regimental Returns of Births and Baptisms of Soldiers' Children (1761–1924) (see page 57): the indexes should cover all the regiments and the records most certainly do specify the regiments.

Muster rolls and pay lists

- At **TNA**, class WO 12 covers 1878–98 and class WO 15 covers 1760–1872, with a few stragglers going back to 1708. Those records for artillery, engineers and others are in class WO 10, 11, 14 and 15. They were compiled quarterly.

Description books

- These cover the period 1795–1900, with a few dating back to 1756, and are in **TNA** classes WO 25 and 67, arranged by regiment and then by initial letter of the surname.

Discharge and pensions

- Until the late 19th century, pensions were paid through the Royal Hospitals at Kilmainham, Dublin, founded by Charles II (1679) and Chelsea, opened in the reign of William and Mary (1692). Those resident there are called Kilmainham or Chelsea Pensioners, while all other non-officers in receipt of a pension for disability or completion of their term of service were called Kilmainham or Chelsea Out-pensioners.

⎆ Discharge documents of pensioners 1782–1854 for Chelsea (in **TNA**, WO 121) have been indexed online in **www.catalogue.nationalarchives.gov.uk**. They complement WO 97 and are particularly useful for tracing 18th- and early 19th-century soldiers.

⎆ Soldiers discharged in Ireland were paid via Kilmainham, regardless of where they subsequently lived. There are many records relating to pensions. In-pensioners are recorded in **TNA**, class WO 23.

⎆ Kilmainham In- and Out-pensioners admission registers are in **TNA**, class WO 118 (1704–1922).

⎆ Chelsea long-service admissions are at **TNA** in WO 116 1823–1920 and disability pensions WO 118 1715–1913. In-pensioners' regimental registers are in WO 120 (from 1715).

Regimental returns

⎆ The returns of soldiers who were discharged to pension are in **TNA**, class WO 120, covering 1715–1843 (with a second series going up to 1857), arranged chronologically. They are also partially indexed by J. D. Beckett's *An Index to the Regimental Registers of the Royal Hospital, Chelsea, 1806–1838* (Manchester and Lancs FHS, 1993).

⎆ From 1842, pensions were paid through a series of local pension offices throughout the British Isles. If you know where your ancestor lived, you can examine the registers of the most local office at **TNA** in WO 22.

Attestation and discharge papers

⎆ Records of men who paid to leave before their term of service was over for the period 1817–70 are in **TNA**,

△ **British troops leaving for France, 1915.**

class WO 25, arranged by regiment. However, the best records are in WO 97, with some others in WO 121, 122 and 131. They cover soldiers who were discharged to pension, who completed their term of engagement or paid to leave early, in the period 1760–1913. From 1883 there is one single alphabetical series, with a supplementary one covering entries that were misfiled. Fortunately, these records are now included in **www.catalogue.nationalarchives.gov.uk** for the period 1760–1854.

⎆ A **Soldiers Index** for 1855–72 is held, and can be searched for a fee, by Ms S. Davis.

CASUALTIES AND DESERTERS

⎆ Casualties and deserters are listed at **TNA** in class WO 25 in several categories covering 1797–1817 and 1809–1910.

⎆ Casualty rolls for specific wars between 1857 and 1898, published

and unpublished, are listed in S. Fowler's *Army Records for Family Historians* (PRO Publications, 1998).

DESERTERS AND COURTS MARTIAL

⎆ **TNA** class WO 25 contains records of deserters 1799–1852. Those caught and disciplined for desertion – or for a host of other intriguing offences – appear in records of military courts, dating from 1688 and catalogued in WO 71–2 and 81–93, with officers (1806–1904) in WO 93/1B. Deserters are also listed in the *Police Gazette*

QUICK REFERENCE

See also main sources in Useful Addresses, page 306

ROYAL MILITARY COLLEGE
Sandhurst
Camberley GU15 4PQ
☎ **01276 63344**
www.atra.mod.uk/atra/rmas

SOLDIERS LIST
Ms S. Davis
18 Manor Road
East Molesey
Surrey KT8 9JX

△ **The British Cavalry passing Albert Cathedral during the First World War.**

and *Hue and Cry*, copies of which are at **TNA**.

PRISONERS OF WAR

🗗 Records from 1793 are at **TNA**. Those for the First World War are detailed in **TNA** information leaflet 72 and those for the Second World War are in leaflet 111. WO 345 is a card index of 57,000 of those captured by the Japanese.

🗗 The **International Welfare Department of the British Red Cross** can deal with humanitarian enquiries, but not those made purely for family history purposes.

THE FIRST WORLD WAR

🗗 Some 6 million men served in the 'Great War', mostly after the introduction of conscription in 1916. The records of 15% of officers were destroyed in Second World War bombing but a supplementary series of records of varying degrees of completeness – about 85% - survives divided between WO 339 and WO 374 (searchable in **TNA** catalogue) with an index at **TNA** in WO 338 and searchable online at **www. catalogue.nationalarchives.gov.uk**. If you do not find what you are

looking, for the officer may have served beyond 1922, so contact the MoD at Kentigern House.

🗗 Many non-officer's records were destroyed in the same bombing but about 2 million of the latter still survive at **TNA**, covering men who died or were discharged between 1914 and 1920, arranged in approximate alphabetical order. These are the misleadingly named 'burnt' documents (WO 363), now available online at **www.ancestry.co.uk**.

🗗 Be aware that between 1914 and 1920 each regiment numbered its own soldiers, and so men in different regiments ended up with the same number.Furthermore, when battalions and regiments were partially or almost entirely annihilated, the survivors were assimilated into others so a long-serving soldier might have served with several regiments by the end of the war.

🗗 There are also unburnt documents, at **TNA**, such as WO 364 covering non-commissioned officers and other ranks that claimed pensions for war services from 1914 to 1920.

🗗 There are supplementary files at **TNA** for 140,000 officers in WO 339, arranged numerically (an index to find an officer's number is in WO 338), and WO 374, concerning some 80,000 Territorial Army soldiers. The files vary in detail from full service papers to just date of death. You can also consult pension records 1914– 20 in PMG 4, 9, 42–7 and PIN 26.

🗗 9000 surviving service records of the Women's Army Auxiliary Corps are in **TNA** in WO 398.

🗗 Where service records do not survive, the medal rolls (c. 1914–22) will at least tell you the campaigns in which your ancestor fought, and Officers' War Diaries may mention their acts of heroism, or at least provide some background to their service. All the former and some of the latter are on **www.nationalarchives.gov.uk/ documentsonline/default.asp**.

🗗 For identifying First World War soldiers' regiments also use N. Holding's *More Sources for World War I Army Ancestry* (FFHS, 1991).

🗗 The Great War Section of the **Veterans Agency** may also be able to provide details of a soldier's regiment. Electoral registers (see page 164) for autumn 1918 and spring 1919, for the soldier's home, include most men waiting to be demobilised, and name their regiment.

🗗 First World War armed forces deaths are at **TNA** and **www.familyrelatives.com** and **www.findmypast.com**. However the most accessible source is the **Commonwealth War Graves Commission** website, covering 25,600 First and Second World War memorials and cemeteries all over the world, with about 1.8 million names (see box, right).

⊟ Soldiers whose deaths were registered by the Belgian and French authorities are at **TNA** in RG 33/45–69, arranged alphabetically by first letter of surname.

⊟ Many soldiers' names appear alphabetically by battalion in *Soldiers Died in the Great War* (Naval and Military Press, 1989), and a similar work for officers (1919), available in good **genealogical libraries**. There are 81 of the volumes on a CD-Rom version, which has a name-search facility.

⊟ Many names appear on local war memorials and in rolls of honour, which were produced by localities and institutions, all listed in N. Holding's *The Location of British Army Records,*

QUICK REFERENCE

See also main sources in Useful Addresses, page 306

INTERNATIONAL WELFARE DEPARTMENT OF THE BRITISH RED CROSS
9 Grosvenor Crescent
London SW1X 7EJ
☎ 020 7201 5153
www.redcross.org.uk

VETERANS AGENCY
Norcross
Blackpool
Lancashire FY5 3WP
☎ 0800 169 2277
www.veteransagency.mod.uk

COMMONWEALTH WAR GRAVES COMMISSION
2 Marlow Road
Maidenhead
Berkshire SL6 7DX
☎ 01628 634221
www.cwgc.org

THIS IS A TYPICAL entry from the Commonwealth War Graves Commission's excellent website, **www.cwgc.org.uk**.

Debt of Honour Register
In Memory of ADOLPHUS OLATUNJI OSUN
Lance Corporal,
NA/87476
Nigeria Regiment, R.W.A.F.F.
who died on Sunday 15 April 1945.

CEMETERY: ENUGU MILITARY CEMETERY, Nigeria
GRAVE OR REFERENCE PANEL NUMBER: African Mohd. Plot. Row E. Grave 4.
LOCATION: Enugu, the capital of the Eastern Region, is 193 kilometres north of Port Harcourt on the main railway line to Kaduna and Kano. The Military Cemetery is situated on the left of the main road to Onitsha, just below Milliken Hill, and is 2 kilometres from the railway station.
HISTORICAL INFORMATION: The cemetery contains 90 Commonwealth burials of the 1939–1945 War, 1 of whom is unidentified. There are also 24 post-war graves. The cemetery is circular and is divided by radial paths into separate plots. A Cross of Sacrifice has been erected near the centre. The three United Kingdom soldiers are buried in the European plot on the southern perimeter of the cemetery. The war graves of the African soldiers are in denominational plots.

COMMONWEALTH WAR GRAVES COMMISSION

WHERE TO SEARCH

A National Directory of World War I Sources (FFHS, 1999). Of particular note are the *National Roll of the Great War 1914–1918* (National Publishing Company, 1918–21, and now at www.familyrelatives.org), compiled with information on about 150,000 men, alive or dead, mostly supplied by their families. The Marquis de Ruvigny's *The Roll of Honour, a Biographical Record of Members of His Majesty's Naval and Military Forces who Fell in the Great War 1914–1918* (LSE, 1987) covers about 25,000 deceased soldiers, including names of fathers and sometimes of mothers. Many entries are accompanied by a photograph.

There is also a useful website, www.great-war-casualties.com, and an index to many soldiers who died in the First World War kept by **Robert Base**, giving battalion number, places of birth and enrolment, residence, service number, rank, and date and place of death.

The best sources for general information about conditions, battles and so on are the archives and associated publications of the **Imperial War Museum**. At **TNA** in class WO 95 are war diaries for each infantry battalion. Men mentioned tend to be officers, but the relevant diary will still tell you exactly what your ancestor's battalion was doing, and when. Some soldiers, especially officers, kept their own diaries. MH 106 contains about a tenth of the soldiers' hospital records that survived.

RECORDS AFTER 1926

Soldiers' records after 1926 are held at the **Army Records Centre.** They are not open for public searching, but you can apply for a service record of a deceased forbear, so long as you can prove they are deceased and you are the next of kin. On application, you will be sent a form to fill in and you must also pay £20 for a search and send your evidence.

The **FRC** holds army deaths and the Commonwealth War Graves Commission website www.cwgc.org includes British soldiers who have died in wars since 1918. See also www.great-war-2-casualties.com.

THE SECOND WORLD WAR

For the Second World War there are rolls of honour, including place of birth and normal address, at Westminster Abbey and **TNA**, also available on CD-Rom from the Naval and Military Press.

Second World War war diaries are in **TNA** classes WO 165–79, 215, 218 and 257. The **Army Medals Office** holds records of medals awarded for Second World War service.

Other **TNA** sources are outlined in J. D. Cantwell's *The Second World War: A Guide to Documents at the PRO* (PRO Publications, 1998).

HOME GUARD

Records of the real life 'dads' army', the Home Guard, are in **TNA** classes WO 199, 166 and also in PREM 3. An article on their records is in *Practical History*, July 2007.

SCOTSMEN

Scots in the British army appear in military records after the Act of Union (1707). Prior to then (and aside from Scots who happened to fight in English regiments) the records of the ad hoc Scottish armies are sparse, and what survives in terms of musters are at the **NAS** and listed in J. Gibson and A. Dell's *Tudor and Stuart Muster Rolls: A Directory of Holdings in the British Isles* (FFHS, 1991). A fine secondary source is C. Dalton's *The Scots Army 1661–1688* (Naval and Military Press, 1989).

THE ARMY OVERSEAS

AUSTRALIA

First World War army records for Australia are at the Australian Archives.

INDIA

The Honorable East India Company (HEIC) maintained armies in each of the three Indian presidencies, comprising regiments of Indians, called Sepoys, led by British officers, and also regiments of British soldiers. In 1861 some of these troops were amalgamated into the British Army (records at **TNA**) and the rest were formed into the Indian Army (records at the **India Office Library**, except officers' commissions, which are at **TNA** in HO 51; WO 25/1–88 and WO 31), under the direct control of the Viceroy. Most records relating to these soldiers are also in the India Office Library. The records include HEIC court minutes, including indexed cadet papers (1789–1860), which usually include a birth or baptism

A HARD-WORKING SUBADAR

QUICK REFERENCE

See also main sources in Useful
Addresses, page 306

ROBERT BASE
15 Appleford Close, Hoddesdon
Hertfordshire EN11 9DE

IMPERIAL WAR MUSEUM
Lambeth Road
London SE1 6HZ
☎ 020 7416 5320
www.iwm.org.uk

ARMY RECORDS CENTRE
Ministry of Defence
Historical Disclosure
Mail Point 400
Kentigern House
65 Brown Street
Glasgow G2 8EX
☎ 0141 224 3030
www.mod.ulc

ARMY MEDALS OFFICE
Government Office Buildings
Worcester Road, Droitwich
Worcestershire WR9 8AU
☎ 01905 772323
www.army.mod.uk

INDIA OFFICE LIBRARY
British Library
96 Euston Road
London NW1 2DB
☎ 020 7412 7513
www.bl.uk/collections/
orientalandindian.html

NATIONAL ARMY MUSEUM
Royal Hospital Road
Chelsea
London SW3 4HT
☎ 020 7730 0717
www.national-army-museum.ac.uk

NATIONAL ARCHIVES OF NEW ZEALAND
10 Mulgrave Street
Thorndon
Wellington
New Zealand
www.archives.govt.nz

THE JALIL FAMILY who live in the Midlands knew that their immediate forbear was born in Bihar and that his father, Saiyid Mohammod Jalil, born in 1905, was the son of Abdul Majeed Mugurjalil Cahman, a doctor in the Indian Army. Many Indians living in the 19th century do not appear in records, but because of his involvement with the British, there was a good chance that Abdul would appear in the records of the India Office Library, part of the British Library, in London. And indeed he did.

In the 1910 Indian Army List, under 'Medical Services: Indian Subordinate Medical Department (Bengal)', we find listed Abdul Majid, born on 1 April 1882, who entered the service, proficient in English, to serve in the 19th Punjab Regiment, on 2 April 1903 – in other words, immediately after his 21st birthday. He became a 3rd class hospital assistant on 2 April 1908 and subsequent directories show his steady rise, no doubt through extremely hard work, to become a sub-assistant surgeon, 1st class, serving with the 125th Rifles, by the outbreak of the First World War.

Later directories show that, for his service in the war, he won the Indian Distinguished Service Medal. In 1926 he was 'specially promoted' to the rank of 'subadar', which was the equivalent to the rank of captain within the hierarchy of Indian warrant officers. Had he been white, he would no doubt have become a high-ranking surgeon – but this was as far as the British were prepared to promote Indians. Yet at least he was recorded in such a way that we can find this much about him.

certificate and all providing parents' names.

🗐 Records of the British officers serving under the HEIC 1796–1841, with some records relating to officers' and soldiers' pensions, are at **TNA** in classes WO 23 and 25. The **National Army Museum** has a card index to them, and both the **India Office Library** and **SoG** have army lists and biographical dictionaries detailing their promotions, where they served and usually when and where they died. The **SoG** also holds its own collection of material relating to the British in India.

NEW ZEALAND

🗐 Militia and army records for New Zealand are at the **National Archives** in Wellington.

THE ROYAL NAVY

GENERAL

Henry VIII made the navy the responsibility of the Lord Admiral in 1546. Naval records up to 1660 are scattered among the State Papers (Domestic), Privy Council, Exchequer and Admiralty, but, if you are lucky, you will find mention of ancestors who served as officers.

- From the Restoration in 1660 and until 1832, records are mainly in the Navy Board and Admiralty records at **TNA** and exclusively in the Admiralty records (ADM) for 1833–1926.

- The very best guide to **TNA**'s holdings is B. Pappalardo's *Tracing Your Naval Ancestors* (TNA, 2003). After 1926, if you can prove you are the next of kin of a deceased sailor, you can apply for their records to the **Naval Personnel Records Office**.

- Naval museums will give you a true flavour of what life was like for your nautical forbears. The main one for naval history (Royal and Merchant) is the **National Maritime Museum** and there is also the **Royal Naval Museum**. Both have complete sets of the Navy Lists from 1797.

OFFICERS

The main ranks of commissioned officers were admiral, rear admiral, commodore, commander, captain and lieutenant. Below them came warrant officers, who were in charge of functional aspects of the ship, such as master, engineer, sailmaker, gunner, boatswain, surgeon and carpenter.

- Commissioned officers serving 1660–1814 are outlined in D. Syrett

and R. L. DiNardo's *The Commissioned Sea Officers of the Royal Navy 1660–1815* (Naval Records Society, 1994), which draws on a wide variety of sources and includes details of officers commissioned by 1815 but whose careers continued long after.

- Also worth checking is J. Charnock's *Biographia Navalis, Or Impartial Memoirs of the Lives and Characters of Officers of the Navy of Great Britain from 1660 to the Present Time* (R. Faulder, 1794–8). N. Hurst's *Naval Chronicle 1799–1818: Index to Births, Marriages and Deaths* (N. Hurst, 1989) is useful for the Napoleonic period. Coming forwards to 1835 is J. Marshall's *Royal Naval Biography, Or Memoirs of the Services of all the Flag-officers ... whose Names Appeared on the Admiralty List of Sea Officers at the Commencement of the Present Year [1823], or who have Since been Promoted* (Longman, 1823–35).

- Finally, there is W. R. O'Byrne's *A Naval Biographical Dictionary; Comprising the Life and Services of every Living Officer in Her Majesty's Navy, from the Rank of Admiral of the Fleet to that of Lieutenant* (John Murray, 1861). This details the careers of officers often including correspondence between author and subject, detailing officers living in 1845 and also 600 who died in that year. In many cases the father's name and residence is given, making this particularly useful to genealogists.

- Most First World War officers will appear in the *Naval Who's Who* (1917). There are also lists of officers published occasionally from 1700 and consistently as Navy

Lists from 1782. These include warrant officers. They are available at **TNA** and **SoG**, and will enable you to build up a picture of your ancestor's career.

- Useful original sources at **TNA** include classes C 215/6, oaths of allegiance to Charles II taken by officers and men, and a similar list for oaths made to William III in 1696, is in C 213. Lieutenants' passing certificates, 1691–1902 (ADM 6, 13 and 107), arranged alphabetically, include baptism and later birth certificates, with a similar series for warrant officers.

- Commissioned and warrant officers' service records, c.1840–1920, some of which include dates of birth, marriage and death, are at **TNA** in ADM 196. Chronological registers of commissions are in ADM 6 (1695–mid-19th century). Records of commissioned and warrant officers on full pay are mainly in ADM 24 (1795–1872) and half-pay in ADM 25 (1693–1926); the latter may record the officer's residential address.

- Class ADM also contains records of courts martial, wounded officers' pensions, widows' pensions (including letters of application, proof of marriage and baptism of children) and so on, all detailed in N. A. M. Rodger's *Naval Records for Genealogists* (PRO Publications, 1998).

RATINGS

- Before 1853, ordinary sailors (ratings) were discharged after each voyage and could (and did) serve on merchant ships, so can be very difficult to find in records. Sailors who served from 1853 onwards can be easily traced

◁ **Thomas Potter's continuous service agreement. Note that Thomas's mother got confused and wrote her name where his should have been.**

THE NATIONAL ARCHIVES has a new database of resources for the Battle of Trafalgar (1805) at www.nationalarchives. gov.uk/ trafalgardatabase.

Pensions for 1802–94 may be found at **TNA** in ADM 29, for which there is an index. Remember that after 1853 sailors who had served for 20 years could leave and receive a pension even if they carried on working outside the navy for decades to come.

The hospital at Greenwich was established in 1695 to care for naval pensioners and their families. Records of its admissions and discharges (1704–1869) are in at **TNA** in ADM 73. N. A. M. Rodger's *Naval Records for Genealogists* (PRO Publications, 1998) outlines the hospital's many other records, including that of its school for sailors' children.

through the indexed continuous service engagement books at **TNA** in ADM 139 (1853–72) and ADM 188 (1873–1923), fully indexed in ADM 188/245–67.

Once you find a ship on which your ancestor served, you can examine its muster rolls at **TNA** in ADM 36–9 (1740–1808, with some for the period 1688–1739). Your ancestor's first and last musters on a ship should tell you the previous vessel on which he had served, and the one to which he was transferring, or whether he was being discharged, or had died. With luck, therefore, you should be able to track his whole naval career.

Pay books

Pay books covering 1691–1856 are in **TNA**, classes ADM 31–5. They can be used to substitute gaps in the musters and may also name next of kin, such as the sailor's wife or parents who received the pay on the sailor's behalf.

Ships' logs

Some of these survive from the 17th century. They are in classes ADM 50–5 at **TNA** and will provide much useful background. They may even mention your ancestor, especially if he had an accident or was killed.

Seamen's effects papers

These are at **TNA** in class ADM 44 (1800–60). Other wills may be found in ADM 48 (indexed in ADM 142). In ADM 171 are medal rolls for all ranks covering 1793–1972, arranged by ship and not indexed. Description books are in ADM 38.

Pensions

The Chatham Chest (in **TNA**, ADM 82) was a fund set up in 1590 to pay pensions to wounded sailors or the families of sailors killed in action. Registers survive for 1653–7 and 1675–1799 (indexed from 1695). From 1803, these pensions were paid through the Royal Naval Hospital at Greenwich.

QUICK REFERENCE

See also main sources in Useful Addresses, page 306

NAVAL PERSONNEL RECORDS OFFICE
Ministry of Defence
CS(RM)2 Navy Search
Bourne Avenue
Hayes
Middlesex UB3 1RF
☎ 020 8573 3831
www.mod.uk

NATIONAL MARITIME MUSEUM
Park Row
Greenwich
London SE10 9NF
☎ 020 8858 4422
www.nmm.ac.uk

ROYAL NAVAL MUSEUM
Buildings 1–7, College Road
HM Naval Base
Portsmouth
Hampshire PO1 3NH
☎ 023 9272 7562
www.royalnavalmuseum.org

△ Shipyards, from the Clyde to Chatham, provided employment for many from the Middle Ages but especially in the 19th and early 20th centuries.

WHERE TO SEARCH

Courts martial

⊟ Courts martial 1680–1913 are at **TNA** in class ADM 1.

RESERVE SAILORS

⊟ Some peoples' ancestors became reserve sailors, such as the Sea Fencibles, raised to help defend the country against France between 1798 and 1813, and many Merchant Navy sailors were also members of the Royal Naval Reserve (RNR), created in 1859. The records of members of the **RNR** who served in the First World War are in **TNA** in class ADM 337.

DOCKYARDS

⊟ The main naval dockyards in Britain were at Portsmouth, Woolwich, Deptford, Chatham, Sheerness and Plymouth. If you discover a record of the baptism or marriage of an ancestor in one of these places, he could well have had naval connections and, if you loose sight of him, look in the parish records of other dockyard towns. It may be worth considering the other British dockyards abroad at Halifax, Nova Scotia; Port Royal, Jamaica and Gibraltar.

⊟ Many men worked in the dockyards as clerks or tradesmen. Their records are in the ADM series too at **TNA**, particularly paybooks 1660–1857 (ADM 42, 32, 36 and 37) and books containing physical descriptions of tradesmen between 1748 and 1830 (ADM 106).

⊟ The **National Maritime Museum** has a card index compiled from its own holdings and records at **TNA**, especially classes ADM 6 and ADM 11, covering all types of dockyard officers employed in naval dockyards both in this country and abroad for the 17th–19th centuries. The information given is generally confined to periods of employment in a specific job, though if someone died in service the date of death may appear. A project to index the dockyards' letterbooks (ADM 106) is underway and will include names and positions held.

TRINITY HOUSE PETITIONS

⊟ Trinity House issued pensions to retired seamen or their widows and orphans between 1514 and 1854. From 1727 there are registers at

Guildhall Library giving the names and ages of recipients, together with where they were and why they needed help.

⊟ Petitions, including details of the hardships being suffered, often accompanied by certificates proving baptisms, marriages, apprenticeships and so on, survive from 1787. These are at **Guildhall Library** with copies on film at the **SoG**, and indexed in A. J. Camp's *The Trinity House Petitions: A Calendar of the Records of the Corporation of Trinity House, London, in the Library of the SoG* (SoG, 1987).

QUICK REFERENCE

See also main sources in Useful Addresses, page 306

NATIONAL MARITIME MUSEUM
Park Row
Greenwich
London SE10 9NF
☎ 020 8858 4422
www.nmm.ac.uk

JAMES GALLOWAY'S Trinity House petition (see opposite), dated 13 February 1817, shows that he was aged 57 and residing in Marske (Yorkshire) where he had lived for over 20 years as a seaman, and was currently renting a house and working as a day labourer. He went to sea at 17 in a vessel out of the nearby port of Whitby, and served as an 'apprentice to William Maler in the coasting and Baltic trade, latterly in the situation of mate on board the Ship Palion, Captain Livingston, Master, in the Coasting Trade, of which ship John Goodchild Esq. was owner, and in that capacity served for thirty or more voyages'. Galloway's wife was Jane, aged 49, and they had two children under 12, David and Shemelds, and another (unnamed) under 13 who, through infirmity, James could not look after. When the form asked for his property and income, the person filling it in for James (probably Captain Goodchild) wrote '£0-0-0'.

At the foot of the petition is written in bold writing:

> 'NB. The above named James Galloway was in ye voyage wrecked on the coast of Norfolk and the cold he suffered at the time has continued.'

Attached to the petition is a genealogist's dream – original notes signed by parish clergymen confirming James's marriage to Jane Shemelds, by banns, on 10 January 1792 at Whitby, the baptisms of the children, of the wife Jane and of James himself:

> BAPTISM 1759
> August 12 James son of George Galloway. This is a copy of the above Baptism as taken from the parish register of baptisms for the parish of Dunferling in the County of Fife. Richard Thompson, minister, William McKintosh, Eld[er], John Dickison, Eld[er].

The only place with a name similar to this in Fife was Dunfermline, but none of the registers in Dunfermline contained a record of his baptism, nor had any of them ever had a minister with such a name, and nor could elders of the names mentioned be traced. After finding so much fascinating and true information about James, the trail ended with the fake certificate he had probably used to join the merchant navy as an under-age boy. His authentic origins have never been established.

THE MERCHANT NAVY

While the Royal Navy gets most of the press, the majority of Britain's shipping activities were undertaken for trade – by the Merchant Navy. Although not always as glamorous, records of Merchant Navy service can be equally enlightening and make a worthy addition to any family history.

THE MERCHANT NAVY

GENERAL

The best guide to Merchant Navy records is C. and M. Watts' *My Ancestor was a Merchant Seaman* (3rd edition, SoG, 2004).

Many boys and men were trained for the Merchant Navy by the Marine Society, whose indexed registers 1772–1950 are at the **National Maritime Museum**. Many poor boys were apprenticed to the Merchant Navy by their parish (see page 185). Apprentices' indentures were issued from 1824 and are indexed at **TNA** in class BT 150. They include ages and the ship on which the boys sailed.

From 1747 onwards, muster rolls (at **TNA**, class BT 98) were kept, listing the crew of each Merchant Navy ship. Until 1834, they gave each man's home address, date of joining and date of leaving the previous ship. Unfortunately, these musters were deposited at the ports where the ships happened to be, and only those for Shields (1747), Dartmouth (1770), Plymouth (1761) and Liverpool (1772) pre-date the 19th century. Thereafter many more survive and can be searched, provided you have an idea where and when your ancestor set sail, but beware – the records for larger ports may take you a very long time to search.

For the period 1835–57, prospects of finding what you want perk up considerably. In 1835, all merchant vessels came under the control of the Board of Trade, whose records are in class BT at **TNA**. The period 1835–57 is covered by indexed registers of seamen in classes BT 120 (1835–6), 112 and 119 (1835–44), and BT 114

(1845–53), which can lead you straight to the crew lists described above. BT 114 can also be used to look up seamen's tickets (1845–53) in BT 113. There is also an alphabetical register of seamen covering 1853–7 at **TNA** in class BT 116.

After 1857, searching reverts to being as difficult as it was before 1835, until 1913–41, which is covered by a Central Register of Shipping and Seamen at **TNA** on **www.catalogue.nationalarchives. gov.uk**. BT 350 (1918–21) and 348–9 (1921–41) include places of birth and some photographs.

CREW LISTS AND AGREEMENTS

These span the period 1835–60 and are at **TNA** in BT 98. They outline the course of the proposed voyage of a ship and give specific information about each sailor. They are arranged by voyages, so are only easily searched between 1835 and 1857.

TNA also holds the crew lists up to 1861, after which most (up to 1976) have gone to an unusual home – the **Maritime History Archive** in Canada. They offer a search service at $35 (Canadian) per hour. Their collection is indexed for the period 1863–1938. The rest of the records are divided between **TNA**, **National Maritime Museum** and **county record offices** (for which the Newfoundland archive has also produced a single index) and (for the period 1939–50) are with the **Registrar General of Shipping and Seamen**.

DIED AT SEA

If your sailor ancestor died at sea between 1852 and 1889, you can find details of the death, wages due and date and place of joining

the ship at **TNA** in BT 15, indexed in BT 154.

SECOND WORLD WAR

Medals awarded to merchant seamen who served in the Second World War – some 100,000 of them – are now searchable online at **www.documentsonline. nationalarchives.gov.uk.**

LOG BOOKS

These can provide much information about your ancestors' voyages, but survival is patchy and they are divided between **TNA** (BT 165), **National Maritime Museum** and the **Maritime History Archive**. They include details of births, marriages and deaths abroad with a register compiled by the Registrar General of Shipping and Seamen for 1854–87, 1883 and 1890 respectively (BT 158).

CERTIFICATES OF COMPETENCY

Merchant Navy captains were usually referred to as masters, and second-in-commands as mates. From 1845 new masters and mates could – and from 1850 had to – obtain a certificate of competency. These included year and place of birth, and are in registers at **TNA** in classes BT 112 and 123–6, with an index in BT 127. There is also an alphabetical register of masters (1845–55) in BT 115.

Engineers' certificates of competency from 1862 are in **TNA** in BT 139 and 142 (indexed in BT 141). Those to colonial masters and mates are in BT 128, indexed in BT 127, with colonial engineers in BT 140, indexed in BT 141.

Skippers and mates of fishing boats needed certificates from 1883 and these are at **TNA** in BT 129–30, indexed in BT 138.

△ *Merchant Ships under Sail and at Anchor off a Town*
by William Anderson (1757–1837).

⊟ BT 317, 318 and 320 cover
certificates for masters and mates
1917–68, examination registers for
masters, mates and engineers
1913–35 and engineers 1919–29.
Masters are also recorded between
1868 and 1947 in Lloyd's Marine
Collection at the **Guildhall Library**.

SHIPS

⊟ Lloyd's Marine Collection also
contains much information about the
ships themselves, as does **Lloyd's
Register of Shipping**.

SHIP OWNERS

⊟ Many people's ancestors were ship
owners. This was not always as grand
as it sounds, as most ships were
divided into 64 shares of ownership,
some held by investors and others by
craftsmen on the ships, all of whom
expected a share of the profit
accrued by the voyage. Some

records from the 17th century may
be in the **county record office**
covering the ship's home port.

⊟ From 1786 to 1854, registers for
ships over 15 tons, listing the ship
owners and their home addresses,
are in **TNA** class BT 107. For 1855 to
1889, see BT 108. An index to the
ships in both is in BT 111. Records
after 1889 are in BT 110.

EAST INDIA COMPANY

⊟ Records of the Honourable East
India Company's fleet of merchant
and warships (the latter was known
as the 'Bombay Marine' and later the
Indian Navy) are in the **India Office
Library**, including information about
captains, masters and mates, and
logs of voyages covering 1605–1856.
You are unlikely to find records of
East India seamen listed before the
mid-19th century.

QUICK REFERENCE

See also main sources in Useful
Addresses, page 306

NATIONAL MARITIME MUSEUM
Park Row
Greenwich
London SE10 9NF
☎ 020 8858 4422
www.nmm.ac.uk

MARITIME HISTORY ARCHIVE
Memorial University of New
Foundland
St John's
Newfoundland A1C 5S7
Canada
☎ 00 1 709737 8428
www.mun.ca/mha/about.html

**REGISTRAR GENERAL OF SHIPPING
AND SEAMEN**
Anchor House
Cheviot Close
Parc Ty Glas
Llanishen
Cardiff CF14 5JA
☎ 029 2044 8800

LLOYD'S REGISTER OF SHIPPING
71 Fenchurch Street
London EC3M 4BS
☎ 020 7709 9166
www.lr.org

INDIA OFFICE LIBRARY
British Library
96 Euston Road
London NW1 2DB
☎ 020 7412 7513
www.bl.uk/collections/
orientalandindian.html

THE ROYAL MARINES

Charles II created the Marines in 1665 to serve as soldiers on board Royal Navy ships, acting as sentries and additional labour in peacetime and providing musket fire in sea battles. The force was disbanded in the early 18th century and reformed in 1755: they were known as 'Royal' from 1802.

◁ 'Captain, Flag Officer and Commander' from *Costume of the Royal Navy and Marines*, engraved by L. and E. Mansion (19th century).

WHERE TO SEARCH

THE ROYAL MARINES

⊟ Records of Marines are arranged by three divisions: Chatham, Plymouth and Portsmouth. The records, which are in most respects identical to those of the army, are at **TNA** in the Admiralty records (class ADM). **TNA** has a card index to many (but not all) attestation forms (ADM 157/1–659) in the Research Enquiries Room and has several information leaflets, especially no. 46, 'How to find a division', to guide you through the records.

⊟ Lists of marine officers 1757–1850 and 1760–1886 are at **TNA** in ADM 118/230–336 and ADM 192 respectively, fully indexed from 1770. Marine officers are listed in the Navy Lists. Further information may be obtained, especially concerning officers who were appointed after 1926, from the Commandant General at the **Royal Marines** and the **Royal Marines Museum**, which details the whereabouts of service records before and after 1926.

⊟ Like army and navy records, post-1926 service records are confidential but can be applied for by proven descendants from **Royal Marines Historical Records and Medals**. The best book on Marines is G.Thomas' *Records of Royal Marines* (PRO Publications, 1994).

QUICK REFERENCE

See also main sources in Useful Addresses, page 306

ROYAL MARINES
Commandant General
Ministry of Defence (Navy)
Whitehall
London SW1
☎ 0870 607 4455
www.royalnavy.mod.uk

ROYAL MARINES MUSEUM
Eastney Barracks
Southsea
Hampshire PO4 9PX
☎ 0239 281 9385
www.royalmarinesmuseum.co.uk

ROYAL MARINES HISTORICAL
RECORDS AND MEDALS
HRORM
Room 038
Centurion Building
Grange Road
Gosport
Hampshire PO13 9XA
☎ 023 9270 2126
www.mod.uk

THE ROYAL AIR FORCE (RAF)

The army founded the Royal Flying Corps (RFC) in 1912, only nine years after the first powered flight, followed two years later by the Royal Navy's Royal Naval Air Service (RNAS). The two were unified as a third branch of the military in 1918. The force then numbered 291,000 officers, rising to a million men and women during the Second World War.

WHERE TO SEARCH

THE ROYAL AIR FORCE

- Records up to 1918/20 are at **TNA** in classes WO 363, 364 and ADM 273, with further records in WO 339 and 374 (RFC officers who left before 1918) and other ranks in WO 363 and 364.

- Records of RNAS officers who left before 1918 are at **TNA** in class ADM 273 and other ranks in ADM 188. RAF officers who left by 1926 are in AIR 76 and some airmen for the same period are in AIR 79, indexed in AIR 78.

- Women's RAF records for the First World War are at **TNA** in AIR 80.

- After 1926, the same confidentiality rules apply as to army and navy records. If you can prove you are the next of kin of a deceased serviceman you can contact the **RAF Personnel and Training Command**. Those for the Fleet Air Arm are at the **Ministry of Defence**. W. R. Chorley's *Royal Air Force Bomber Command Losses of the Second World War* (Midland Counties Publications, 1992–3) is also worth searching.

- Officers were included in the published Army and Navy Lists until the formation of the RAF, which subsequently published its own Airforce Lists. W. Spencer's *Air Force Records for Family Historians* (PRO, 2002) is a useful guide to discovering more about the airforce careers of members of your family. The **RAF Museum** has a useful website.

QUICK REFERENCE

See also main sources in Useful Addresses, page 306

RAF PERSONNEL AND TRAINING COMMAND
Branch PG 5a(2) (for officers) and P Man 2b(1) (for non-officers)
RAF Innsworth
Gloucestershire GL3 1EZ
☎ 01452 712612
www.mod.uk

MINISTRY OF DEFENCE
CS(R)2
Bourne Avenue
Hayes
Middlesex UB3 1FR
☎ 0870 607 4455
www.mod.uk

RAF MUSEUM
Grahame Park Way
Hendon
London NW9 5LL
☎ 020 8205 2266
www.rafmuseum.org.uk

◁ RAF flyers in England during the Second World War.

CHAPTER TWENTY-THREE
TAX & OTHER FINANCIAL MATTERS

Since the Norman Conquest, the state has been ruthless in its efforts, efficient or otherwise, to tax us. But what was bad for our ancestors is good for us, because not only were vast amounts of taxes raised but detailed records of them were made and still survive today.

For the 12th and 13th centuries, tax records indicate how surnames were spelled, at the very period in which they were becoming hereditary, and therefore help us to work out what they originally meant. For the period before parish registers (up to 1538), they provide one of the best sources for determining who was alive, and when. They do not tell you how people were related, but the disappearance of one person from a series of tax lists and his replacement by another with the same surname can indicate a possible father–son relationship.

Tax records add a little colour to family history, indicating how much people's houses or landholdings were worth, how many windows and fireplaces they had, and so on. They can also be invaluable if you do not know where an ancestor came from. A county tax list for the period when the ancestor was likely to have been born can provide a list of parishes where people of the same surname lived, and thus where your ancestor may have been born.

QUICK REFERENCE

See main sources in Useful Addresses, page 306

WHERE TO SEARCH

TAX RECORDS AND GENEALOGY

⊟ Some **county record offices** have card indexes to many of their tax lists, including lay subsidies, hearth tax, window tax and so on. Many sections of tax lists have been published, especially by **county record societies**, as listed in E. L. C. Mullins' *Texts and Calendars: an Analytical Guide to Serial Publications* (RHS, 1958 and 1983).

⊟ M. Jurkowski, C. L. Smith and D. Crook's *Lay Taxes in England and Wales 1188–1689* (PRO Publications, 1998) is a comprehensive survey of national taxes, ranging from poll tax to land tax, subsidies and forced loans, many of which survive in class E 179 at **TNA**. The same text is on **www.nationalarchives.gov.uk/e179/**. Be aware that these are not transcriptions or indexes of the lists themselves – they still need to be searched manually.

THE MAIN TAX LAWS

The main taxes you are likely to encounter, and which you should be able to use yourself for tracing your family tree, are as follows.

LAY SUBSIDIES

These were taxes chargeable on movable goods. The clergy were exempt – hence the term 'lay' – as were the poor, and some goods, such as knights' armour, were not taxable. Lay subsidies list names from the late

12th century, although in practice few survive from before 1327. From 1334 only the places and sums raised were recorded. In 1523, with Henry VIII's Great Subsidy, names of all those aged 16 or more with land or goods worth £2, or annual income of £1 or more, were recorded. Lay subsidies continued to be raised periodically until the end of the 17th century.

POLL TAX (1377–1703)

Centuries before Margaret Thatcher, poll taxes were causing misery and unrest throughout England and Wales. They were raised in 1377, 1379 and 1381(resulting in the Peasants' Revolt), then in 1641, and 18 times between 1660 and 1703. All men aged 16 or over who were not paupers were liable to pay a set amount.

SHEEP TAX (1549)

This was a tax raised by Edward VI on flocks of sheep. Ewes kept on enclosed land were changed at 3d a head, shear-sheep on such land 2d a head and shear-sheep on commons 3½d. Even though sheep owners only had to pay if the amount assessed exceeded what they had paid in a subsidy on goods earlier that year, the tax caused great

SHEEP TAX

THERE ARE A FEW surviving returns listing flock-holders' names at TNA in E 179 listed under 'poll tax on sheep'. See my article in *Ancestors* (TNA's magazine), August 2004, pp. 50–5 and note on returns for newly-found Breconshire returns in *Ancestors*, October 2004 edition, page 7.

QUICK REFERENCE

See main sources in Useful Addresses, page 306

WHERE TO SEARCH

THE MAIN TAX LAWS

LAY SUBSIDIES

⊡ Some records are in **county record offices**, but most are at **TNA** in class E 179, listed in S. Colwell's *Family Roots; Discovering the Past in the PRO* (Weidenfeld & Nicolson, 1991). Many have been published by **county record societies**. E 179 also contains other Tudor taxes, such as assessments for forced loans of 1522–3, which were raised from men aged 16 or over.

⊡ These records are particularly useful when they pre-date the registers of the parish where your ancestors lived. If you are lucky, you will find surviving tax lists for every couple of years, showing people with your surname, indicating who earlier generations may have been.

⊡ Some Irish subsidy rolls survive, particularly for Northern Ireland, at the **PRONI**.

POLL TAX

⊡ The 13th- century returns are in **TNA** class E 179 and sometimes provide not just names but also occupations and relationships. They are being published: vol. 1 is C. Fenwick's *The Poll Taxes of 1377, 1379 and 1381* (OUP for the British Academy, 1998). The 17th- and 18th-century lists survive only patchily. The 1641 survivals are listed in J. Gibson and A. Dell's *The Protestation Returns 1641–42 and other Contemporary Listings* (FFHS, 1995) and those from 1660 are in J. Gibson's *The Hearth Tax, and other Later Stuart Tax Lists and the Association Rolls* (FFHS, 1996).

⊡ Scottish poll tax records 1693–99 are at the **NAS** and listed in Gibson, and some for Northern Ireland are at the **PRONI**.

LIFETIMES: AN ARQUEBUSER IN THEIR ANCESTRY

A FEW YEARS AGO, I successfully traced the Chard family back through a number of parishes on the Devon–Somerset border, to Thomas Chard of Hemyock, whose children, Elizabeth, William, Oliver, Edward and Cornelius, had been baptised there between 1692 and 1705. Thomas himself was baptised in Hemyock in 1667, son of a John Chard, but the registers of that parish showed no sign of his baptism, or indeed any other Chards. It seemed likely, therefore, that the family had come from somewhere else. To establish where this might have been, we examined the printed 1582 Lay Subsidy returns. These gave three references to the surname:

St Mary Church	John Charde	goods	5d
Clayhidon	John Charde	goods	12d
Crediton	Walter Charde	goods	3d

Clayhidon adjoined Hemyock, and in the Clayhidon registers were records of the following baptisms:

1648, 18 December,	Anne d. of John Chard
1642, 20 May,	Oliver Chard s. of John Chard jnr
1639, 13 March	John s. of John Chard jnr

The occurrence of the name Oliver here was pretty conclusive and this, coupled with the absence of a burial for John, indicated that the boy baptised in 1639 was the person who later settled in Hemyock.

John junior's baptism does not appear in the registers, but they only started in 1634. A few years' worth of bishops' transcripts survived, however (see page 114), and these indicated other children of John senior, including Grace (1626), Richard (year unspecified) and William (1620). John senior appears as a churchwarden of Clayhidon in 1640/1, and is listed in the Protestation returns of 1641.

Earlier, there is a Richard Chard listed in the 1569 muster roll (see page 208) for Clayhidon as an 'harquebusier' – an arquebus was a large and rather clumsy gun – and he was, in turn, son of the John who paid his taxes in 1581. This earlier John also appeared in the muster roll, recorded as having to provide an 'almain rivet', two bows, two sheafs of arrows, two steel caps and a bill, in case of Spanish invasion. There are even earlier tax lists, such as the 1332 Devonshire Lay Subsidies, which list three Chardes, Walter and John in Broadwoodwidger and Richard in 'Athens' St Mary, and even a John de Charde in Otterton – possible forbears of the Chardes of Hemyock.

resentment and contributed to rebellion that summer. It was repealed in November.

SHIP MONEY (1634–40)

Charles I's raising of ship money – a tax ostensibly for the navy, which he could raise without Parliament's agreement – was a major cause of the argument between the King and Parliament that led to the Civil War.

CONTRIBUTIONS FOR IRELAND (1642)

In autumn 1641, a Catholic rebellion broke out in Ireland, and in February 1642 the King and Parliament agreed to send an army out to protect the Protestant settlers. To raise funds for the army, the wealthy were asked to lend money at 8% interest, while all men were invited to make 'gifts' of money via the overseers of the poor and churchwardens, and this was done between June and the following April. Some of the resulting lists of contributors survive.

△ *Charles I in Three Positions*, painting by Carlo Maratta after Van Dyke (1625–1713).

COMMITTEES FOR ADVANCE OF MONEY AND COMPOUNDING (1642–60)

From 1642 onwards, a Parliamentarian committee forced people, Royalist and Parliamentarian alike, to loan money to the Commonwealth. From 1646, only defeated Royalists had to make these loans although, to be fair to Parliament, efforts were made to pay the money back with interest.

From 1643 onwards, a Parliamentarian committee called the Committee for the Sequestration of Delinquents' Estates sat in judgement on landowners who had supported the King, and seized their land. The Committee for Compounding, which was not wound up until the Restoration, then gave the land back in return for an oath of loyalty to the Commonwealth and a hefty fine.

FREE AND VOLUNTARY PRESENT (1661)

This pseudo-tax, which was theoretically voluntary, although the well-to-do were expected to pay, was raised for the newly restored – and heavily indebted – Charles II in 1661.

WHERE TO SEARCH

SHIP MONEY
Surviving returns for the period 1634–40 are in **TNA** class SP 16 and SP 17.

FREE AND VOLUNTARY PRESENT
Lists of some 130,000 names, usually with occupations, are in **TNA** class E 179.

QUICK REFERENCE

See main sources in Useful Addresses, page 306

SPINNING WHEEL PREMIUMS

IN THE NAPOLEONIC WARS, the Navy needed much linen. The flax needed to make linen made heavy demands on the soil, so farmers were reluctant to grow it. The Government introduced an incentive scheme in the north of Ireland whereby farmers growing flax received a spinning wheel for every quarter acre or a loom for a full acre. The lists, especially for 1796, survive at the National Archives, PRONI and Mormon Family History Library.

△ *The Quillwinder*
by John Harden (1772–1847).

HEARTH TAX RETURNS (1662–89)

The hearth tax was one of the Restoration government's chief methods of raising extra income. Assessments of how many fireplaces were in each house in the realm were made by constables, and enrolled at the Quarter Sessions, and the householders taxed at 1s per six months per hearth. Those occupying property worth less than 20s in yearly rent, or had less than £10 worth of movable goods, or were receiving poor relief or alms, were let off, as were charitable institutions, alehouses, kilns and furnaces and blowing houses. After May 1664, those with two hearths or more had to pay regardless.

Because the law empowered constables to enter houses to search for hearths, the tax was rightly detested as an unwarranted intrusion on Englishmen's 'castles' and was repealed in 1689.

LAND TAX (1693–1963)

Land tax replaced earlier, random taxes, particularly hearth tax and subsidies. It was levied from 1693 to 1963, but most records survive from between 1780 and 1832. They are arranged by parish within hundreds and list all landholders with property worth 20s or more and (from 1772) tenants, although if more than one tenant lived in a building, only one will be listed. The property may also be described briefly.

MARRIAGE DUTY ACT (1695–1706)

This Act, introduced in May 1695 to fund one of our many wars with France, taxed all births, marriages and burials – and just to be fair, it also taxed widows without children and bachelors aged over 25! Paupers were let off.

WINDOW TAX (1696–1851)

This tax was introduced in 1696 and, despite being very unpopular, was not repealed until 1851. Paupers were exempt (not many paupers' cottages had windows anyway), but when records survive most other ancestors appear in the records – mostly at county record offices.

OTHER FINANCIAL RECORDS

Taxes record the removal of our ancestors' money, but there are some happier records showing what they did with their remaining pennies. For the more nosy-minded among us, there is nothing more fascinating than finding out exactly how many pennies our ancestors (or, indeed, other people's) actually had.

WHERE TO SEARCH

COMMITTEES FOR ADVANCE OF MONEY AND COMPOUNDING

The records of the committee's highly intrusive activities from 1642 have been indexed and calendared in Mary Anne Everett Green's *Calendar of the Proceedings of the Committee for Advance of Money, 1642–1656, Preserved in the State Paper Office of Her Majesty's Public Record Office* (1888).

The original records for the Committee for Compounding, called Royalist composition papers, are in **TNA** class SP 23 and have been calendared and indexed in Mary Anne Everett Green's *Calendar of the Proceedings of the Committee for Compounding, etc, 1643–1660* (1889–92).

HEARTH TAX RETURNS

Generally, the parish assessments give names, sometimes with the inclusion of 'senior', 'junior', 'widow' and so on, and the number of hearths, annotated with what was actually paid. Those exempt are sometimes listed. Most records at **TNA** are for 1662–6 and 1669–74. To find what has survived, you can search on **www.nationalarchives.gov.uk/e179/**.

Also check J. Gibson's *The Hearth Tax, and other Later Stuart Tax Lists and the Association Rolls* (FFHS, 1996), which will indicate what is in **county record offices** and what has been published. Their main use is in finding out in which parish people of your surname lived just after the end of the Civil War, complementing Protestation Returns and Covenant Records (see page 220), which show who was where when the disruption started.

Scottish hearth taxes survive for 1661–95 and are at the **NAS**.

Those for Ireland, called hearth money rolls, have survived in places, as listed in J. G. Ryan's *Irish Records – Sources for Family and Local History* (Ancestry, 1997). Those for Dublin are at **www.irishfamilyresearch.co.uk.**

LAND TAX

Returns mainly survive for the countryside and are in Quarter Session records (see page 232). An almost complete record for England and Wales for 1798 is in **TNA** class IR 23. After 1798, the tax could be commuted by a lump-sum payment equivalent to 16 years' tax. Records of those 'exonerated' are in IR 22. Whereabouts of records is in J. Gibson, M. Medlycott and D. Mills' *Land and Window Tax Assessments* (FFHS, 1998).

MARRIAGE DUTY

The **county record offices** hold those relatively few assessments which have survived – details are in J. Gibson's *The Hearth Tax, and other Later Stuart Tax Lists and the Association Rolls* (FFHS, 1996). Where they do survive – mainly borough records and a handful of Wiltshire parishes – they will tell you who the householders in the parish were.

WINDOW TAX

The records are mostly at **county record offices**. Details of surviving records are in J. Gibson, M. Medlycott and D. Mills' *Land and Window Tax Assessments* (FFHS, 1998). The assessments state name, address, number of windows and amount payable – an interesting side-light on a family history. Many old houses still have windows, which were bricked up to lessen the amount of tax due.

Scottish returns, at the **NAS**, are mainly for 1748–98, and provide occupiers' names. The series is almost complete and includes records of the properties not liable to tax.

▽ **A hearth tax return from 1664.**

QUICK REFERENCE

See main sources in Useful Addresses, page 306

TITHE APPLOTMENT BOOKS & GRIFFITH'S VALUATION

TWO IMPORTANT SOURCES for Irish research are the Tithe Applotment Books and Griffith's Primary Valuation. The tithe records date from 1823 to 1837 and record, parish by parish, the occupiers of all agricultural land, the name of the land, the landlord and the amount of tithes deemed to be payable. The original records are at the National Archives of Ireland and those for Northern Ireland at the PRONI.

The primary valuation of Irish landholdings was overseen by Sir Richard Griffith, a civil engineer who served as Commissioner of Valuation in Ireland from 1828 to 1868, whose work created a resource of immense value to family historians. Griffith's task was to record all those liable to pay the poor rate and assess how much they should pay. To this end, his team worked throughout the Irish counties from 1847 to 1865, recording the landlords and occupiers of all buildings and land, noting the nature of the holding, with precise size and rateable value within each poor law union. The original records are at the National Archives of Ireland, with some copies at locations such as the SoG and IHGS, and full, indexed copies on CD-Rom, produced by Heritage World and the Genealogical Publishing Co. Inc. It is also searchable online at **www.irishorigins.com**.

Besides the obvious fascination of seeing exactly what land and buildings your ancestors tenanted, Griffith's valuation is an excellent way of locating families. Say your ancestor James Crowley turned up in Liverpool in the 1870s, but you have no idea where he came from. At best you might find him through the index, tenanting his smallholding in the 1860s. Even if he is not listed himself (only heads of households were listed), you can learn where in Ireland the majority of Crowleys lived, and then you can look for heads of households with the same Christian name, giving you a good idea as to which parish registers to search for your James.

Maps showing the location of the properties in Griffith's valuation are at the Valuation Office. The Valuation Office at 6 Ealy Place, Dublin, also has the surveyors' notebooks, which sometimes provide extra information about the individuals recorded in the valuation, later valuations, made in 1865 and 1968, and books recording changes in ownership and occupation since the original valuation was made.

For landowners, you can also search in *A Return of Owners of Land of One Acre and Upwards* (HMSO, 1876), which contains 32,000 people, listed alphabetically by county.

More details on these records and how to use them are in my book, *Collins Tracing Your Irish Family History* (Collins 2007).

OTHER FINANCIAL RECORDS

BANK ACCOUNTS

A surprising amount of records have survived for ancestors' bank accounts. The best are in the **Bank of England Archives**.

During the 17th and 18th centuries, many small banks were established, most of which either folded or were swallowed up to create the present big high-street names. Records of small local banks can sometimes be found in the local **county record offices**.

FIRE INSURANCE

Was your ancestor prudent enough to insure their property against fire? From 1696 onwards, records exist, many among the papers of the Sun Fire Office (papers at **Guildhall Library**, indexed 1816-24 at **www.a2a.org.uk**), whose 'sun' plaques are still to be seen on many old buildings. There are some records in county record offices but, because most insurance firms were based in the City, many are at Guildhall Library, which has indexes to some of the 18th-century records. The records will usually tell you your ancestor's occupation, the address of the property being insured and, of course, the amount.

TONTINES AND ANNUITIES

Public annuities were established by the state as a means of raising capital. People were encouraged to pay a lump sum in return for which a nominated person (who could be the person who made the payment or a dependent) would receive a guaranteed annual income for life. Similar schemes were tontines, whereby a group of people invested money into a scheme and shared the income: as they died, the survivors got a greater share of the income. Tontines were especially popular in Ireland and amongst Huguenots.

Various schemes were organised between 1693 and 1789 and records of these are at **TNA** in classes NDO 1–3 and E 401, 403 and 406–7. See also F. Leeson's *A Guide to the Records of the British State Tontines and Life Annuities of the 17th and 18th Centuries* (Pinhorns, 1968). There is an index to participants in some of the 18th-century schemes is in F. Leeson's *Index to the British State Tontine and Annuities 1745–1779* (SoG microfiche, 1994).

LOTTERIES

Records of the Million Lottery, established in 1694, is in **TNA** class C 46.

QUICK REFERENCE

See also main sources in Useful Addresses, page 306

BANK OF ENGLAND ARCHIVES
Threadneedle Street
London EC2R 8AH
☎ 020 7601 5096
www.bankofengland.co.uk/
archive.htm

TAXING THE RICH

THIS IS NOT a modern Socialist idea, but one deeply embedded in Hanoverian policy. Taxes devised to raise money from the middle and upper classes included:

➤ Carriages: 1747–82
➤ Silver plate: 1756–77
➤ Male servants: 1777–1852 (except those working in farming, trade or industry)

The SoG has an index to the employers listed in the 1780 returns.
➤ Game: 1784–1807
➤ Horses used for transport: 1784–1874
➤ Female servants: 1785–92
➤ Coats of arms: 1793–1882
➤ Hair powder: 1795–1861
➤ Dogs: 1796–1882
➤ Empty houses: 1851–1924
➤ Income: (for the very wealthy only) 1789, 1803–16 and 1842–present

The only surviving pre-1842 records are of those who failed to pay.

Surviving records, listing the tax payers only – and the survival is very patchy – are in TNA classes E 182 and T 47, but many more will be found in county record offices and are always worth a search. The NAS hold many comparable lists.

CHAPTER TWENTY-FOUR
SWEARING OATHS

The 17th century was one of bitter civil war. Traditional loyalty to the state could no longer be assumed, so it had to be sought – or demanded – by public oaths, each of which are described in this chapter. Short it may be, but the information is nonetheless of relevance.

THE MAIN OATHS

The surviving lists of oath takers are immensely helpful because they show who was where at a definite time (and can also give you an indication of where people's loyalties lay) or, at least, where they wanted the state to believe they were.

PROTESTATION RETURNS AND THE COVENANT (1641–2)

In 1641, as tension rose between Charles I and Parliament, a number of Royalist conspirators, led by Henry Jermyn, and including a number of prominent Catholics, hatched a plot to bring the King's northern army down to London to rescue the Earl of Strafford from the Tower and restore royal authority. The plot was discovered, the plotters fled and Parliament devised an oath promising 'to live and die for the true Protestant religion, the liberties and rights of subjects, and the privilege of Parliament'. It was the last bit that really mattered, of course, though the bit about supporting Protestantism also had the effect of excluding all Catholics, or at least those with strong consciences, effectively driving them into the arms of the Royalists.

The oath was imposed on all Members of the House of Commons on 3 May 1641. Parliament wanted to impose the oath on all Englishmen, but this was rejected by the House of Lords (whose members included a strong minority of Catholics). But, on 30 July, the Commons declared that anyone who refused to swear the oath was unfit to hold office.

In January 1642, Charles I marched into Parliament intending to arrest his five most vociferous opponents. It was from this time on that conflict really started to escalate towards Civil War and it was under these circumstances that the Commons imposed the oath on the whole of England and Wales. Copies of the oath were sent to every parish priest, who read out the text and lists were made of everyone who

QUICK REFERENCE

See also main sources in Useful Addresses, page 306

HOUSE OF LORDS RECORD OFFICE
Palace of Westminster
London SW1A 0PW
☎ 020 7219 3074
www.parliament.uk

signed – and also everyone who didn't. The surviving returns provide an excellent form of 'census', and are reasonably complete. Some types of people were omitted – women, including widows, were let off, as were men under 18 years of age. It is worth bearing this in mind if you are using the protestation returns as a means of seeing which surnames turned up in which parishes in a certain area. If the father had died just before the oath was taken, leaving a widow and a whole brood of boys about to turn 18 and start breeding prolifically, the surname won't show up at all, yet by the time of the Hearth Tax returns (see page 216), the parish could be teaming with people bearing it.

Some areas are poorly covered. The returns for Leicestershire and Norfolk have not survived at all, and there is nothing for the wapentakes of Staincross or Stafforth and Tickhill.

But for all this, when it comes to leaping back across the Commonwealth Gap to see where your ancestors were living before the massive disruption of war, protestation returns are a real winner. Furthermore, as well as simply pinning people down to a particular place, you can also get a feel for how they may have felt about the great issues burning around them from whether they appear in the list as signatories or refusers.

TEST AND CORPORATION OATHS (1661–1823)

These oaths, introduced in 1661 and 1672/3 and not repealed until 1823, were designed to keep Catholics out of public office by making all office holders, civil and military, swear to uphold the King as the head of the Church of England and deny the Catholic doctrine of transubstantiation.

ASSOCIATION ROLLS (1695/6)

This was a register of oath takers introduced in 1695/6 in response to a Jacobite plot to kill William of Orange. Swearing an oath of allegiance was obligatory for all public office holders, from clergy to army and navy officers, but in fact most men (and some female householders) of reasonable social standing took it anyway.

WHERE TO SEARCH

THE MAIN OATHS

PROTESTATION RETURNS

⊟ The lists of Protestant contributors in 1642 are in **TNA** classes E 19 and SP 28 and are listed in J. Gibson and A. Dell's *The Protestation Returns 1641–42 and Other Contemporary Listings* (FFHS, 1995). Some lists, such as the surviving two-thirds for Buckinghamshire, have been printed: in John Wilson's *Buckinghamshire Contributions for Ireland 1642 and Richard Grenville's Military Accounts 1642–1645* (Buckinghamshire Record Society, no. 21, 1983).

⊟ Most surviving protestation and covenant lists are in the **House of Lords Record Office** with some in the relevant parish chest. They are therefore now likely to be in the local **county record office**, and some have been published.

⊟ The surviving Kent returns (about 25%, mainly for the northeast of Kent) have been transcribed and indexed and are available on microfiche from the **IHGS**.

TEST AND CORPORATION OATHS

⊟ Records of men taking these oaths are mainly in the Quarter Sessions and at **TNA** in classes C 224, E 196 and KB 22.

ASSOCIATION ROLLS

⊟ Arranged parish by parish, the surviving parish returns can be studied at **TNA** in class C 213 and are listed by C. Webb in the *Genealogists' Magazine*, December 1983.

CHAPTER TWENTY-FIVE
LEGAL ACCOUNTS

There are many different types of court, divided into two main categories – criminal courts (see below) and civil courts (see page 226). From 1875 the judicial system was reformed and so, after that date, there are other types of court records to explore. These are outlined from pages 224 onwards.

WHERE TO SEARCH

LEGAL ACCOUNTS

⊟ The **London Borough of Camden Public Library** is especially good for law reports. Many are included in the *All England Law Reports*, which include cases going back to 1558, indexed in I. Bridgeman and C. Emsley's *A Guide to the Archives of the Police Forces of England & Wales* (Police Historical Society, 1990). A substantial index to over 100,000 reports is *The English Reports, Index of Cases A to K* (Professional Books, 1986, with another Vol. L–Z).

⊟ A major collection of pamphlets has been published and fully indexed in microfilm: C. Healey's *British Trials 1660–1900*.

QUICK REFERENCE

CAMDEN PUBLIC LIBRARY
88 Avenue Road
London NW3 3HA
☎ 020 7974 6522
www.camden.gov.uk

Many ancestors of ours appeared in court cases, either as plaintiffs, bringing action against others, defendants or respondents, answering the charges, or as witnesses or jurors. However, you are unlikely to know that an ancestor was involved in a court case unless you look, so legal records are generally a lucky dip to consult if you have the time, or are really stuck. Aside from the emerging indexes outlined below, the records can be very hard to search, and details of most crimes and trials are generally more easily sought through newspaper reports (see page 144). Church court and Quarter Session records can be found in county record offices and most other court records are at TNA.

WHERE TO START

You may be lucky enough to find that a case involving your ancestor was summarised in a printed and indexed law report. Law reports apply to all courts and can be searched in law libraries. Although original records are relatively hard to search, many trials were reported, often in much more detail than in the court records, in contemporary pamphlets. These could include verbatim transcripts of what was said, especially when the cases involved prominent people, highwaymen, duelling, cruelty, theft and forgery. Trials of radicals, Chartists and trades unionists were also popular. Civil trials received widespread interest if they involved sexual scandals, divorce, libel and disputes between corporations.

CRIMINAL COURTS

Court cases come in two types – civil cases between private individuals, and criminal cases, in which the state enforced its laws on individuals. Many genealogists hope to find the proverbial ancestor who was 'hanged for sheep steeling'. It is nestling among the records of criminal court cases that you might just find him (see Where to Search, overleaf).

A SMART MOVE TO SMARDEN

Assize records do not have to say 'x was son of y' to be useful to family trees. William Harvey was a husbandman in the Wealden parish of Smarden, Kent, and died there in 1654, the year his wife Mary proved his will at the Commonwealth Will Registry, which had temporarily replaced the Prerogative Court of Canterbury (see page 129). William's origins were a mystery until the following summary of a Kent assize record was found:

George Weldishe jr, baker of Goudhurst, and others including clothiers, who assembled illegally at Cranbrook and attended the conventicle in the house of William Hervey, 23 July 1642.

This tells us that William was in trouble for hosting illegal religious meetings, and the assizes go on to relate how in 1652 Cranbrook was seized by a witch purge resulting in five women being burned. Add to this the fact that William's previous wife, Phoebe, had been buried in Cranbrook in 1647, and it's small wonder that William decided to settle in the quieter atmosphere of Smarden. Subsequent research proved that the two Williams were definitely one and the same.

BETWITCHED

Some assize records have been printed, such as those for Kent in J. S. Cockburn's *Calendar of Assize Records: Kent Indictments* (HMSO, 1975–97). These include many ancestors mentioned simply as members of the grand jury (evidence at least that they were alive and adult at the time) along with plenty of unlicensed alehouses and 'tippling-houses', burglaries and deaths, such as the sad tale of Jane Streete of Cliff, spinster, heard at Maidstone Assizes on 21 September 1644. It seems that she gave birth to a 'bastard' on 18 December 1642, but left it in a bundle of straw in an outhouse, where the poor thing was smothered. Fortunately for her – and surprisingly, perhaps – she was found not guilty of infanticide.

Less lucky, though, was the widow Alice Jenkyn of Hinxhill. In December 1594 she was accused of bewitching three pigs worth 15s and four heifers worth 30s belonging to Arnold Back, and they dropped dead. Worse, she had previously 'bewitched' another Arnold, Arnold Fynne of Hinxhill, who fell into a 'languishing state', from which he died in February 1595. Within five days she had been dragged to the assizes, found guilty of murder and executed.

▷ An all-too familiar scene from a 17th-century witch hunt.

CRIMINAL COURTS

GENERAL

The most detailed information on searching for criminal trials and their consequences is D. T. Hawkings' *Criminal Ancestors: A Guide to Historical Criminal Records in England & Wales* (Sutton, 1992).

Besides records of the trials themselves, there are also some useful records of payments to sheriffs made by the Treasury for their expenses in catching criminals, which name many people accused of felony. These are indexed in **TNA** in class T 53 (1721–1805) and T 54 (1806–27).

EYRE

Derived from the Latin *iter*, meaning journey, this term describes the visitations of the King's judges to administer justice in the counties between the 12th and 14th centuries. The records, covering 1194–1348, cover a vast range of criminal and civil matters and are mostly in **TNA** class JUST 1-4 and many have been translated and published and listed in E. L. C. Mullins' *Texts and Calendars: an Analytical Guide to Serial Publications* (RHS, 1958 and 1983).

ASSIZES

These replaced the Eyres and continued until superseded in turn by Crown Courts in 1971. Surviving records are in **TNA** classes JUST and ASSI 1–54 (England) and 57–76 (Wales), except for those for London and Middlesex, and those which have been lost.

The judges operated either under royal commissions of 'oyer and terminer' (meaning they could hear felony cases in the provinces rather than in London), or 'gaol delivery' – hearing cases against prisoners awaiting trial in local gaols. Records include calendars of indictments, describing the accused and giving residence and alleged crime; gaol books detailing those in prison and their charges; and gaol delivery calendars giving the barest details of the trial.

Middlesex and the City of London's criminal justice system was administered by the Lord Mayor, recorder and aldermen sitting at the Old Bailey. Brief records, detailing the accused and their offence survive from 1684, with verdicts and sentences from 1791. Trial records concerning the City of London are at the **Corporation of London Records Office** and those to do with Middlesex at the **London Metropolitan Archives**.

In 1834, this system was replaced by the Central Criminal Court, which sat at the Old Bailey and whose records are in **TNA** class CRIM. Some have been published and indexed in J. Cordy Jeaffreson's *Middlesex County Records* (GLC, 1975).

Searching for Old Bailey trials has recently become a lot easier with the launch of **www.oldbaileyonline.org**, which contains more than 100,000 trials for the period 1674–1834.

WELSH COURTS

From its conquest by England in 1282, Welsh justice was administered by county courts called Great Sessions, and the Welsh marches were covered by courts held by the Marcher lords. Following the abolition of the Welsh marches in 1540, the whole of Wales was covered by a Court of Great Sessions which visited each county twice a year, and Justices of the Peace. Its records are at the **National Library of Wales**.

In 1830, the Welsh counties were incorporated into the English system of assizes, with its own circuit, which was then split into two, for North and South Wales, in 1876. The post-1830 records are at **TNA** in class ASSI 57–77.

SCOTTISH COURTS

Serious crime, such as murder, arson, rape and robbery, were dealt with by the King's Justiciar and his assistant justiciars and by the High Court of Justiciary, which sat in Edinburgh then, from 1708, travelled around the country hearing cases in different towns and cities. Its records, at the **NAS**, survive in part from 1572.

Less serious cases tended to be heard in sheriff courts, with minor ones appearing in the burgh and franchise courts and those of the Justices of the Peace. For more information on these records see my book, *Tracing Your Scottish Family History* (Collins, 2008).

IRISH COURTS

The bombing of the Four Courts in 1922 destroyed most Irish legal records. What little survived is in the **National Archives of Ireland**, which also holds vast collections of solicitors' papers.

As with England, however, cases are easier and better reported in newspapers and law reports. Butterworth have produced several hundred volumes of the *Irish Reports*, starting in 1838 and working forwards towards the present. There are also plenty of legal records at **TNA** concerning Ireland, such as the Court of Chancery of Ireland, which are in class C 79.

FORFEITED ESTATES (1715)

The Forfeited Estates Commission was established to punish those who had supported the 1715 rebellion and its records are in the **NAS**, while those for English and Welsh rebels are at **TNA** in FEC1 and 2, indexed by name in *The Records of the Forfeited Estates Commission* (HMSO, 1968).

QUICK REFERENCE

See also main sources in Useful Addresses, page 306

CORPORATION OF LONDON RECORD OFFICE
c/o London Metropolitan Archives
40 Northampton Road
London EC1R 0HB
☎ 020 7332 3820
www.cityoflondon.gov.uk

LONDON METROPOLITAN ARCHIVES
40 Northampton Road
London EC1R 0HB
☎ 020 7332 3820
www.cityoflondon.gov.uk

▽ The bombing of the Four Courts in Dublin in 1922 destroyed most Irish court records, wills and many Protestant parish registers. However, some records survived – and they are still available to be searched!

CIVIL COURTS

The civil courts do not record criminal behaviour. Instead, they record the quarrels and disputes that raged among our ancestors. The records bring out an extraordinary range of ways in which human beings can fall out with each other, and provide many useful genealogical details into the bargain.

WHERE TO SEARCH

CIVIL COURTS

CHANCERY RECORDS

⊟ The Court of Chancery, whose records date from the late 14th century, provided merciful justice that was not constrained by the severe rules of the common law courts. In 1875 the Court of Chancery became the Chancery Division of the High Court, and still exists today. The records are at **TNA**, chiefly in class C, and some in class J. They concern disputes over money and land, often between relations, and can therefore provide a cornucopia of family history information.

⊟ The records are usually filed per category, so pleadings, evidence and decisions (see box, opposite) are seldom found together, and unfortunately the records are very far from comprehensively indexed. Remember that many cases dragged on for years (sometimes bankrupting either or both parties) and many never ended. Therefore, you may find a complete set of records for a case involving your ancestor, or you may simply be lucky enough to find a reference to an ancestor in an index to one of the foregoing categories of records, and thus learn something more about them than you knew already.

⊟ The best finding aids to Chancery cases are **TNA**'s new online index **www.catalogue.nationalarchives. gov.uk**, now covering 15th and early 16th century cases, with cases from 1558 not yet so well covered.

⊟ There is also the Bernau Index, compiled by Charles Bernau, which covers over 4 million parties and witnesses up to and including the 18th century, and which can be searched in microfilm at the **SoG** and **Mormon Family History Centres**. Bear in mind, though, that this only scratches the surface of what is available in the original records.

⊟ A comprehensive list of Chancery records and available finding aids is given in M. Herber's *Ancestral Trails* (Sutton Publishing and SoG, 2000).

EXCHEQUER RECORDS

⊟ Exchequer records seldom pre-date 1558, by which time the court, originally for disputes between the Crown and its subjects over money, had taken on a role very similar to that of the Court of Chancery. Indeed, in 1841, the two were amalgamated. The records are in **TNA** class E. The cases generally take the form of pleadings – with production of evidence and witnesses' statements, which include age, address and occupation – and decisions.

⊟ Many of the records are indexed in the Bernau Index at the **SoG** (including all deponents and defendants in E 134, though the index is not thought to be complete). **www.catalogue.nationalarchives.gov.uk** indexes class E 134, covering plaintiffs, defendants and subjects but not deponents (nor does it cover London or any cases not involving depositions). **TNA** information leaflet 19 covers this in detail.

KING'S COUNCIL

⊟ This was known in Latin as *Curia regis* and the records, kept in rolls, survive for the 12th and 13th centuries and are in **TNA** class KB 26. Some have been printed and are listed in E. L. C. Mullins' *Texts and Calendars: An Analytical Guide to Serial Publications* (RHS, 1958 and 1983).

COURT OF COMMON PLEAS

⊟ This mainly dealt with land and money. Records 1194–1875 (after which it became part of the Common Pleas division of the High Court of Justice) are in class CP at **TNA**.

PLEA ROLLS

⊟ These record common law actions in the courts of Common Pleas, King's Bench, Exchequer and others. Most are at **TNA**: the City of London's, at **Guildhall Library**, have been translated and published from their original Latin and French in volumes covering 1298–1482, including A. H. Thomas' *Calendar of Plea and Memoranda Rolls Preserved among the Archives of the Corporation of the City of London at the Guildhall a.d.1413–1437* (CUP, 1943).

QUICK REFERENCE

See main sources in Useful Addresses, page 306

COURT OF KING'S BENCH

Court of King's Bench (class KB) contains such things as writs of *habeus corpus*. There are some indexes to defendants (London and Middlesex, 1673–1845) and provincial defendants 1638–1704, 1765–1843) in **TNA** in class IND 1.

COURT OF REQUESTS

This dealt mainly with disputes over money and land of the poor 1493–1642, for which **TNA** has indexes in class REQ.

STAR CHAMBER

This court, presided over by the monarchs and privy counsellors, sat in a chamber whose ceiling was painted with stars, from 1487 to 1641. Despite being infamous for its trials of nobles and others for treason, heresy and rebellion, it also heard appeals from common people seeking justice that they felt unable to obtain in other courts. Surviving records are in **TNA** class STAC and some have been printed in E. L. C. Mullins' *Texts and Calendars, An Analytical Guide to Serial Publications* (RHS 1958 and 1983).

PALATINE COURTS

Cheshire, Durham and Lancashire were each run entirely separately from the rest of the country, as palatines, with their own courts for chancery, equity and criminal cases. Almost all records are at **TNA** in classes CHES, DURH and PL respectively. There was also a court for the Royal Duchy of Lancaster, which heard disputes over land within the duchy, whose records are in class DL.

COURT OF WARDS AND LIVERIES

This existed from 1541 to 1660 and is in **TNA** in class WARD. It oversaw the rights of children under 21 who were orphaned heirs to land held direct by franchise from the Crown.

HIGH COURT OF ADMIRALTY

Set up in the 14th century, this dealt with maritime matters, from piracy to sailors' claims for prize money – their share of the profits from captured enemy ships. Vice-admiralty courts were also established to deal with similar affairs in coastal counties and colonies abroad. Their records are in **TNA** in class HCA and are described in C. T. Watts and M. J. Watts' *My Ancestor was a Merchant Seaman: How can I find out more about him?* (SoG, 1991).

PALACE COURT

This operated from 1630 to 1849 for small debt claims within 12 miles of Westminster and records are in **TNA** in class PALA.

COURT OF DIVORCE & CAUSES

See page 95.

COURT OF CHANCERY RECORDS

THE RECORDS generally take the form of:

Pleadings: a bill of complaint, in which the aggrieved party stated their case, and the defendant's answer, followed by any replications and rejoinders by the two parties.

Evidence: depositions taken from witnesses including their ages, residences and occupations.

Court decisions: the cases were then generally reviewed by the Masters in Chancery, or the six Chief Clerks on their behalf, who gave their view on who was right and who was wrong, and an order could be given stating the outcome of the case.

COURTS AFTER 1875

HOUSE OF LORDS

The Upper House could hear appeals from the Court of Appeal, especially in matters relating to divorce and probate between 1858 and 1875. These are chronicled along with all other business of the House, in the *House of Lords Journal*, which is held with the rest of the Upper Houses's records in the **House of Lords Record Office**.

PRIVY COUNCIL

The Privy Council grew out of the King's Council in the 14th century and comprised the monarch's chief ministers, household officials and bishops. The main records are in **TNA** class PC 2 covering 1540 onwards. These have been printed in facsimile form 1631–45 and printed and indexed in *Acts of the Privy Council 1542–1631*. The Privy Council dealt with affairs of state but also heard appeals and petitions on all sorts of matters involving ordinary people. Scottish Privy Council papers 1545–1691 have been published as listed in E. L. C. Mullins' *Texts and Calendars: An Analytical Guide to Serial Publications, Vol. 1* (RHS, 1958).

COUNTY COURTS

Established in 1846 to deal with civil matters, their records are in **county record offices**.

COURT OF AUGMENTATIONS

This sat between 1536 and 1554 and dealt with Henry VIII's dissolution of the monasteries. Records include receipts of rent from monastic tenants while the land was in Crown hands. Records are in **TNA** class SC and there are some in Exchequer records (see page 226).

CIVIC COURTS

Many cities and boroughs had their own courts, whose records are in **county record offices**. The City of London's courts, including the Court of Hustings and Mayor's Court, whose records go back to the 14th century, are at the **Corporation of London Record Office** and some early records have been published. The Fire Court was established in 1666, for which see P. E. Jones's *The Fire Court: Calendar to the Judgements and Decrees of the Court of Judicature Appointed to Determine Differences between Landlords and Tenants as to Rebuilding after the Great Fire* (William Clowes & Sons, 1966–70).

SCOTTISH COURTS

The records are at the **NAS** and are very well catalogued at **www.nas.gov.uk**. Civil cases were generally heard in the Court of Session, whose minute books date from 1557 and are printed and indexed annually from 1782. These, in turn, can lead you to a court's acts and decrees, providing further details of the case.

However, civil cases could also be heard by the Scottish Privy Council (until 1707), the Courts of Exchequer, which had jurisdiction over cases involving revenue 1708–1859 and the Admiralty Court, which oversaw maritime cases. Many more civil cases were heard at the sheriff courts, though their records tend to be patchy until the late 18th century.

Burgh courts, known as Bailies, are worth considering for civil and criminal matters, though during the 18th century their use declined greatly and the **NAS**'s holdings are sparse. The same applies to franchise courts, such as Barony and Regality Courts, which were courts held by landowners by franchise from the Crown.

QUICK REFERENCE

See also main sources in Useful Addresses, page 306

HOUSE OF LORDS RECORD OFFICE
Palace of Westminster
London SW1A 0PW
☎ 020 7219 3074
www.parliament.uk

CORPORATION OF LONDON RECORD OFFICE
c/o London Metropolitan Archives
40 Northampton Road
London EC1R 0HB
☎ 020 7332 3820
www.cityoflondon.gov.uk

COURTS AFTER 1875

In 1875 the judicial system was reformed and amalgamated into the Supreme Court of Judicature, divided into the High Court of Justice and Court of Appeal, and then into divisions to cover Chancery, probate, common pleas and so on. There are full details in the *Guide to the Contents of the Public Record Office* (HMSO, 1963 and 1968).

▽ *House of Lords* by T. Rowlandson (1756–1827) and A. C. Pugin (1762–1832), the most senior Court of Appeal until 1875.

BANKRUPTCY IS THE official winding up of the affairs of people unable to meet their debts. Initially it was available to those in trade or business: many insolvent gents, therefore, would describe themselves as tradesmen, usually chapmen, in order to qualify. In 1861, bankruptcy was available to all. The Lord Chancellor dealt with bankruptcy from 1571 until 1831, when the Court of Bankruptcy was formed. This established district courts, whose work was transferred to county courts in 1861, and the Court of Bankruptcy became the High Court of Justice in Bankruptcy in 1883.

Records from the 18th century are in TNA class B, but the *London Gazette* and local newspapers make much easier and often more detailed reading. Details of sales of some 3000 bankrupt Irish estates 1848–80 whose cases passed through the Encumbered Estates Court are at TNA.

BANKRUPTCY

LIFETIMES: PERRY NURSEY GOES BANKRUPT

PERRY NURSEY was a Suffolk landscape artist whose expensive tastes led to him collecting more of other peoples' paintings than selling his own. This, and the severe slump in the agricultural economy which decimated the income from his small estate, ruined him. This is the harrowing process that followed, all described in minute detail in a succession of reports in his local newspaper, the *Ipswich Journal*, whence they were extracted at the Suffolk Record Office in Ipswich.

Towards the end of 1833, Perry's creditors made an affidavit before one of the Masters of Chancery, pleading that he was so much in debt he should be made bankrupt. The Lord Chancellor agreed, granting a commission of bankruptcy on 21 December – just in time to ruin Perry's Christmas – and appointing five commissioners, who in turn appointed two solicitors to handle the affair. The announcement appeared in the local paper and the *London Gazette* at the beginning of the next year. Perry, as the contemporary expression had it, had been 'gazetted'. Because bankruptcy was only available to tradesmen, Perry, who formerly described himself as 'Esquire', was now termed an 'architect, builder, dealer and chapman'.

SALE OF POSSESSIONS

On 14 January Perry 'surrendered' himself to the solicitors and his creditors, by pre-advertised arrangement, at a local hotel. Both sides produced their relevant accounts and the creditors appointed three assignees of their number to oversee the sale of Perry's possessions, using the proceeds to repay the debts and also make Perry an allowance of 5% of the value raised to a value not exceeding £300, a small mercy available to all but gamblers. Several subsequent meetings were held to decide whether to sell or retain the leases of two of his farms, to regain another from the landlord, Lord Bristol, who had himself repossessed it, and decide whether Perry was eligible for his certificate of bankruptcy.

In the meantime, starting on 14 February, a series of auctions were held to dispose of his goods and other leases, each item meticulously described in the paper and in specially printed and widely circulated catalogues. His art collection was auctioned in April, with advertisements circulated in London to attract the best dealers. Ironically, having neglected to sell many of his own paintings over the years, his creditors now did an excellent job marketing him, so as to raise the highest prices: even unfinished works were sold off.

STARTING OVER AGAIN

By May, Perry was free from claims by any further creditors. That December, the assignees paid the creditors 2s 4d for each pound originally owed. Perry himself was left with his clothes, the tools of his trade, including his paintbrushes and the ability to contract new debts, should anyone be ill-advised enough to lend him money or supply goods on credit. A friend lent him a cottage and he started a new life, as an art teacher, though age, financial worries and probably a great sense of failure contributed to his death a mere seven years later.

It is a sad story, but the detailed lists of his belongings, musical instruments, books and paintings was fascinating and would never have been made had he not been a bankrupt. Posterity, ultimately, was better served by Perry having been bankrupt than had he remained solvent.

ECCLESIASTICAL COURTS

Church courts dealt with practical matters relating to the church, such as tithe payments or drunken priests; religion, such as heresy and witchcraft; and morality. In fact the courts dealt mainly with sexual misconduct in all its many and varied forms, and for this reason they were known as the 'bawdy courts'. Sadly, the records are in Latin and few have been published – the county record office staff can tell you if anything relevant to your searches is in print. For all that, the original records are still worth searching for a chance mention of your ancestor as a last resort if you are stuck, or if you have plenty of time, in the hope of finding some salacious tales to embellish your family history.

Cases were usually heard in the archdeaconry courts, with appeals being made to the bishop's court. The lawyers who practised in these were proctors and advocates.

Cases were usually opened following a presentment by the churchwardens of a parish, often made during the annual archdeacon's visitation of the parishes, or the triennial bishop's visitations. Cases took the form of civil action between two individuals, called instance cases, and actions by the church against individuals, called office cases. Evidence might be heard orally, in which case few records will survive, or by written evidence, and these can result in detailed records.

The records can provide useful information for genealogists, such as ages and places of birth of witnesses, and how long they had lived in the parish. They may also describe relationships (especially in cases of adultery, illegitimacy and so on) and religious denomination – many cases were brought against non-conformists for non-attendance at church or refusal to pay tithes.

WHERE TO SEARCH

ECCLESIASTICAL COURTS

The organisation of church courts, the location of their records, their role in proving wills and dealing with subsequent disputes over them, is explained above.

⊟ Appeals against sentences could be made to the Court of Arches (with records at **Lambeth Palace Library**, indexed in J. Houston's *Cases in the Court of Arches 1660–1913* (BRS, vol. 85, 1972)), and the Chancery Court of York (records at the **Borthwick Institute**), depending on the province in which your ancestor lived.

⊟ Final appeals were made to the Pope and, after the Reformation, to the High Court of Delegates (mostly indexed in **TNA** class DEL 11).

QUICK REFERENCE

See also main sources in Useful Addresses, page 306

LAMBETH PALACE LIBRARY
Lambeth Palace Road
London SE1 7JU
☎ 020 7898 1400
www.lambethpalacelibrary.org

BORTHWICK INSTITUTE
St Anthony's Hall
Peasholme Green
York YO1 7PW
☎ 01904 642315
www.york.ac.uk/inst/bihr

LIFETIMES: A LITTLE OF WHAT YOU FANCY

A. TARVER'S *Church Court Records: An Introduction for Family and Local Historians* (Phillimore, 1995) provides many salacious (and not unfamiliar) examples of our ancestors' sex lives.

Mr St John Haynes, for example, was horrified when his servants told him his wife Mary had been having sex with Dr Joseph Berrington in the small parlour next to the kitchen in their house in Willoughby, Warwickshire. He sent her away to a boarding house in Chelmsford, under the strict chaperoning of a servant, Mary Webb. This measure did not quell Mrs Haynes' libido, however, and before long Mary Webb, finding black hairs in the bed of her blonde mistress, realised more hanky-panky was afoot. Mr Haynes obtained a separation from his wife, but neither she nor he, despite being the wronged party, were permitted to remarry while the other one lived.

QUARTER SESSIONS

Quarter Sessions dealt with a vast amount of business, criminal and civil, that, indirectly or not, touched the lives of most of our ancestors. They are a fabulous resource for family history, and the only reason they are not much more widely used is that, on the whole, they tend not to have been transcribed or indexed. I imagine this will change over next few decades.

Quarter Sessions were courts held from 1361 to 1971 in each county four times a year, and on other occasions called 'divisions', when they were petty sessions. They were presided over by Justices of the Peace (JPs), also called magistrates, who still deal with cases in Magistrates' courts. Like them, quarter sessions tended to deal with less serious crimes than the assizes (see page 224), such as theft and poaching, and were also concerned with many matters of local government, especially licensing inns; prosecuting Catholics; enforcing the poor law; taking of oaths; overseeing matters relating to apprenticeship and qualification of craftsmen; policing local militias; maintenance of roads and bridges; and overseeing tax collection.

THE RECORDS USUALLY COMPRISE THE FOLLOWING:

➤**Books** (or, earlier, rolls) for orders detailing the JPs' decisions and orders; minutes or processes, recording what happened at each sitting.
➤**Indictments with details of criminal charges** and information about the accused in terms of residence, alleged offence and perhaps some information about the victim.
➤**Other documentation brought to or issued by the hearings,** such as sworn statements; lists of prisoners, jurors, people born abroad (from 1792), voters and freemasons; licences for the likes of alehouse keepers, itinerant traders and gamekeepers; bonds and sureties; tax returns; enclosure awards; and lists of householders liable for paying county rates.

CRIMINALS

Once people were found guilty in court –– whether they were really guilty or not – they generated a new set of records, which can tell you about their lives as convicted criminals.

PRISONERS

The fate of many of our criminal ancestors was either branding and flogging, execution or transportation. Public execution, usually by hanging, was a commonplace event, a cheap form of entertainment in

WHERE TO SEARCH

QUARTER SESSIONS

The records were kept by the Clerk of the Peace and are in **county record offices**, and those for Scotland are in the **NAS**. They are detailed in J. Gibson's *Quarter Sessions Records for Family Historians: A Select List* (FFHS, 1995), which also notes the relatively little that has been published on the subject.

You may be able to work out when an ancestor was likely to appear in the records (if he was an alehouse keeper, for example), or you may wish to approach the records simply as a 'lucky dip' and see if you run across any forbears by chance. If you do, you will most likely open up new windows on their lives offering riches you could never have anticipated.

QUICK REFERENCE

See main sources in Useful Addresses, page 306

▽ *Execution of John Thurtell at Hertford Jail* in 1824 (anon).

LIFETIMES: BAPTISED ON THE 4TH OF JULY

IT WAS KNOWN that William Seal was transported to America in 1747 and a published compilation of sources, *English Convicts in Colonial America*, cited the Middlesex Sessions of Gaol Delivery, at Greater London Record Office, as the source. The original record told us:

'That William Seal late of the parish of Enfield in the County of Middlesex Labourer ... on the 8th Nov in the 21st year of the reign of our sovereign Lord George ... and with force & arms at the parish aforesaid ... one Plough Chain of the value of 2 shillings and one Iron Bolt of the value of sixpence of the goods & chattels of one Samuel Wyburn then & there being found feloniously did steal take and carry away against the peace of our said Lord the King ... his dignity.

This got us back to Enfield. Although William's baptism was not found in the registers of Enfield, Essex, the IGI revealed that there was a baptism in the neighbouring Hertfordshire parish of Cheshunt, for William and Thomas, twin children of Robert Seale, baptised on 4 July 1726 – what an appropriate date for someone later sent to America.

the days before television, and many hangings were recorded in souvenir pamphlets and prints. It was abolished in 1868, by which time the death penalty was rarely applied for offences other than murder.

In the Middle Ages, prisons were generally used for those awaiting trial, and it was only in the 16th century that Houses of Correction started to be built to hold criminals (and other 'wrongdoers', like vagrants and pregnant women) for punishment. But with so many hanged or transported for the most minor of thieving offences, prisons of the sort we know today did not really come into being until during the 19th century.

△ Interior of the Debtors' Prison, Whitecross Street in the 1830s.

TRANSPORTEES

Many people who were not executed for their misdemeanours were transported to British colonies. Indeed, many early settlers in America and the Caribbean were transportees and once the American War of Independence put paid to this, prisoners were sent to Australia instead.

WHERE TO SEARCH

CRIMINALS

PRISONERS

⊟ From 1823, records relating to prisons often appear in Quarter Session records while gaolers' journals, usually providing names and dates of admission and discharge, and what the offence was, will be found in **county record offices**.

⊟ Criminal registers arranged year by year, county by county, for England and Wales 1805–92, with date and place of trial and details of the verdict and punishment are at **TNA** in HO 26–7. These are partially indexed on disk by S. Tamblin's *Criminal Register Index, 1805–40*, which can be viewed at **www.fhindexes.co.uk**. The registers for London and Middlesex go back to 1791 and those to 1802 give place of birth and a physical description as well.

⊟ Different categories of calendars of prisoners, some dating from as early as 1774, can give you the age and occupation of the prisoner, as well as details of the alleged crime. At **TNA** (in HO 7, 8, 9, 23 and 24, and PCOM 2, ADM 6, KB 32, T 1, T 38 and WO 25) and also the **county record offices** are many prison registers, which provide name, birthplace, age, details of the crime and punishment, and often a physical description. From the mid-19th century you may even find a photograph. If your ancestor was imprisoned on a hulk – old navy ships used as prisons – or petitioned for pardon, their records may also be found at **TNA**. Full details of **TNA** and county record office holdings are given in D. T. Hawkings' *Criminal Ancestors: A Guide to Historical Criminal Records in England & Wales* (Sutton, 1992). Criminals' petitions 1819–39 are in HO 17.

⊟ A useful site for British prisons and their records (and many other institutions such as orphanages, hospitals and prisons) is **www.institutions.org.uk**.

⊟ Scottish prisoners' records are at the **NAS**, though few survive from before the mid-19th century.

TRANSPORTEES

⊟ The main sources for pre-Australian transportation have been collated and indexed in P. W. Coldham's *The Complete Book of Emigrants in Bondage, 1614–1775* (GCP, 1990), but there are many others. Those in print include J. C. Hotten's modestly titled *The Original Lists of Persons of Quality, Emigrants, Religious Exiles, Political Rebels, Serving Men Sold for a Term of Years, Apprentices, Children Stolen, Maidens Pressed and Others who went from Great Britain to the American Plantations 1660–1700 from MSS Preserved in the State Paper Department at the PRO* (GCP, 1962) and W. M. Wingfield's *The Monmouth Rebels 1685* (Somerset Record Society, 1985), which lists the men caught and sentenced to transportation (as opposed to execution under Judge Jeffries) after the Monmouth rebellion in 1685.

⊟ Hawkings' *Criminal Ancestors* (see left) lists the **TNA** sources for those sent to Australia; the main one being the registers of convict transportation 1787–1867 in HO 11, which are sadly unindexed.

⊟ Most records of transportees will tell you where they were convicted, but not where they originated. If you are lucky, though, their place of conviction will be near their place of origin, enabling you at least to narrow your search to a particular geographic region. Of great interest for people with Scottish ancestry are the uprisings of 1715, in favour of the exiled prince James Stuart, and 1745, in favour of his son, Bonnie Prince Charlie. Much information appears in the calendared and indexed State Papers (Domestic) and (Scotland) series at **TNA**, while records of trials of rebels are in the King's Bench records, KB 8. Other cases appear in assize, palatine and treasury papers listed in **TNA** information leaflet 4.

QUICK REFERENCE

See main sources in Useful Addresses, page 306

CHAPTER TWENTY-SIX
EDUCATION! EDUCATION! EDUCATION!

Records of education are of best use to genealogists when they provide ages and father's names, not least when the father himself went to the same institution. Records of schools exist across the world and the main sources are listed overleaf.

For *Extraordinary Ancestors*, we visited a school in Gujarat to try to find out more about Ari Alibhai's grandfather. The headmaster produced the old school records, and, sure enough, there he was. We were delighted to note one of his classmates who went on to become famous – Mohamed Ali Jinnah, the future president of Pakisan!

▷ Claude Lorraine Richard Wilson Nursey (1816–73), headmaster of Belfast School of Design.

▽ A Stonyhurst speech day programme from 1833, including my cousin Richard Havers.

LIFETIMES: JOSEPH ADOLPH

SCHOOL RECORDS CAN PROVIDE all sorts of wonderful detail about our forbears' formative years. Besides school and team photographs, a host of details can be learned. The following is what was discovered about my grandfather, Joseph Albert Stanislaus Adolph, from the school magazines and other records at St George's, Weybridge:

He arrived at St George's on 16 September 1920 and was numbered 1756 in the list of pupils. He was preceded there by his father (1890–97), who had been numbered 278, and three of his father's four surviving brother, Albert (1890–94), Arthur (1890–95) and William (1896–8). In 1925, in the Literary and Dramatic Society he gave a recitation of 'The Hammer and the Nail', and a humorous reading, 'Hickleton Fair', and in the Musical Society in December he sang 'Little Brown Jug' and in March 'Drink Puppy Drink'. In the school's mock House of Commons he was the Member for Croydon and Clerk to the House and always took a very active part, being reported in The Georgian as 'a bright and intelligent speaker'. Joe was also a member of the KBS of the OTC and the Sodality of Our Lady, and in his final year was President of the Debating Society and also the sub-editor of The Georgian, together with Maurice Lucie-Smith (1920–28).

1925 saw the beginning of the 'House System' and Joe was put into Kilmorey House. He played in the 2nd XI Cricket ('a good bowler'), the 2nd XI Hockey ('very useful in the final line of defence') and won his junior Rugby Colours in the 2nd XV.

In the Lower Fifth he won 2nd prize with an average of 69% and a 1st in geography and maths. He was also 2nd in the Miss Kean Apologetic Prize and came 2nd in the Prize Debate. He left St George's in 1926.

SCHOOLS

I used to live barely a mile from the oldest school in England, the King's School, Canterbury, which was founded in AD 597. Early, fee-paying schools were founded by the church, and later by private benefactors and guilds, and many of these survive to the present as grammar, private or public schools.

Schools for the poor tended to focus on children up to about 13, and were relatively uncommon before the 19th century. There were some charity schools founded from the 17th century onwards, and during the 18th century some workhouses started providing elementary education for the children in their care. From 1810 onwards, many more schools for the poor began to be founded, such as Dame Schools, Ragged Schools and many founded by religious groups, such as the Society for the Promotion of Christian Knowledge. Many were established following the Education Act of 1870, but they often charged small fees, thus putting the poor off, even after an Act of 1880 made attendance for under-13s

OVERSEAS STUDENTS

SOME BRITISH STUDENTS went abroad, particularly to Leyden or Heidelberg University if they were Protestants, but there were other destinations. *Family Tree Magazine* (July 2003) contains J. Titford's transcript of British students at Franeker University in Friesland, 1585–1811 and 1816–44.

Catholics went, whenever they could, to Catholic universities on the Continent, such as those in Spain, Portugal, France and Italy. Much material covering these has been published by the Catholic Record Society (see page 258).

compulsory, although some exemptions were made for children over ten. Free secondary education, for children up to about 18, existed in some places from 1880 but did not become normal until after 1902.

For these reasons, many people could not read or write. But it is important not to think of everyone below the middle class as a herd of illiterates: many children were taught a lot at home, or by members of the gentry or clergy. Sometimes, I hear people saying, 'But great-grandfather was so well educated: his parents couldn't have been labourers.' The truth, though, is that bright children could learn a great deal at even the smallest village schools, enabling them to rise from labouring backgrounds to join the middle class.

UNIVERSITIES

The only two universities in England before the establishment of Durham University in 1832 were those of Oxford and Cambridge. Registers of those who attended Oxford and Cambridge – including most of the Anglican clergy – have been published. Later universities, such as Durham and London (founded in 1836) also have published registers and all universities have archivists who can be consulted.

WHERE TO SEARCH

SCHOOLS

⊡ School records, such as reports, team photographs and leaving certificates, are often found in family papers. School archives may also contain information about your ancestors, such as admission books, records of clubs, log books, school magazines and much else.

⊡ If you know the name of the school, you may find it is still there and in possession of its own archives, or if not, the records may be in the local **studies library** or **county record office**. You can work out where your ancestor may have been educated by consulting contemporary directories (see page 82). Registers of many public schools have been published and will usually give you age or date of birth and father's occupation and residence. They may include team photographs and information about what the pupil did later in life. Remember to look up not just your ancestor, but anyone else of the same name, as many families tended to use the same school generation after generation. There are good collections of printed registers at the **SoG**.

⊡ An excellent source of background information is C. R. Chapman's *The Growth of British Education and its Records* (Lochin Publishing, 1992).

⊡ Scottish schools were generally maintained by burghs and parishes, and many were founded by the Society in Scotland for Propagating Christian Knowledge, whose records are at the **NAS**. School boards were established in 1872, with records variously at the **NAS**, **regional record offices** or **local council archives**.

⊡ There are some published records of Irish grammar schools dating back to the 17th century. Irish primary education started in 1831, and registers can provide names and ages of pupils, with their fathers' addresses, occupations and denomination, mainly held by the schools themselves. Most for Northern Ireland are at the **PRONI**.

QUICK REFERENCE

See main sources in Useful Addresses, page 306

EDUCATION! EDUCATION! EDUCATION! 239

UNIVERSITIES

Cambridge is covered by J and J. A. Venn's *Alumni Cantabrigiensis: A Biographical List of all known Students, Graduates and Holders of Office at the University of Cambridge from the Earliest Times to 1900* (CUP, 1922–7 and 1940–54), with sometimes quite detailed biographical notes about the graduate's subsequent career.

The period before 1500 is supplemented by A. B. Emden's *A Biographical Register of the University of Cambridge to 1500* (CUP, 1963).

Oxford is covered by J. Foster's *Alumni Oxoniensis: The Members of the University of Oxford 1500–1714; their Parentage, Birthplace, and Year of Birth, with a Record of their Degrees* ... (James Parker & Co., 1891) and *Alumni Oxoniensis: The Members of the University of Oxford 1715–1886* (James Parker & Co., 1888–91) both available on CD from **www.archivecdbooks.org**, supplemented for the 16th and previous centuries by A. B. Emden's *A Biographical Register of the University of Oxford to AD 1500* (OUP, 1957) and another volume *1501–1540* (OUP, 1974).

By the Reformation, Scotland had four universities, St Andrew's, Aberdeen, Glasgow and Edinburgh, all of whose matriculation lists have been published. The universities hold many further records.

The only university in Ireland was Trinity College, Dublin, whose registers have been published in G. D. Burtchaell and T. U. Sadlier's *Alumni Dublinenses: A Register of the Students, Graduates, Professors, and Provosts of Trinity College, in the University of Dublin* (Williams and Norgate, 1924).

▷ My great-great-grandfather, Rev. Patrick Henry Kilduff, a clergyman in Tottenham, who trained at Trinity College, Dublin.

SHILPA MEHTA was the co-presenter of our Channel 4 series *Extraordinary Ancestors*. Not surprisingly, she became interested in her own family, and I helped her find out more from her father and cousins in America and India.

△ Shilpa's great-grandfather, Laxmilal Mehta (centre), in charge of a construction site near Bombay.

Twenty years ago, there was a terrible flood in the city of Bhavnagar, in Gujerat. Among the damage done was the destruction of a venerable house, known as the House of Pilewala in the street called Diwanpara. On the wall of the house was a great family tree, drawn in European style, as a tree, containing all the names of the Pilewala family, who were also known by their nickname, derived from their centuries-old occupation (see below) – Mehta. After the waters receded, the tree was found to have been washed away.

Had this disaster occurred in Europe, the loss of the family tree would probably have meant the loss of all family knowledge. What the waters could not wash away, however, were the excellent memories of the Mehta family, which were already used to holding a considerable amount of family knowledge. And so, the family tree of the Mehtas came to Europe in the form of oral history, and then here, to the printed page.

THE NAGAR BRAHMINS

Within Gujerat, the most prestigious of the Hindu castes were the Nagar Brahmins. They were Brahmins, although some simply styled themselves Nagars to indicate that they were not priests. They were generally landowners or high-ranking state officials, and from their number come many of the high-ranking literary figures of modern Gujerat.

It was from among the Nagars living in the city of Bhavnagar that the Maharajah of Bhavnagar picked his political administrators, called 'mehtas'. More interested in their hedonistic lifestyles and in spending, rather than raising, taxes, the Maharajahs relied heavily on their mehtas, particularly those drawn from the House of Pielwala. Indeed, so many of the men in the family served as mehtas that Mehta became a substitute surname for the family, and that is how they became known.

Memories of the family tree go back to the end of the 17th century, to Bhanji Mehta, born in about 1690. From him, a clear line comes down to the present day, as shown overleaf. One famous Mehta who does not appear on the family tree, but who could be related to Shilpa's ancestors, was Narsingh Mehta. He lived 500 years ago, in Junagadh (about 100 miles from Bhavnagar). Having fulfilled his duties as a husband and father, he retired to study, meditate and compose hymns and poems. So highly regarded was his mysticism that he became regarded as a holy man – a saint.

THE FAMILY BACKGROUND

In the 18th century, Bhavnagar was a proud independent state, surrounded by plenty of other proud, independent states, constantly at war with each other, with a strong army including Rajputs and Arabs, with Indo-Portuguese men from the south manning the city's formidable batteries of artillery.

S. M. Edwardes' *Ruling Princes of India: Bhavnagar* (Bombay, 1909) tells us that when the British arrived in 1807–8 all this started to change under Colonel Walker. Thereafter, British interference in Bhavnagar was extensive, holding back attempts at internal reorganisation. From 1863, however, Colonel Keatinge introduced the police of British non-interference in the region and the port of Bhavnagar was placed solely in the state's hands.

Now that the state was not held back by external interference, the Maharajah's prime minister, or Diwan, Azam Gavrishankar Oza, started an energetic programme of reforms – roads and harbours were built, land was reclaimed from the sea, mass education and vaccination was encouraged, laws were codified, prisons built and a proper police force was instituted. Azam Gavrishankar (Azam was a title) was aided by a council of seven administrators, including Shilpa's 4x great-grandfather Azam Vajeshankar Gulabrai Desai, who became deputy administrator, and who is shown in an old photograph, and also Savilal Somji Mehta, Shilpa's 3x great-grandfather, who was Karbhari in charge of the state's political department.

Thus, Bhavnagar became the most orderly and progressive state in the region, working closely with but not dominated by the British, and Shilpa's ancestors had a great deal to do with it. Subsequent Diwans included Azam Samaldas Parmanandas Mehta and Vithaldas Samaldas Mehta, who belonged to an extended branch of Shilpa's family, while

△ Shilpa's maternal grandfather, Damodar Thakker, and his teacher, Atre Acharya, striding off to meet Ghandi on his famous march against salt tax.
◁ Laxmilal Mehta overseeing the construction of a railway.

Azam Harilal Savailal Mehta, who was Shilpa's 3x great-uncle, was a deputy prime minister, shown in white seated on his own and in the group photograph seated immediately to the left of the Diwan (who is in the centre, in white).

MOVING ON

Shilpa's great-grandfather Laxmilal Mehta, born in 1877, broke the mould and trained as a consulting civil engineer. Continuing the Mehtas' policy of modernisation, however, he built the port of Bhavnagar under the Maharajahs. It is from Laxmilal's son Krishnavadan Mehta, born in 1909, that Shilpa may derive

△ Shilpa with her brother and father, in Zambia, where their father was temporarily stationed.

some of her flare as a presenter. In the days before film and television, he loved the theatre and directed numerous plays, including the first three-act play ever performed in Gujerat, in 1935. His work as an engineer for the Indian Hume Pipe Company took him away from Bhavnagar, to places as far-flung as Delhi, Karachi, Mumbai and Chinnai. His work also took him to Porbunder, where his son Shailendra Mehta, Shilpa's father, was born in 1931.

Porbunder was also the birth place of Mahatma Ghandi and, having spent several centuries working with the British, many members of the Mehta family joined Ghandi's struggle for Indian freedom. Several were imprisoned for civil obedience, most notably Shilpa's great aunt Akhileshwari and her husband, but in the end their cause was won and India achieved independence in 1947.

Ironically, when Shilpa went to Gujerat to film Ari Alibhai's family for *Extraordinary Ancestors* (see page 236) her journey took her to within minutes' walk of the house where her father was born. By the time the Mehtas settled there, Ari's family had migrated to East Africa, but relatives of his would almost certainly have known the Mehtas.

SHILPA'S MATERNAL ANCESTRY

In 1955, eight years after Indian Independence, Shilpa's father settled in England where he worked for 40 years as a specialist advisor, essentially performing the same task for the British government as his forbears had done for the Maharajahs.

Shilpa and her brother Shayur Mehta were both born here. Shayur, who played Prince Jhoti in *The Far Pavilions* and Crown Prince Chululongkom in *The King and I*, and Shilpa have also inherited strong artistic genes from their mother, Nivedida Thakkar, who is an actress, a radio artist and an Indian classical dancer. Nivedida's mother was Vidushi Kumair Omkarnand, an early Indian feminist. Besides being Principal of the Baroda Women's College, she was also an ardent disciple of Swami Vivekananda, whose cult she promoted in southern Africa in the 1920s, travelling there by dhow. Her husband, Shilpa's grandfather, was Damoder Thakker, a leading light of Nehru's Congress Party in Thane, Mumbai, while his grandfather, Shilpa's

△ 'British Indian Passport' of Shilpa's grandmother, Miss Vidushi Kumari Omkarnand.

maternal great-great-grandfather, was Valji Thakker, a botanist and agriculturalist in Kutch, Gujerat, whose portrait is said to hang in the main entrance of the agricultural college at Puhna.

The thing about Shilpa's ancestry that I find most remarkable is that so much is still known within the family, despite the flood and the fact that they now live thousands of miles away from India.

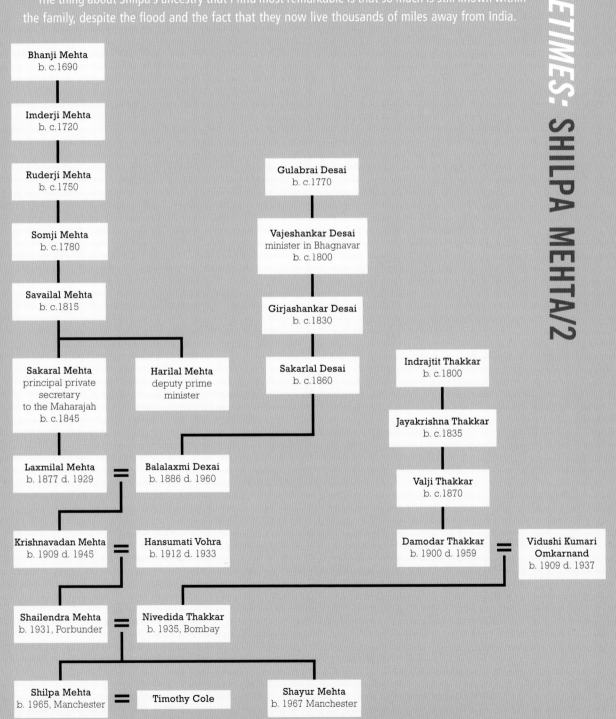

Bhanji Mehta
b. c.1690

Imderji Mehta
b. c.1720

Ruderji Mehta
b. c.1750

Somji Mehta
b. c.1780

Savailal Mehta
b. c.1815

Sakaral Mehta
principal private
secretary
to the Maharajah
b. c.1845

Harilal Mehta
deputy prime
minister

Laxmilal Mehta
b. 1877 d. 1929

Balalaxmi Dexai
b. 1886 d. 1960

Krishnavadan Mehta
b. 1909 d. 1945

Hansumati Vohra
b. 1912 d. 1933

Shailendra Mehta
b. 1931, Porbunder

Nivedida Thakkar
b. 1935, Bombay

Shilpa Mehta
b. 1965, Manchester

Timothy Cole

Shayur Mehta
b. 1967 Manchester

Gulabrai Desai
b. c.1770

Vajeshankar Desai
minister in Bhagnavar
b. c.1800

Girjashankar Desai
b. c.1830

Sakarlal Desai
b. c.1860

Indrajtit Thakkar
b. c.1800

Jayakrishna Thakkar
b. c.1835

Valji Thakkar
b. c.1870

Damodar Thakkar
b. 1900 d. 1959

Vidushi Kumari
Omkarnand
b. 1909 d. 1937

EMIGRANTS

Many people migrated from Britain, mainly to inhabit new colonies, either voluntarily as settlers or involuntarily as convicts. Generally, emigration from Britain was poorly recorded, though many countries of arrival kept records of incomers, such as the Ellis Island records of immigrants to New York, which can be accessed at **www.ellisisland.com**.

EMIGRANTS

- Many towns and cities founded by emigrants have excellent archives including memoirs of settlers, describing how they got there and where they came from, and often the most useful of these will have been published. Such a book may not mention your ancestor, but it may still help if it indicates where most original settlers started their journeys – always bear in mind that people preferred to travel in groups with people (often relatives) already known to them. It is also worth looking for obituary notices, especially from the late 19th century onwards. Even if the obituary is of the grandchild of an emigrant, it may give some information on the family's origins – or reputed origins – in Britain or Europe (see page 144).

- At **TNA** in class T 1 are Treasury Board records 1557–1920, calendared 1557–1775, containing many references to emigrants to the colonies. Passenger lists of ships leaving Britain generally survive only from the 1890s and are in BT 27 (see also page 255). You will need to know from where and have pretty good idea of when someone left to make the search feasible – and they will only give name, age, occupation and place of destination – not place of birth.

- Some 16th- and 17th-century travellers applied for licences to pass 'beyond the seas': these can be sought in **TNA** classes E 157 and CO 1. Applications for and issue of passports 1794–1948, including details of where the applicant wanted to go, are in FO 610, in date order but partially indexed for the periods 1851–62 and 1874–1916 in FO 611, now indexed 1851–1903 at **www.nationalarchivist.com**. However, passports were not compulsory, and therefore very few were issued, before the start of the First World War.

- At **TNA**, the Colonial Papers (CO 1) and Board of Trade Minutes 1675–1704 (CO 391) have been calendared and indexed by HMSO, and you may also find references to migrant ancestors or relatives in the *Calendar of State Papers Colonial, America and West Indies 1574–1738* – a lucky dip, but relatively easy to search at **TNA**, **British Library** and many other major **libraries**.

- From 1890, the Board of Trade kept passenger lists for people leaving for destinations outside Europe (**TNA** class BT 27), including names, ages and occupation and usually last place of residence – but they are arranged by port and ships. They include *Titanic's* ill-fated passengers and are being indexed at **www.findmypast.com**.

- Records of assisted emigration of the poor, who had their passage paid for them in return for agreeing to work as indentured servants for a term of years after their arrival, are at **TNA** and Guildhall Library, and many such records have been printed in P. W. Coldham's *The Complete Book of Emigrants in Bondage, 1614–1775* (GCP, 1988). Other details of emigrants whose dispatch to the colonies was considered less irksome than supporting them at home are in parish vestry minutes (see page 166) and, after 1834, in Poor Law Union records (both at **county record offices**), while lists of many who emigrated under the latter system are in **TNA** class MH 12.

- Once they had arrived in their new homes, migrants started keeping records, which are generally still in those countries. However, many Anglican communities abroad sent their original registers, or copies of bishops' transcripts, to the Archbishop of Canterbury and Bishop of London, and these are now divided between **Lambeth Palace Library**, **Guildhall Library** and **TNA**. Holdings are listed in G. Yeo's *The British Overseas: A Guide to Records of their Baptisms, Births, Marriages, Deaths and Burials available in the United Kingdom* (Guildhall Library, 1994). **TNA** holds a substantial collection of miscellaneous foreign returns, from all over the world, in classes RG 32–6 and RG 43, dating back to the 17th century but mainly for the 19th century.

- **TNA** also holds many Foreign Office records of baptisms, births and so on, some but not all of which are included in the **GRO**

▷ Migrants to America. *In the Land of Promise* by Charles Frederic Ulrich (1858–1908).

consular returns. If the entry you want is not there, you might yet find it in the unindexed returns in the FO papers at **TNA**. A search in **www.catalogue.nationalarchives.gov.uk** under the city or country where you think the event took place should tell you if returns for the right period are available.

🖿 **www.theshipslist.com** is a website of previously unpublished resources, including passenger records; contemporary immigration reports; newspaper records; ship wreck information and ship pictures.

POPULAR DESTINATIONS FOR EMIGRATION

THE AMERICAS

🖿 Emigration was also a favoured way of dealing with orphans or children of paupers. Many were sent to Virginia from the 17th century onwards by Christ's Hospital in London, and are listed in P. W. Coldham's *Child Apprentices in America from Christ's Hospital, London, 1617–1778* (GPC, 1990). Parish Guardians of the Poor were permitted to dispatch orphans and poor children to the colonies from 1850, and many charities like Dr Barnardo's did so as well, Canada being one of the most popular destinations. P. Bean and J. Melville's *Lost Children of the Empire* (Unwin Hyman, 1989) provides further information for those with such children in their family tree.

🖿 Also worth mentioning is **TNA** class T 47/9–12, a detailed and unique register of emigrants from Britain to the Americas 1773–6 containing name, age, occupation, last place of residence and dates of departure and destination.

🖿 A formidable compilation of records relating to migrating to the Americas is given in P. W. Coldham's *The Complete Book of Emigrants* (GPC, 1987–93), also available on CD-Rom.

🖿 Assisted emigration to Australia, North America and the West Indies was also encouraged by free passage and grants of land to willing settlers, by the Colonial Land and Emigration Office, which was founded in 1833. It became the Colonial Commission of Land and Emigration and its records, to 1896,

are at **TNA** in CO 384, with further records in CO 386 (emigration entry books) and CO 327–8 (North American emigrants registers 1850–68). Many Australian records of assisted immigrants have been indexed, and are accessible through the relevant **state archive office**.

QUICK REFERENCE

See also main sources in Useful Addresses, page 306

LAMBETH PALACE LIBRARY
Lambeth Palace Road
London SE1 7JU
☎ 020 7898 1400
www.lambethpalacelibrary.org

WHERE TO SEARCH

CATHOLICS

GENERAL

Catholics are generally well recorded both in their own records and in state records of their persecution. Much of both have been published by the **Catholic Record Society (CRS)**, and a good collection is at the **Catholic Central Library**. There is also an excellent **Catholic Family History Society**.

A good source for London and London-area marriages of Catholics is Fr Godfrey Anstruther OP's *Catholic Marriage Index*, which I have written about fully in *Family History*, New series 105, at present looked after by the **IHGS**. It covers some 30,000 marriages from the late 19th century back as far as the registers go (in some cases to the 18th century). One of its great virtues is that its compiler added many notes from his personal knowledge, and its arrangement also facilitates searching through all marriages under a surname looking for others with the same parents. Its corresponding Converts index is described in *Family History*, New series 114.

The whereabouts of the main records described here can be found through M. Gandy's *Catholic Family History: Bibliography of Local Sources* (M. Gandy, 1996) and D. Steel's 'Sources for Jewish and Catholic Family History', *National Index of Parish Registers*, Vol. 3. Another useful reference work for Catholic ancestry is J. Gillow's *A Literary and Biographical History, or Bibliographical Dictionary of the English Catholics; from the breach with Rome in 1534 to the present time* (Burns & Oates, 1885–1902). **www.catholic-genealogy.com** is a portal for British Catholic ancestry.

An index to English Catholics 1700–1837 is being compiled by Bro. Rory (br_rory@yahoo.com.au).

16TH AND 17TH-CENTURY CATHOLICISM

Annual returns of resulting fines, levied under 16th and 17th-centuries anti Catholic legistration. The Recusant Rolls, are in **TNA** class E 367 and 377 (1592–1691), though in practice these tend only to record the well-to-do. In the early years of the Restoration the fines for non-attendance at church were fairly strictly enforced: transcripts of surviving records are given in J. Gillow and J. S. Hansom's 'A List of Convicted Recusants in the Reign of Charles II' in Vol. 6 of the **Catholic Record Society**'s publications.

Persecution records include those fined £100 under the Act of 1606 which compelled everyone to have their children baptised as Anglicans: documentation is sometimes found in Ecclesiastical Courts (see page 231).

The Protestation Returns of 1641 (see page 220) and 1643 Covenant contain many Catholics, as do the Royalist Composition Papers and records of the Committee for the Advance of Money (see page 215) generated by the Civil War.

Many Catholics joined James II in his exile at Saint-Germain-en-Laye near Paris in 1689. Many later returned, but not before they had married or had children baptised there – your 'missing ancestors', perhaps. The best sources are C. E. Lart's *Saint-Germain-en-Laye: The Parochial Registers: Jacobite Extracts 1689–1720* (St Catherine's, 1910) and the Marquis de Ruvigny's *The Jacobite Peerage* (Charles Skilton, 1974).

The 1715 rebellion in favour of James II's son generated some very useful records when the state ordered the registration of well-off Papists' estates and wills. Original records are in Close Rolls of the Chancery courts (**TNA**, C 54) and Recovery Rolls of the Court of Common Pleas (CP 43), listed in a series of articles in *The Genealogist*, new series, vols. 1–3, and Quarter Sessions (those for Lancashire are indexed at the Lancashire Record Office). Printed records are in E. E. Estcourt and J. O. Payne's *The English Catholic Nonjurors of 1715* and Payne's *Records of the English Catholics of 1715* (1889) and *'Cosin's List'– The Names of the Roman Catholic Nonjurors and others, who Refus'd to take the OATHS to His Late Majesty King George* (J. Robinson, 1862).

The 1767 national census of Catholics has been published as E. S. Worrall's *Returns of Papists 1767: Diocese of Chester* (CRS, 1980) and *Dioceses of England and Wales except Chester* (CRS, 1989).

Because of death penalties, priests went about incognito and only a handful of registers survive for the 17th and 18th centuries, but the Catholic embassies in London and chapels of the Vicars Apostolic kept registers which contain names of many English Catholics. Most surviving material has been published by the **CRS**.

After Hardwicke's Marriage Act (1754, see page 99), Catholics had to marry in the Church of England, although they also conducted separate Catholic marriages of their own. Because enforcement of penal legislation had become negligible, priests now started keeping registers of baptisms. Most Catholic registers are still with the parishes which created them: an essential tool is M. Gandy's *Catholic Missions and Registers 1700–1880* (M. Gandy, 1993) and his *Catholic Parishes in England, Wales and Scotland: An Atlas* (M. Gandy, 1993). Although some Catholic priests kept notes of members of their congregation who had died, burial registers were rare until the 19th century. Most Catholics were buried at night in parish churchyards (which had, after all, been consecrated before the Reformation) but without the Anglican burial service. Records of such burials may nevertheless be found in Anglican burial registers.

From 1768 English Catholics were served by the Laity's Directory, which included many death announcements, succeeded by the Catholic Directory in 1837, copies of which can be seen at the **Catholic Central Library**.

19TH-CENTURY CATHOLICISM

The 'Oxford Movement' of the 1830s saw a wave of conversions to Catholicism, and waning Catholic numbers were vastly increased by the Irish who migrated here due to the potato famine of 1847. **Crook's Liverpool Marriage Index** aims to identify all Irish marriages that took place there, and includes many other foreign marriages of Spaniards, Genoese, Chinese, Polish, French and so on.

SCOTLAND

In Scotland, Catholicism was made illegal in 1560, but it remained a small but potent force north of the border, as was demonstrated by the risings of 1715 and 1745, which contained strong Catholic elements. Both rebellions caused severe repercussions for Catholics, the latter continuing until 1793. Most of the surviving pre-1855 Catholic registers are at the **NAS**, and those kept subsequently are with the churches.

IRELAND

Irish Catholicism is covered on pages 178–9, and in my book, *Collins Tracing Your Irish Family History* (Collins 2007).

QUICK REFERENCE

See also main resources in Useful Addresses, page 306

CATHOLIC RECORD SOCIETY (CRS)
c/o 12 Melbourne Place
Wolsingham
Co. Durham DL13 3EH
☎ 01388 527747
www.catholic-history.org.uk/crs

CATHOLIC CENTRAL LIBRARY
St Michael's Abbey
Farnborough Road
Farnborough
Hampshire
GU14 7NQ
☎ 020 7732 8379
www.catholic-library.org.uk

CATHOLIC FAMILY HISTORY SOCIETY
The Secretaries
45 Gates Green Road
West Wickham
Bromley
Kent BR4 9DE

CROOK'S LIVERPOOL MARRIAGE INDEX
25 Gerneth Road
Speke
Liverpool L24 1UN

▽ *Landscape in Spring, with a Nun Walking among Daffodils* by John Sowerby (1876–1914). Many Catholic girls became nuns; an index to these is being compiled by the Catholic Family History Society.

DR WILLIAM'S LIBRARY

IN 1742 THE BAPTISTS, Presbyterians and Independents formed a General Register of the births of children of Protestant Dissenters of the three Denominations at Dr William's Library – an idea copied by the Methodists in 1818. The Dr William entries, which are generally considered to be very accurate, are mainly for Londoners but there are many entries from all over the country and abroad. They provide the full names of both parties, father's residence and occupation, and the mother's and father's name and residence. They run from January 1743 to June 1837 – a total of 48,975 births, mainly concentrated in the late 18th and early 19th centuries. They take the form of a duplicate parchment certificate signed by the parents and witnesses, one copy of which was lodged at the library and the contents copied into a register, and the other returned with a note affirming that the information has been registered. From 1768 onwards, baptisms were recorded as well, not least because some Anglican clergy refused burial when proof of baptism could not be produced. The Library entries are now indexed in the VRI and online at **www.bmdregisters.co.uk**.

From 1837 legally recognised marriages could be performed in Catholic churches with a registrar present, but in some cases the practice of a double marriage, one in a Catholic church one in an Anglican one (or now in a registrar's office) continued until Catholic priests could themselves be licensed to perform legally binding marriages in 1898. It was not until 1926, however, that it ceased to be technically illegal for a Catholic clergyman to wear a habit in public.

PROTESTANT NON-CONFORMISTS

Protestant non-conformity arose through groups splitting off from the Church of England. The 'three denominations' of Congregationalists, Baptists and Presbyterians trace their roots to the Elizabethan Puritans within the Church of England, who broke away completely after the failure of the Savoy Conference in 1661. Quakerism was founded by George Fox in the 1640s and, in the 18th century, Unitarianism broke off from the three denominations and Wesleyan Methodism split away from the Anglican church. Because people often changed denomination, sometimes leaving the Church of England, at other times returning to it, you can never predict what you will find in your ancestry. Among the most useful guides to this subject is D. J. Steel's *Sources for Non-conformist Genealogy and Family History* (Phillimore for the SoG, 1973).

CONGREGATIONALISTS, BAPTISTS AND PRESBYTERIANS

During the 17th century, Protestant non-conformists were most likely to be recorded in records of persecution, especially in Quarter Sessions (see page 232) and church courts. This is especially so following the 1662 Act of Uniformity, which excluded all non-Anglican clergy, schoolmasters and fellows of colleges from practising, and the 1664 Conventicle Act, which imposed first fines and then imprisonment and transportation on people attending non-Anglican religious assemblies numbering over five. In 1672 the Declaration of Indulgence allowed non-conformist teachers and ministers holding assemblies ('conventicles') to apply for licences – 1061 ministers did so.

The Toleration Act of 1689 guaranteed religious freedom to Protestant non-conformists. Thousands of meeting houses, mainly of Independents, were built for the now legal conventicles, licences being granted by the Quarter Sessions. Baptist congregations proliferated, mainly in towns. The subsequent rifts and reunions of the various denominations and their sub-sects are too complicated to detail here, but in general terms they succeeded at the expense of the Church of

LIFELINES: LOUISA JENKINS

FOR *EXTRAORDINARY ANCESTORS*, I was asked to find the original name of Louisa Jenkins' ancestor, Mark Brown. Louisa knew he came from Italy, and that he had changed his name to avoid the prevalent anti-Italian feeling in Edinburgh at the time. But what had it been before? The first surprise was when his daughter Theresa's 1876 Edinburgh marriage record was obtained, giving the father as Stack Brown, a figure maker. The censuses indicated he was born in Italy, and that he had a son Charles born in 1855. This was the annus mirabilis for Scottish genealogy because of the wealth of information contained on certificates made in that year alone. Charles's birth record told us that Stack Brown was born in Milan and that he married Theresa Brady (from Dublin) in 1839 in Edinburgh. An Italian marrying an Irish girl called Theresa pointed clearly to Catholicism, and Catholic registers of Edinburgh rewarded us with the marriage record of Theresa Brady and Eustachio Bruni.

Directories (see page 82) showed there were several Italian figure makers in Edinburgh at the time: the *figuristi di gesso* like Eustachio made the beautiful plaster statues that ornament many of Edinburgh's grandest houses and public buildings.

The photographs here are of Eustachio Bruni and Theresa Brady's descendents, down the female line, through their daughter Theresa Turnbull (née Brown), Eliza Mackenzie (née Turnbull), to Louisa Jenkins (née Mackenzie).

△ (top) Louisa's Aunt Anna, sister of Eliza Mackenzie, daughter of Theresa Turnbull.

△ (above) Aunt Julia and Uncle Jim Turnbull, Louisa's mother's brother.

▷ (right) Eliza Mackenzie (née Turnbull), mother of Louisa Jenkins, with her son William and daughter Eliza.

▷ (far right) Louisa Jenkins (née Mackenzie), daughter of Eliza Mackenzie, daughter of Theresa Turnbull.

LIFELINES: RUBY WAX

WHEN I WAS TRACING Ruby Wax's ancestry, for her BBC 1 show, *Ruby*, I came across a number of references to people called Wachs in the area of Eastern Europe where she knew her family originated. Included among the recorded memories of survivors of the Holocaust was the following (www.jewishgen.org). I do not know if this was a member of Ruby's family, but from the way she was behaving I would not be at all surprised if it was:

The Rebbetzin, the wife of Rabbi Yechezkel, was from the well-known Wachs family, which was renowned for its riches and piety. They were landowners ... and they enabled the rabbi to turn his home into a place where guests would be received on a constant basis. [There were] many guests from all parts of Poland, who came to prostrate themselves at the grave of Rabbi Elimelech of holy blessed memory. Amongst them were needy people who lacked money for food. Such people knew the address of the rabbi ... and approximately twenty people would eat at his table every day, receiving their meals as if they were members of the household. It is said that once a guest arrived late after everyone had finished eating, and was turned away by the Rebbetzin with the comment,

'There is nothing to eat, Mr tardy Jew'.

However, as he left, she changed her mind,

'Why is he guilty that twenty people came before him?'

She immediately asked him to return, and told him that she did not have any meat left, but that nobody starves [in her house], and she gave him other food to eat. When he left, he said to her,

'Rebbetzin, you should know that I have eaten a Simchat Torah feast here'.

JEWS

- The main records are those of the synagogues and are in Hebrew, so it is advisable to hire a researcher with knowledge of that language. You can expect to find birth registers, and middle-class Jews sometimes paid to have their children's births registered in parish registers too.

- Boys were usually circumcised eight days after birth and records of circumcision (*brit milah*) were kept by surgeons, but can be very hard to locate.

- Marriage contracts (kethubot) are in synagogue records and many were announced in the *Jewish Chronicle*, published (with a gap June 1842–September 1844) from November 1841.

- Synagogues also recorded deaths, and many were announced in the *Jewish Chronicle*.

- Many prosperous Jews' births, marriages and deaths were also announced in *The Times* and *Gentleman's Magazine*, and many of these were copied in the Collyer-Fergusson manuscripts (at the **SoG**), which also includes will abstracts. A useful list of Jewish wills in the **PCC** (see page 129), references to obituaries and facsimiles of Jewish bookplates (mainly for the Sephardic community) are in Anglo-Jewish notabilities (see below).

- Synagogues may also have other records such as offering books, listing donations made by all males save the very poor, commemoration books recording charitable bequests from wills, synagogue membership lists. A full list of pre-1837 Jewish synagogue registers is given in D. Steel's 'Sources for Jewish and Catholic Family History', *National Index of Parish Registers Series*, Vol. 3. Many London records are now at the United Synagogue Record Room and the Court of the Chief Rabbi, although most have been moved to the Archive Office of the Chief Rabbi, where public access is no longer possible.

- A useful guide to the records is I. Mordy's *My Ancestors Were Jewish: How Can I Find More About Them?* (SoG, 1995) and A.Kurzweil's *From Generation to Generation: How to trace your Jewish Genealogy and Family History*, reissued

△ **The Jewish cemetery in Worms, Germany.**

2004 by Jossey-Bass (Wiley). For the better-off sort, there is also *Anglo–Jewish Notabilities* (Jewish Historical Society of England, 5709/1949), which covers *London Magazine* notices of Jewish births, marriages and deaths 1732–85, Anglo–Jewish wills and administrations in the **PCC**, Anglo–Jewish coats of arms, including many facsimile bookplates and a collection of biographical references.

- There are few areas of genealogy in which the internet has had such a revolutionary impact as Jewish research. **www.cyndislist.com** contains a formidable array of Jewish resources. Useful too is the index to the Poor Jews Temporary Shelter at Leman Street, Whitechapel, containing 43,000 names at **www.chrysalis.its.uct.ac.za/shelter/shelter**. There is also **www.jgsgb.org.uk/info1.shtml**, which provides a gateway to many British and foreign Jewish and general research websites, but foremost is **www.jewishgen.org**, which includes a discussion group, a database of 300,000 surnames and towns, the 'Family Tree of the Jewish People' with over 2 million people and 'ShtetLinks' for over 200 communities. Many Jewish communities were destroyed by the Holocaust, but survivors wrote memoirs of their own experiences and recorded as much as they could about their original communities and family history. Harrowing though they can be to read, they are a magnificent historical and genealogical resource.

QUICK REFERENCE

See main sources in Useful Addresses, page 306

Family history has many intriguing byeways. Do you belong to a clan? Have you a coat of arms? What does your surname mean? Can DNA tests or even psychics help you learn yet more about your family's past? This section tells you how to find out.

CHAPTER TWENTY-NINE
GENETICS

We all inherit our appearance from our ancestors. Sometimes all you need to do is look at someone and, by studying their hair, eye or skin colour and facial features, you can make a few reasonable assumptions about where they may or may not have originated.

HOW GENES OPERATE

Eye and hair colour are determined by combinations of both parents' genes and work rather like mixing watercolour paints – the darker colour being dominant over the paler. So, if one partner is dark-eyed and the other pale eyed, then their children are likely to be dark-eyed – but not necessarily. Each child inherits an eye-colour gene from each parent, and it is up to the laws of chance which one will be passed on to their children. The dark-eyed partner might, therefore, have inherited a dominant dark-eyed gene from one parent and a hidden, pale-eyed gene from the other. If they, in turn, pass on their pale-eye gene to their child, and this matches with a pale-eyed gene from the other partner, then the child will have pale eyes. However, if you put it the other way around, a couple who both have pale eyes, such as blue or grey, cannot be carrying a 'hidden' dark-eyed gene, because, logically, if one of them had such a gene, they would have dark, not pale, eyes. Thus, such a couple are highly likely to produce only pale-eyed children.

Similar principles apply to hair colour – blonde mixed with brown or black tends to make paler brown or black, or sometimes red, while the fairer both parties' hair, the fairer the children's are likely to be. Red and red almost always produce red. Curly or wavy hair tends to dominate over straight. Among black people, very curly hair tends to be dominant. In Caucasian–African unions this usually results in at least half of the resulting offspring having curly hair. Thick lips and large ear lobes, likewise, dominate over thin ones. But these are only generalisations.

GENES FOR DNA TESTS

One of the most exciting things about tracing family history at the beginning of the 21st century is the advent of DNA technology. Up to the

◁ Until quite recently, the double helix of DNA was an impenetrable scientific mystery. Now it is a dynamic genealogical tool.

last decades of the 20th century, genealogy had remained relatively unchanged for centuries. Records had become much easier to access, and computer indexing had had a major impact, but genealogy was still based on what people could remember, or upon written records. Then, suddenly, DNA technology became accessible to genealogists, providing an entirely new way of adding to or detracting from the burden of proof in family trees – not by historical records – but by the very stuff of which our bodies are composed.

DNA is deoxyribonucleic acid, a major constituent of our chromosomes and carrier of the genetic information that makes us what we are. There are two sorts of DNA test. One is to see if your DNA matches someone else's, thus helping to prove or disprove a presumed genealogical connection. The other is to see how your DNA matches (or is similar to) samples already taken from populations around the world, helping you pinpoint where in a country or on the globe your distant genetic roots lie.

THE LIMITATIONS OF DNA

Exciting though DNA testing sounds, there are some big limitations. First, you can't test for relationships with simply anyone in your family tree. At present, tests are only possible with direct male-to-male or female-to female lines, and thus with people with whom you have, or suspect, a male-to-male (A) or female-to-female line link (B). In other words, you can have a comparative test with someone who you think is your father's father's brother's son (A), but there is no point having a comparative test with your father's father's sister's son (C), because his father's Y chromosome will have come from a different source to yours.

The reason for these limitations is that the only DNA on which the test is practical is the 'Y' chromosome, which is passed from fathers to sons (but not daughters), and the mitochondrial DNA within the 'X' chromosome, which is passed from mother to both her sons and daughters, but then only from the daughters, not the sons, to their own offspring. Thus, men can have their direct male and female line DNA tested, but women can only have their female line DNA tested. If a woman wants to know about her male-line ancestry, she must secure a DNA sample from a brother, father or other direct male-line male relation (D).

➤**If two people who fit these criteria have their DNA tested and find it matches exactly, they can be sure they are related.**

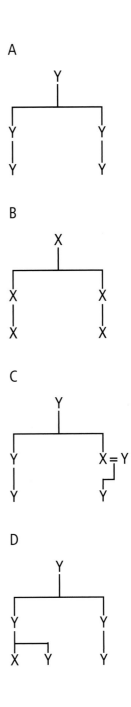

Key
Y = male
X = female

TAKING A DNA TEST

DNA TESTS are simple and generally cost around £100–£150 per person. There are several firms in Britain and America (I find www.FamilyTreeDNA.com and www.familygenetics.co.uk to be very good). They will send you a kit, including a little brush which you use to rub off a small skin sample from the inside of your cheek and post back to them. The firm then performs their test (make sure the firm you use has a rigorous privacy policy) and produces a table giving numerical figures for the number of times certain 'markers' within the chromosome are repeated. Because DNA mutates very slightly over long periods of time, the closer the markers in two people's DNA are, the more likely they are to be related. A very close match indicates a strong change of a male-line relationship. You can enter results in sites such as www.ysearch.org to seek genetic relatives who have already submitted their results. For best results go for the highest number of markers available. For paternity testing see www.lgc.co.uk/ paternity, www.identitytesting.net and www.paternityexperts.com.

> If there are only small discrepancies between their results, they can assume they are related, but through a more distant connection.

But 'How far back?' is a question geneticists cannot answer. If DNA matches perfectly, there is a 50% chance that the most recent common ancestor lived within the last seven generations, but a 50% chance that the ancestor they share in common lived up to 30 generations ago, while slight discrepancies tend to indicate cousinship through ancestors living even further back.

So, if two people trace their family tree and think they are descended, male-to-male, from a set of brothers born in the 1650s, a positive 'Y' chromosome match will confirm that they are related. But it won't confirm that their genealogy is accurate – the relationship may actually have come through any two other male members of the same family, possibly hundred of years before or after 1650. However, if the genealogical link is pretty certain, and the DNA test comes back positive, then it is an excellent piece of circumstantial evidence that the tree is correct.

Equally, DNA cannot be used to prove a family tree is wrong. If our two researchers find their DNA is completely dissimilar, their record-based genealogical research might be completely accurate but, at some point in the history of either line, an undisclosed fostering, adoption or illegitimacy might have occurred to alter the biological link.

SOME TEST CASES

I have seen DNA tests used in a number of highly effective ways. A group of people with a fairly unusual Irish surname (let's call it O'Boru) had spent decades trying to match oral traditions with the decidedly patchy records of early 19th-century Donegal to work out their family tree, but nothing tied in properly. I suggested DNA testing and a dozen O'Borus took one. On a 12-marker test of their 'Y' chromosomes, four matched exactly and four others fell into a group with only slight dissimilarities, indicating that the first four had a 50% chance of being related within the last seven generations and were definitely related within the last 30. They were more distantly connected (that is, almost certainly more than seven generations ago) to the second four. Everyone matched closely enough to show that their branches had split *away* after the surname had arisen – in other words, after Boru himself had lived. That's a bit hazy still, I know, but it introduced a great deal more clarity than before, when nobody knew for certain how closely or not anyone was to any of the others.

LIFETIMES: VIKING DNA

◁ A typical Norwegian port, whence the Vikings set sail.

MUCH WORK has also been done on Viking DNA. When a Mr Jones from Cardiff approached *Extraordinary Ancestors* and said he thought he had Viking blood on the basis that he believed he looked a bit like some Scandanavians he had met, I was extremely sceptical, but we commissioned a DNA test to see what the results would be. By taking extensive samples from modern Scandanavians, geneticists have been able to establish a profile of what Viking DNA would have been like, and then see if it matched people living in the areas settled by Vikings – northeastern England, Iceland, Dublin and, as it turns out, Cardiff. It transpired that Mr Jones was right and I was wrong. While his male-line ancestors had acquired a Welsh surname, probably in the last couple of hundred years, his 'Y' chromosomes were indeed a positive testimony to his remoter Norse forbears. Conversely, when geneticists tested the Icelandic population, which was supposedly pure Viking, they found a quarter of the population was originally of Irish descent!

Another case is that of Nicholas Betts-Green Esq., formerly Nicholas Green. His persistent family tradition was of an illegitimate Green fathered by 'the lord of the manor'. Research suggested that the culprit could have been a 19th-century army major, George Betts of Wortham Hall, but there were no documents to prove this for certain. Poor Mr Green might have spent the rest of his life wondering, but a test on his 'Y' chromosomes and those of a co-operative legitimate descendant of Major Betts showed that they matched, adding a vast weight of circumstantial evidence to the genealogical findings and prompting Mr Green, very properly I think, to add 'Betts' to his surname.

DEEP ANCESTRY TESTS

The second use of genetics is in your 'deep' ancestry. This can determine where your distant male and female line ancestors lived tens of thousands

DNA GUIDES

THE BEST GUIDES TO DNA testing is C. Pomery's *DNA and Family History: How genetic testing can advance your genealogical research* (TNA, 2004) and *Family History in the Genes* (TNA, 2007),with a supporting website www.dnaandfamilyhistory. com. It includes links to other sites on which DNA test results can be analysed.

LIFETIMES: HEMOPHILIAC HERITAGE

SOMETIMES, DNA CAN THROW an established family tree into question. Queen Victoria's family's hemophilia is a case in point. Before DNA was understood, her carrying of hemophilia was regarded as simple bad luck, but now we know that, whilst it can arise as a birth-defect it is, in most cases, genetically inherited. This suggests that instead of the Duke of Kent, who was not a carrier of hemophilia, Victoria's real father might have been a passing and, as yet, unidentified hemophiliac (and yes, hemophiliacs could produce children – Victoria's son Leopold did, and thus passed the affliction on to his daughter Alice). This does not mean that Victoria was illegitimate – she was born within wedlock and was thus the legal heir of her mother's husband – but it does mean that her genetic roots might not have been what we once thought they were. If such genetic discoveries then lead to proven academic research into her true genetic origins, then all well and good.

◁ Queen Victoria, seen here with her mother, passed hemophilia on to some of her descendants, but neither her mother nor her supposed father had a history of it in their families.

△ The Tsarina Alexandra, a granddaughter of Queen Victoria, who passed hemophilia on to her son, the Tsarevich Alexei.

of years ago. You may be surprised to find that they came from the other side of the world, but more likely, if you are of British origin, you will find that you belong to one of the core genetic populations of the British Isles, descended from the original Palaeolithic population of Europe, the Cro-Magnons 'cavemen', who came here about 10,000 years ago.

Whatever your results, you will learn how you fit into the story of the human race, which genetics, combined with studies of linguistics and archaeology, is constantly refining. Ultimately, all genetic lineages outside Africa go back to a tiny band of people, probably numbering only a few dozen, who left Africa about (very roughly) 65,000 years ago. Together with the lineages that remained in Africa, geneticists have found that every single member of the human race goes back in the male-line to one man who lived in Africa about 70,000 years ago, dubbed the 'genetic Adam'. Equally, all female-line lineages (including that of Adam's mother) ultimately go back to the 'genetic Eve', who lived in Africa between about 100,000 and 140,000 years ago.

Both Adam and Eve were descended from the original tiny core of *Homo sapiens*. Our species evolved in Africa about 200,000 years ago out of earlier *Homo* species, probably *Homo Helmei*, themselves descended from *Homo Heidelbergensis*. Other descendants of *Homo Heidelbergensis* included the Neandertals, who lived in Ice Age Europe up to at least 28,000 years ago, and the three foot tall *Homo floriensis*, dubbed 'Hobbits', whose remains were found on the south-east Asian island of Flores in 2004 and who lived until at least 18,000 years ago – possibly more recently.

OUR EARLIEST ANCESTORS

Homo Heidelbergensis evolved over 2 million years ago, out of earlier Homo species, who were themselves descended from our *Australopithecene* forbears about 2.5 million years ago. These diminutive, hairy ancestors of ours lived in southern and eastern Africa. They walked upright and made use of stones and bones as primitive tools and weapons. They were closely akin to the ancestors of modern apes and monkeys. And so it goes back. There were single-celled organisms floating about in the primordial seas 200 million years ago who are no less ancestors of yours than your beloved granny.

EXHUMATION

More realistic is the possibility of making a comparative DNA test between someone living and a deceased ancestor's (or supposed ancestor's) DNA, using surviving hair, dried blood or even exhumed bones. The mitochondrial DNA within 'X' chromosomes usually survives much better than 'Y' chromosomes, but exhuming a body (if that's what it takes) requires permission from the legal heir both of the deceased and the original grave-owner, the burial authority and a permissive licence from the Home Secretary. The total cost can be vast, but it can be worth it. The technique was used to identify the presumed body of the murdered Tsarina Alexandra when it was exhumed at Ekaterinburg in 1991, by comparing her mitochondrial DNA with that of Prince Philip, whose mother's mother was Alexandra's sister. The DNA in the remains did indeed match Prince Philip – the identification was thus positive.

CHAPTER THIRTY
WHAT'S IN A NAME?

Both forenames and surnames can tell us a lot about the ancestry and cultural origins of their bearers, both of which are discussed in this chapter.

△ Winston Churchill, whose popularity spawned a generation of boys called Winston.

△ *The Blacksmith* from *Le Livre des Echecs Moralises* by Jacques de Cessoles. Many medieval blacksmiths' children ended up surnamed 'Smith'.

FORENAMES

Forenames, called Christian names in Christian countries, can be chosen randomly, as they often are now in the Western world. They can tell us a little about the parents' tastes – my mother, for example, is a devout Catholic with a particular devotion to St Anthony. Many parents choose names of the moment: children called Kylie and Elvis hint strongly at their parents' musical tastes, and in centuries to come genealogists may be able to guess that an ancestor called Kylie was unlikely to have been born before the mid-1980s, when Kylie Minogue first appeared in *Neighbours*. Equally, names like Winston and Horatio reflect our ancestors' admiration for earlier wartime heroes, and again help us to set the earliest likely date when children so named would have been born. Monarchs and their spouses have always been a source of inspiration for naming children. There were very few Victorias in Britain before 1837 and not too many Alberts before the queen married her beloved consort in 1840.

Going back only a few generations, however, we find that families tended to have had a more regimented system for giving names to children. The presence of people called Ignatius in a family usually suggests Catholicism, as do names like Timothy, Ambrose, Stanislaus and Theresa. Old Testament names like Aaron, Joshua and Rachel suggest Protestant non-conformist links. Catholic names can often suggest Irish connections, while names like Mungo, Murdoch and Christian (for a female) suggest Scottish or Protestant Northern Irish roots.

Outside Europe, most cultures have customs governing how names are chosen for children. Many children are named after ancestors, especially grandparents, not least among Hindus, for whom the new-born child may be regarded as the living incarnation of an earlier generation. Children are often given similar names to their fathers, such as a name with the same prefix or suffix. Other Indian names are chosen from gods, places, professions, plants or animals, or words with positive connotations.

△ Krishna Mehta with his sons Dhairendra and Shailendra. The surname Mehta is Hindu, meaning political administrator: his forename was chosen to venerate the Hindu god Krishna.

THE MEANINGS OF NAMES

➤**European forenames** all mean something. Some are Anglo-Saxon (Edmund, Edward, Alfred and so on) in origin and others are French or German (like Robert and Ludwig) or Greek (like Anthony). However, the majority of European forenames come from the Bible, and don't you think it extraordinary, on reflection, that the bulk of the indigenous population of Western Europe are walking about using names derived from a tiny tribe who lived in the Middle East over 2000 years ago, and from whom most are not descended? The actual meaning of the names now, however, seldom has any relevance for their bearers. George means 'farmer' in Greek, but I doubt anybody giving that name to their child in the last two millennia has done so because they were agriculturalists.

➤**Many Hindu names** are derived from Sanskrit and are taken from gods, especially those whose stories are told in the Bhagavad Gita (such as Krishna and Arjun) and the Ramayana, such as Sita, Janaki, Lakshman and Rama. In many cases, the choice of names is dictated by caste too – hence names connoting spirituality for the Bhahmins, power for the Ksatriyas (warriors), wealth for the Vaisyas (merchants) and servitiude for the Sudras (labourers and peasants).

➤**Buddhist names,** because of their Sanskrit roots, are not always easily distinguished from Hindu ones. Some popular ones, however, are Tara (the name of a Mahayan godess), Mani and Padma, derived from the tantric mantra *om mani padme hum* – 'the jewel is in the lotus'.

➤**Islamic names** are mostly derived from vocabulary words still in use: as Mona Baker wrote in P. Hanks and F. Hodge's *A Dictionary of Christian Names* (OUP, 1990) – and without any apparent hint of irony – 'Arabs

NAMING PATTERNS

IN CATHOLIC FAMILIES, a child's name was often that of their same-sex godparent. My German Catholic ancestors followed this practice to an absurd degree when a forbear of mine was given the names of both godparents, his cousin William Adolph and his uncle Adolph Fischer. They called him William Adolph Adolph.

Scottish Presbyterian families usually named the eldest son after his paternal grandfather, the second son after the maternal grandfather and the third after the father. They would name the eldest daughter after the maternal grandmother, the second daughter after the paternal grandmother and the third after the mother. If you have a complete list of a Scottish Presbytarian couple's children, therefore, you can make a pretty good guess at what the couples' parents were called.

THE BEST CASE of alterations I have encountered is that of a Brazillian family called Pudwell. The surname sounds completely English, but the family knew their ancestor migrated to South America from Germany. There are indeed Pudwells and Pudwills in Germany, and over the Polish border there are Budwills, and heraldic records confirm that the Budwills belonged to the Sulima family group (somewhat akin to a Scottish clan) and were well established in eastern Germany. The older version was Budywil, derived from the Slavic *budi* meaning 'awaken, inspire', a word derived directly from the self-same Sanskrit word which gave the epithet 'enlightened one' to the 5th-century BC Prince Gautama Siddhartha – the Buddha himself!

and Watmough mean brother-in-law of Richard ('Hick') and Walter ('Watt') respectively.

The parents' name sometimes appeared as just that, hence 'Thomas' meant 'son of Thomas'. But in many cases, especially in the north, where there was a greater Scandanavian influence, it was suffixed 'son', sometimes shortened to '-s', thus Sanderson and Saunders both meant 'son of Alexander'. In the case of Norman names, 'fitz' was added as a prefix for 'son of', so Fitzgerald means 'son of Gerald'.

Sometimes, the original forename was modified before it became a surname. Now, to be familiar, we often shorten a name and by adding a 'y' to it, so Thomas becomes Tommy. Our medieval ancestors tended to use 'cock' and 'kin' (both perhaps due to Dutch influence), thus Tomkin, which might then become someone's surname. Metathesis is when two letters in a word are swapped around. I was very taken when I came across John Giblet of St George's, Hanover Square, in 1765 working – of all things – as a butcher. It turns out that his gorily appropriate surname meant 'son of Giblet', a metathesised version of Gilbert!

Occupational or metonymic surnames

This group of surnames is derived from peoples' occupations. If surnames were still fluid, we would have plenty of people surnamed Enginedriver, Typist and Programmer. As it is, British occupational surnames tend to reflect what people were doing here in the Middle Ages. Some, such as Smith, Farmer and Serjeant are obvious. Others, such as Fletcher and Fuller, require more detailed knowledge of old occupations – these two examples mean 'arrow maker' and 'cloth bleacher' respectively.

Locative surnames

These derive from the place someone lived in or came from. They are the most popular type of surname in England. Originally, they were often prepositioned 'de', so John de Prescot was John of or from Prescot: he may have owned the place, or simply lived at Prescot – or he may even have come from Prescot and only acquired the surname once he had moved elsewhere.

Some feudal lords who had several different landholdings used different surnames according to where they were. If John de Prescot owned Prescot and Redwood, he might call himself John de Prescot whilst in residence at Prescot and John de Redwood whilst in residence at Redwood. Confusing, but unavoidable.

Topographical surnames

These arose from a geographical feature that distinguished the person's home. Originally, they often were often prepositioned 'atte' or 'at', so Clement who lived in or by a meadow would have been Clement atte Lee. The prepositions were usually shed by the 14th century but, where they were not, surnames such as Atlee arose.

Working out what surnames means often involves some knowledge of Saxon, Norse and so on – *lee* is a Saxon word. Others are more obvious because words have not changed – Wood, Church, Brook and so on are as clear now as they were almost a thousand years ago when they described where ancestors of ours lived.

Sobriquets or nicknames

Such surnames describe someone's dominant characteristic, often starting, as in school playgrounds to this day, as a jest or taunt. Black, Redhead; Wiseman and Little are all examples, but remember that nicknames were sometimes used ironically – Robin Hood's chum Little John was absolutely enormous!

EVOLVING LANGUAGE

One factor to be aware of when studying surnames is the way they can change over time through pronunciation or translation, or simply be written down in an unusual way, such as Rebecca Oldfield in the example on page 169.

Surnames do not have 'correct' and 'incorrect' spellings. They have changed over time and will probably continue to do so despite mass

CLAN LOYALTIES

TARTANS AROSE through regional variations in weaving patterns and, despite claims to the contrary, only became distinctive to specific clans in the late 18th century. Use of tartan is not bound by any official rules, though proper use of it is recorded by Lord Lyon. For more information, see my book *Collins Tracing Your Scottish Family History* (Collins, 2008); Roddy Martine's *Scottish Clan and Family Names: Their Arms, Origins and Tartans* (Mainstream Publishing, 1992); G. Way and R. Squire's *Collins' Scottish Clan and Family Encyclopaedia* (HarperCollins, 1994) and F. Adam's *The Clans, Septs and Regiments of the Scottish Highlands* (revised by Sir Thomas Innes of Learny, Johnson & Bacon, 1984). Useful clan maps are at **www.scotroots.com**.

literacy. People who say 'that person called John Chamberlain cannot possibly be an ancestor of mine because we have always spelt our surname "Chamberlayne"' are buffoons for various reasons. The surname might have been written down on that occasion by someone who did not know how the name should be spelt and it also presupposes John cared or even knew about spelling. My reply is usually, 'If I gave you a cheque for a million pounds and spelt your surname "Chamberlain" you wouldn't throw it away, would you?'

Sometimes, people deliberately adopted unusual spellings to stand out from the crowd. Charles Whyllyames Burton is one of the most extreme I have encountered. When tracing your family tree, always look

GAELIC SURNAMES

GAELIC SURNAMES were often changed by being Anglicised, such as Ó Blathmhaic becoming Blawick, and then further changes sometimes took place to make them more familiar, such as Blawick to Blake. Similarly, some Ó Maoláins became De Moleyn, although there was no ancestral connection with the original Norman family of that name. This can cause great confusion, and the jury is still out in the case of the Dennings of Co. Cavan. Denning derives from the Old English denu which became dean, meaning 'valley'. The Irish Dennings may therefore have come from England, perhaps as planters to the northern Irish counties in the 17th century. However, Denning might be an Anglicised version of O'Dinneen or O'Duinnin, from the Gaelic *donn* meaning 'brown'. Perhaps only a DNA test would clear up the matter for good.

In Scotland, many Gaelic surnames were Anglicised after Culloden to avoid hostility from the English authorities. MacLevy went to Livington, MacDonald to Donald and so on. Equally, many names of Irish immigrants were Caldonianised, such as O'Toole to Doyle and McGrimes to Graham.

out for variant spellings and never be daft enough to reject an entry on the grounds that the parish clerk simply wrote the name down in his own particular way.

Surnames are studied by seeking the earliest possible references to them in records, such as tax lists. By seeing how they were written down around the time when they were first used, it is easier to work out what they really meant. It is not obvious what Atlee, as in my example above, might mean, but the early medieval references to 'at Lee' is much clearer. Similarly, it is a way of avoiding pitfalls. Lucy might seem to mean 'son of Lucy', but early references show it to have been 'de Luci', Luci being a place in Normandy.

Most Indian people have several names, such as a personal name, a patronymic name, a village name and (if Hindu) a caste name: customs vary according to religion and locality and it is not always obvious, on first sight, which is the personal name and which the surname. The Gujerati ancestors of the Alibhai-Brown family, for example, descend from Alibhai Lalji Kanji in the 19th century. Lalji was the caste name, Alibhai was his personal name and Kanji his father's name. His son then took Alibhai as his surname, at which point the family moved to the West and the surname stuck as an hereditary one. In southern India, many people have three surnames – the village name, the father's name and finally the personal name. Westernisation has sometimes caused such patterns to alter, and many Indian families coming to the West will, just like the Welsh coming to England in the Middle Ages, fix their patronymic name as an hereditary surname.

Sikhs usually have three: a personal name; a name to proclaim his identity, usually Singh; and a third name for the particular clan or sect or, if a woman, the name Kaur, which simply denotes female gender.

The Chinese usually have three names, a surname, a generation name and a personal name. Generation names are taken from the words in each family's unique generation poem, the first generation using the first word, the second the second, and so on.

WHERE TO SEARCH

NAMES

🗗 Useful guides to surnames include: P. H. Reaney and R. M. Wilson's *A Dictionary of English Surnames* (Routledge, 1958); J. Rowlands's *Welsh Family History; A Guide to Research* (Association of Family History Societies for Wales, 1997); G. F. Black's *The Surnames of Scotland, Their Origin, Meaning, and History* (New York Public Library, 1946); E. MacLysaght's *The Surnames of Ireland* (Irish Academic Press, 1985); *Irish Families and More Irish Families* (Irish Academic Press, 1985); and the chapter on names in my *Collins Tracing Your Irish Family History* (Collins, 2007).

🗗 To understand the meaning of place names that became surnames, see E. Ekwall's *The Concise Oxford Dictionary of English Place-names* (Clarendon Press, 1960) and the English place name series, published county by county by Leopard's Head Press.

A FINAL WORD OF WARNING

MOST COMPUTER PROGRAMS that print certificates showing you the origin of your 'ancient and distinguished name' are copied straight out of surname dictionaries, usually, it seems, by people with very little understanding of the subject and very low powers of concentration. They mostly contain misleading statements or plain old mistakes.

LIFETIMES: JAMES CHALMERS

BESIDES THOSE who can find lines of descent from royalty, there are also those many more who discover indirect links. The numerous descendants of James Chalmers (1741–1810) may be proud that their ancestor was proprietor and editor of the *Aberdeen Journal*, founder of the *Aberdeen Almanac*. He was a drinking companion of Robbie Burns, too ('A facetious fellow,' Burns called him), but Bishop Skinner, also present at their meeting in 1787, wrote, 'We adjourned for a dram, and though our time was short, we had fifty auld songs through hand, and spent an hour or so most agreeably.'

But there is more – one of James's daughters, Jean, married James Littlejohn, whose grandson David had a daughter Ruth, wife of William Gill. Their daughter Ruth married Lord Fermoy, whose daughter Frances married Earl Spencer. Their daughter was Diana – oh yes! And in fact, illustrative of the point that many more people have royal ancestry than may be suspected, we can also take a line back from James's wife, Margaret Forbes, to her great-grandmother Lady Grizel Stewart, a great-granddaughter of James V of Scotland. This therefore makes the descendants of James Chalmers distant cousins of Prince William, and also more distant cousins of the Queen herself.

△ Through his Chalmers ancestry, Prince William has many close, 'commoner' cousins.

The British nobility is structured as follows. At the top of the pile and nearest in dignity to the Crown are dukes, followed by the ranks of marquis, earl, viscount and baron. Barons were originally those who held substantial amounts of land from the Crown, and subsequently were summoned to sit in the House of Lords, the earliest writs creating hereditary baronies dating back to Edward I.

NOBLES

Among the best works on the peerage are G. E. Cockayne's 13-volume *The Complete Peerage* (Alan Sutton, 1987), known as *'GEC'*, and P. W. Hammond's *The Complete Peerage, Vol 1* (Sutton, 1998), which brings *GEC* up to 1995. These volumes describe the descent of each title, providing great scholarly detail about the bearers and their wives, offices held, places of birth, death and burial, extent and value of their estates, with amusing or enlightening anecdotes given in footnotes. They do not provide details of offspring who did not inherit titles.

For this you will need *Burke's Peerage*, which has been published periodically from 1826: the latest edition is C. Mosley's (ed.) *Burkes' Peerage, Baronetage and Knightage*. Burke's Peerage and Gentry (2003). This includes an index to the living but, excitingly, it can be searched under names, places, dates, schools – whatever you want – at a subscription website **www.burkes-peerage.net**. In Burke's you can see holders of ancient titles such as the Duchy of Norfolk and Barony of Camoys rubbing shoulders with the likes of Jeffrey Archer and Margaret Thatcher.

If a title has become extinct, you will usually find it (besides in *GEC*) in J. B. Burke's *A Genealogical History of the Dormant, Forfeited and Extinct Peerages of the British Empire* (Burke's Peerage, 1964), and L. G. Pine's *The New Extinct Peerage 1884–1971* (Heraldry Today, 1972) or J. Burke's *A Genealogical and Heraldic History of the Extinct and Dormant Baronetcies of England, Ireland and Scotland* (1841).

For European nobility see the *Almanach de Gotha*, (the Holy Roman Empire equivalent of *Burke's Peerage*) and Ruvigny's *Titled Nobility of Europe* (1914). An excellent guide is F. R. Pryce's *A Guide to European Genealogies Exclusive of the British Isles: With an Historical Survey of the Principal Genealogical Writers* (University Microfilms Limited, 1965).

All the families in the Burke's publications are covered by a useful little book, *Burke's Family Index* (Burke's Peerage, 1976). For wider coverage of pedigree sources, see the bibliographies of Whitmore, Marshall and colleagues listed on page 33.

BURKE'S PEERAGE has two virtues over *GEC*. It traces peers' family lines as far back as they are known (regardless of when the title was granted) and includes details of younger sons, and daughters. However, *Burke's Peerage* has two great failings.

First, it does not always include details of all younger sons, and sometimes omits daughters altogether, so the absence of someone from Burke's does not mean they did not exist: the best means of checking is to seek a record of the father's will.

Second, broadly speaking, family pedigrees were printed as submitted by the families themselves, and therefore contain mistakes, inaccuracies, deliberate omissions of family members regarded at the time as black sheep (handicapped children, suicides, daughters who ran off with grooms, and so on), and downright lies, such as claims of descent from non-existent companions of William the Conqueror. These have been weeded out of the modern versions of the book, but not for nothing were the old versions of *Burke's Peerage* described as the greatest work of fiction in the English language after the complete works of Shakespeare!

Peerages created before 1707 were either English or Scottish; peers of Great Britain are those created between 1707 and 1801; Irish peers are all those created before 1801: after 1801, all peers created were – and remain – peers of the United Kingdom. Most peerages pass strictly down to each successive senior male representative of the family in the male line. Some old Medieval titles can be inherited by a woman and passed on to her senior heir, but these are unusual. The recent invention of life peerages means that the majority of titles granted now are for the holder only, and are not hereditary.

CHAPTER THIRTY-TWO
HERALDRY

Heraldry is the use of distinctively painted shields that are passed down within families from father to son. Because of its strictly hereditary nature, heraldry and its records are therefore intimately connected with genealogy.

▽ Arms of my forbears, the Colegrave-Manbys of Cann Hall, Essex, showing an impressive 20 quarterings.

HISTORY OF HERALDRY

It is 14 October 1066. The invading Norman army has succeeded in luring the Saxons down from the heights of Senlac Hill and the pitched battle could go either way. Suddenly, dismay spreads among the Normans – Duke William has been slain! Among those hearing the dismal news is William himself, perfectly unharmed, yet thoroughly alarmed at the wavering courage of his men. He waves his chainmailed arms about and shouts, but to no avail. Then, desperately risking arrow-shot and axe-blow alike, he pulls up his helmet with its wide nosepiece, revealing his distinctive face. Seeing him alive, his men take courage and throw themselves back into the fray.

William won the day, but the solution of how to identify knights on the battlefield eluded both him and his children for 61 years. It was not until 1127 that his son Henry I invested his own son-in-law Geoffrey of Anjou with a blue shield decorated with golden lions, the first recorded coat of arms. The fact that the same arms appear on the tomb of Geoffrey's grandson William Longespee (d. 1226) indicate that the arms were not only personal, but hereditary in the male line. With this, the first recorded hereditary coat of arms, heraldry was born.

◁ Jousting knights from Sir Thomas Holmes' book (English School, 15th century).

COATS OF MANY COLOURS

Over the next three centuries, armoured knights galloped onto battlefields arrayed in ever-more elaborate regalia. Their coats of arms were painted brightly on their shields and embroidered on their banners. Their surcoats, the mantling draped over their massive helms and, of course, the liveries of their squires, matched the principal colour and 'metal' (gold or silver) of the shield. On top of their helms, tied on by a wreath of the main colour and metal twisted together in a 'tort', sat the impressive crest, often the head of the beast calculated to be most intimidating to the enemy. And on a finger, hidden beneath their armoured gloves, was a signet ring also engraved with the arms. By pressing this into wax, they could indicate their assent to legal agreements and letters because, despite all their chivalric splendour, precious few of them could even sign their own names.

respective homes, they administered the system more or less for the benefit of those paying customers whose conscience and sense of history spurred them either to seek a new grant or to update an existing pedigree.

CREST CONNOTATIONS

Heraldic bookplates and stationery had superseded chivalric battledresses, but heraldry was far from declining. In an age when most employment and marriage agreements were dependent on perceived social status, the appearance of a crest – real or bogus – on one's dinner invitations could tip a very real balance between prosperity and poverty. The heraldic stationers or 'bucket shops' of Doctors' Commons were always happy to oblige, looking up the surname (or even a vaguely similar one) in one of the many armorials on the popular market and supplying a coat of arms for a fraction of the cost of a grant of arms from the College of Arms around the corner.

Except in Scotland, where Lord Lyon was and still is a High Court judge, the heralds could do little to curtail such travesties taking place, literally, under their noses. Indeed, some, such as Bernard Burke, cashed in on the growing market, producing the first edition of *The General Armory of England, Scotland, Ireland and Wales, Comprising a Registry of Armorial Bearings from the Earliest to the Present Time* in 1842. The most complete version is Harrison & Sons' 1884 edition (repr. Burke's Peerage, 1961) and updated by *General Armory Two: Alfred Morant's Additions and Corrections to Burke's General Armory* (Tabard Press, 1973).

The egalitarianism of the 20th century saw a mass disappearance of heraldry from letterheads and monuments alike, to be replaced instead by a plethora of commercial logos. Yet despite everything, the heralds still remain part of the Royal Household. Although their theoretical powers to inflict the death sentence on misusers of heraldry were only removed at the end of the century, their control of the Laws of Arms remain intact to this day.

And so heraldry has survived, partially because of its intimate connection with genealogy, but also in its own right, and arms continue to be granted. In December 2002, Paul McCartney was granted a coat of arms showing four black half-flaunches, symbolising the backs of four beetles, two circles alluding to records and CDs, lines for guitar strings and the crest of a 'Liver bird' holding a guitar. You can't get more up to date than that!

WHERE TO SEARCH

HERALDRY

The best overall guide to the subject is A. Fox Davies' *A Complete Guide to Heraldry* (J. P. Brooke-Little, 1969).

The **College of Arms** records, which can be searched for you by the heralds for a fee, are mainly:
- About 10,000 grants and confirmations of arms by the heralds in the 15th–17th centuries, with evidence such as patents, blazons and sketches.
- Pedigrees and sketches of arms from the heralds' visitations, 1530–1687.
- Funeral certificates for the 16th–17th centuries.
- Collections of pedigrees voluntarily submitted from the ending of the visitations to the present day.
- Special pedigree collections such as those of Ralph Bigland.
- Full texts of all grants from 1673.
- Earl Marshal's books, including royal warrants.

The pedigrees recorded in the visitations (see above) are mainly at the **College of Arms** and **British Library** (**www.catalogue.bl.uk**) and many have been published (with or without scholarly notes and additions) by the Harleian Society and indexed in Whitmore and Marshall (see page 33) and C. R. Humphery-Smith's *Armigerous Ancestors and Those who Weren't: A Catalogue of Visitation Records Together with an Index of Pedigrees, Arms* and *Disclaimers* (IHGS, 1997). These pedigrees form the basis for many of those that appear in the Burke's publications (see page 295), but of course they also include the pedigrees of many families whose money had dissipated by the time *Burke's Landed Gentry* started to be published, so these records contain the forbears of very many families of tradesmen and labourers.

🗗 For crests, look at *Fairbairn's Crests of the Families of Great Britain and Ireland* (New Orchard editions, 1986). Inaccurately computerised and widely syndicated, *Burke's Peerage*, and sometimes *Fairbairn's Crests* too, form the basis for the modern 'coat of arms for your surname' booths that clutter modern shopping arcades and seaside piers.

🗗 If you want to identify a coat of arms, you can use J. W. Papworth and A. W. Morant's *An Alphabetical Dictionary of Arms belonging to Families of Great Britain and Ireland Forming an Extensive Ordinary of British Armorials* (T. Richards, 1874), reprinted as *Papworth's Ordinary of British Armorials* (Tabard Publications, 1961). If the arms are European, consult J. van Helmont's *Dictionnaire de Renesse* (Uitgeverij-Editions, 1992).

🗗 738 Court of Chivalry cases are indexed at **www.court-of-chivalry. bham.ac.uk**.

SCOTLAND

🗗 Scottish heraldry is regulated, fairly strictly, by Lord Lyon King of Arms and his or her heralds, who operate from the **Registrar General of Scotland**. The Lyon Court has maintained a 'register of all arms and bearings in Scotland' since 1672, in which all those using arms are supposed to register. Details of all arms granted and/or registered up to 1972 are published in Sir J. Balfour Paul's *An Ordinary of Arms contained in the Public Register of all Arms and Bearings in Scotland* (William Green and Sons, 1903) and *An Ordinary of Arms, Vol. 2* (1977).

IRELAND

🗗 Under British rule, Irish heraldry was regulated by the Ulster King of Arms. Northern Irish heraldry remains under the jurisdiction of the **College of Arms**, while Eire established its own Office of Arms in Ireland, operating from the **Genealogical Office**, whose grants, visitation pedigrees and funeral certificates can be inspected either there or on microfilm at the **National Archives of Ireland** or at **Mormon Family History Centres**.

QUICK REFERENCE

See also main resources in Useful Addresses, page 306

COLLEGE OF ARMS
Queen Victoria Street
London EC4V 4BT
☎ 020 7248 2762
www.college-of-arms.gov.uk

REGISTRAR GENERAL OF SCOTLAND
New Register House
Charlotte Square
Edinburgh EH1 3YT
☎ 0131 334 0380
www.gro-scotland.gov.uk

GENEALOGICAL OFFICE
2–3 Kildare Street
Dublin 2
Eire
☎ 00 353 1 603 0200
www.nli.ie

△ The crest used, with very dubious authority, by my Hammond ancestors. Not all coats of arms and crests are genuine!

USEFUL ADDRESSES

These addresses are divided into main sources (below) and then general addresses, which start opposite. In the main body of the book, the quick reference panels contain the pertinent general addresses, but as the main sources recur so frequently, they only appear in the quick references panels on their first mention. Thereafter the reader is guided to these pages.

All addresses are in alphabetical order and those for Ireland, Scotland, the Isle of Man and the Channel Islands are on the follow pages:

- ☒ Ireland – see page 310
- ☒ Scotland – see page 311
- ☒ Channel Islands – see page 311
- ☒ Isle of Man – see page 311

MAIN SOURCES

ASSOCIATION OF GENEALOGISTS AND RECORD AGENTS (AGRA)
29 Badgers Close
Horsham
West Sussex RH12 5RU
Website www.agra.org.uk

BRITISH LIBRARY
96 Euston Road
London NW1 2DB
☎ 020 7412 7676
http://blpc.bl.uk

FEDERATION OF FAMILY HISTORY SOCIETIES (FFHS)
PO Box 2425
Coventry CV5 6YX
☎ 024 7667 7798
www.ffhs.org.uk

GENERAL REGISTER OFFICE (GRO)
Smedley Hydro
Trafalgar Road
Southport PR8 2HH
☎ 0870 243 7788
www.gro.gov.uk

GUILDHALL LIBRARY
Aldermanbury
London EC2P 2EJ
☎ 020 7332 1868
www.cityoflondon.gov.uk

HISTORIC MANUSCRIPTS COMMISSION (HMC)
See National Archives
www.archon.nationalarchives.gov.uk/hmc/

INSTITUTE OF HERALDIC AND GENEALOGICAL STUDIES (IHGS)
79–82 Northgate
Canterbury
Kent CT1 1BA
☎ 01227 768664
www.ihgs.ac.uk

MORMON FAMILY HISTORY CENTRES
Locations can be found on www.familysearch.org or in your local phone book. The main one is:
Hyde Park Family History Centre
64/68 Exhibition Road
South Kensington
London SW7 2PA
☎ 020 7589 8561
www.familysearch.org

NATIONAL LIBRARY OF WALES (LLYFRGELL GENEDLAETHOL CYMRU)
Panglais
Aberystwyth
Ceredigion SY23 3BU
☎ 01970 632800
www.llgc.org.uk

SOCIETY OF GENEALOGISTS (SoG)
14 Charterhouse Buildings
Goswell Road
London EC1M 7BA
☎ 020 7251 8799
www.sog.org.uk

THE NATIONAL ARCHIVES (TNA) (INCORPORATING HISTORIC MANUSCRIPTS COMMISSION)
Ruskin Avenue
Kew
Richmond
Surrey TW9 4DU
☎ 020 8876 3444
www.nationalarchives.gov.uk

IRELAND

NATIONAL ARCHIVES OF IRELAND
Bishop Street
Dublin 8
☎ 00 353 1 407 2300
www.nationalarchives.ie

PUBLIC RECORD OFFICE OF NORTHERN IRELAND (PRONI)
66 Balmoral Avenue
Belfast BT9 6NY
☎ 028 9025 5905
http://proni.nics.gov.uk

SCOTLAND

NATIONAL ARCHIVES OF SCOTLAND (NAS)
HM General Register House
2 Princes Street
Edinburgh EH1 3YY
☎ 0131 535 1334
www.nas.gov.uk
As of 2008, the NAS, General Register House and the Court of Lord Lyon are now part of the new ScotlandsPeople Centre, at the same locations in Edinburgh as before.

GENERAL

A

ADOPTION CONTACT REGISTER (England and Wales)
Smedley Hydro, Trafalgar Road,
Southport, Merseyside PR8 2HH
☎ 0151 471 4830
www.statistics.gov.uk/registration

ARMY MEDALS OFFICE
Government Office Buildings,
Worcester Road, Droitwich,
Worcestershire WR9 8AU
☎ 01905 772323
www.army.mod.uk

ARMY MUSEUM OGILBY TRUST
58 The Close, Salisbury SP1 2EX
☎ 01722 332188
www.armymuseums.org.uk

ARMY RECORDS CENTRE
Ministry of Defence,
Historical Disclosure, Mail Point 400,
Kentigern House, 65 Brown Street,
Glasgow G2 8EX
☎ 0141 224 3030
www.mod.uk

B

BANK OF ENGLAND ARCHIVES
Threadneedle Street,
London EC2R 8AH
☎ 020 7601 5096
www.bankofengland.co.uk/archive.htm

BARNARDO'S AFTER-CARE DEPARTMENT
Barnardo's, Tanners Lane, Barkingside,
Essex IG6 1QG
☎ 020 8550 8822
www.barnardos.org.uk/whatwedo/after
care

BORTHWICK INSTITUTE FOR ARCHIVES
University of York, Heslington,
York YO10 5DD
☎ 01904 321166
www.york.ac.uk/inst/bihr

BRITISH AGENCIES FOR ADOPTION & FOSTERING (BAAF)
Skyline House, 200 Union Street,
London SE1 0LX
☎ 020 7593 2000
www.baaf.org.uk

BRITISH LIBRARY NEWSPAPER LIBRARY
Colindale Avenue, London NW9 5HE
☎ 020 7412 7353
www.bl.uk/collections/newspapers.html

BRITISH LIBRARY, ORIENTAL AND INDIA OFFICE COLLECTIONS
96 Euston Road, London NW1 2DB
☎ 020 7412 7873
www.bl.uk/collections/orientalandindian.
html

BRITISH TELECOM ARCHIVES
3rd Floor, Holborn Telephone Exchange,
268–270 High Holborn,
London WC1V 7EE
☎ 020 7492 8792
www.btplc.com/archives

C

CAMDEN LOCAL STUDIES & ARCHIVE CENTRE
Holborn Library, 32 Theobalds Road,
London WC1X 8PA
☎ 020 7974 6342
www.camden.gov.uk/localstudies

CAMDEN PUBLIC LIBRARY
88 Avenue Road, London NW3 3HA
☎ 020 7974 6522
www.camden.gov.uk

CATHOLIC CENTRAL LIBRARY
New address not available at time of
going to print
☎ 020 7732 8379
www.catholic-library.org.uk

CATHOLIC FAMILY HISTORY SOCIETY
The Secretaries,
45 Gates Green Road, West Wickham,
Bromley, Kent BR4 9DE

CATHOLIC RECORD SOCIETY
c/o 12 Melbourne Place,
Wolsingham, Co. Durham DL13 3EH
☎ 01388 527747
www.catholic-history.org.uk/crs

CHILDREN'S SOCIETY
Post Adoption and Care Project,
91–3 Queen's Road, Peckham,
London SE15 2EZ
☎ 020 7732 9089
www.the-childrens-society.org.uk

CITY OF WESTMINSTER ARCHIVES CENTRE
10 St Ann's Street, London SW1P 2DE
☎ 020 7641 5180
www.westminster.gov.uk/libraries/archives

COLLEGE OF ARMS
Queen Victoria Street, London EC4V 4BT
☎ 020 7248 2762
www.college-of-arms.gov.uk

COMMONWEALTH WAR GRAVES COMMISSION
2 Marlow Road, Maidenhead,
Berkshire SL6 7DX
☎ 01628 634221
www.cwgc.org

COMPANIES HOUSE
21 Bloomsbury Street, London WC1B 3XD
☎ 0870 333 3636
www.companieshouse.gov.uk

COMPANIES HOUSE
Crown Way, Maindy, Cardiff CF14 3UZ
☎ 0870 333 3636
www.companieshouse.gov.uk

CORPORATION OF LONDON RECORD
c/o London Metropolitan Archives,
40 Northampton Road,
London EC1R 0HB
☎ 020 7332 3820
wwwcityoflondon.gov.uk

COURT OF THE CHIEF RABBI
London Beth Din, Adler House,
735 High Road, London N12 0US
☎ 020 8343 6270
info@chiefrabbi.org
www.chiefrabbi.org

CREMATION SOCIETY OF GREAT BRITAIN
Brecon House, 16 Albion Place,
Maidstone, Kent ME14 5DZ
☎ 01622 688292
www.cremation.org.uk

CROOK'S LIVERPOOL MARRIAGE INDEX
25 Gerneth Road,
Speke, Liverpool L24 1UN

PICTURE CREDITS

The publishers wish to thank the following people for use of the following pictures in this book. The other pictures are from the collections of Anthony Adolph and of those listed in paragraph two, overleaf. Where only a picture credit is given, identification details can be found in the caption to the illustration. **BAL** = Bridgeman Art Library; **LMA** = London Metropolitan Archive

Cecilia Doidge-Ripper at TNA in the FRC and Rhys Griffith at the LMA; **12-13** *Portrait of a Family: The Birthday of the Mother* by J. Dastine © Archivo Iconografico, S.A./CORBIS; **26 below** National Gallery, London/BAL; **27 left** *Prosperous Victorian family, three generations united in a garden setting.* Photograph, c.1880. © Bettmann/CORBIS; **27 right** Old portrait of a family. © Andy Washnik/CORBIS; **28** Public Record Office Building in Kew. © London Aerial Photo Library/CORBIS; **34** © Simonpietri Christian/CORBIS SYGMA; **39** Archivio di Stato, Siena, Italy/Alinari/BAL; **41** Cott Nero DIV f.139, British Library, London/BAL; **47** Office of National Statistics; **51** Christopher Wood Gallery, London/BAL; **52** *Gin Lane*, 1751, by William Hogarth/Bibliothèque Nationale, Paris, France, Lauros/Giraudon/BAL; **54** The Edge of Sherwood Forest, 1878 by Andrew MacCallum/Phillips, The International Fine Art Auctioneers, UK/BAL; **63** LMA; **65** Office of National Statistics; **67** Musée des Beaux-Arts, Arras, France, Giraudon / BAL; **68** FRC; **76** Census in 1949. © Hulton-Deutsch Collection/CORBIS; **84** Phone directory of the United Telephone Company, 1885; **85** Mary Evans Picture Library; **86** Guildhall Art Gallery, Corporation of London/BAL; **87** Musée de l'Assistance Publique, Hopitaux de Paris, France/BAL; **88** LMA; **92** LMA; **94** LMA; **96** York Museums Trust (York Art Gallery), UK/BAL; **97** *Lord Cromwell, Wearing the Order of St George* by Hans Holbein (school of)/The Trustees of the Weston Park Foundation/BAL; **102** Christie's Images, London/BAL; **103 above** *Racquets at the Fleet Prison*, illustration from *London Life*, pub. 1809, English School (19th century)/Private Collection, photo: Wingfield Sporting Gallery, London/BAL; **108** Phillimore Publishers; **114** Society of Genealogists; **116-17** *View of New Amsterdam*, 1650–3, Dutch School (17th century)/Museum of the City of New York/BAL; **118** Yale Center for British Art, Paul Mellon Fund, USA/BAL; **119** Great Bealings Manorial Court Book 1746–1803. Suffolk Record Office, Ipswich. Ref 51/2/32/2 p.84; **121** The Berger Collection at the Denver Art Museum, USA/BAL; **122** Fol.10v Biblioteca Marciana, Venice, Italy, photo: Roger-Viollet, Paris/BAL; **124** Fol.195v from *Justiniani in Fortiatum*, French School (14th century)/Biblioteca Monasterio del Escorial, Madrid, Spain, Giraudon/BAL; **125** Hampshire Record Office; **142-143** Sir Arthur Conan Doyle and his Family, 1922. © Bettmann/CORBIS; **154** LMA; **156** Private Collection, photo: The Stapleton Collection/BAL; **157** Private Collection, photo: Michael Graham-Stewart/BAL; **158** Musée des Arts d'Afrique et d'Océanie, Paris, France, photo: Archives Charmet/BAL; **159** © New-York Historical Society, New York/BAL; **160** Detail from Camberwell and Stockwell map, reproduced from the 1913 Ordnance Survey Map; **161 above** Private Collection/BAL; **161 below** Lancashire Record Office; **168** Suffolk Record Office, Ipswich; **170** Hampshire Record Office; **172** Guildhall Library, Corporation of London/BAL; **174** City of Westminster Archive Centre, London/BAL; **175** Royal Holloway, University of London/BAL; **176** Private Collection/BAL; **177** National Gallery, London/BAL; **180** The Maas Gallery, London/BAL; **182** The Postman from *Costume of Great Britain*, 1805, by William Henry Pyne/Guildhall Library, Corporation of London/BAL; **191 left** © Stapleton Collection/CORBIS; **192–3** © Historical Picture Archive/CORBIS; **194** © CORBIS; **195** *The Battle of Isandhlwana*, 1879, by Charles Edwin Fripp/National Army Museum, London/BAL; **197** © Hulton-Deutsch Collection/CORBIS; **198** © Hulton-Deutsch Collection/CORBIS; **199** Unveiling of the Royal Artillery War Memorial, London in 1925. © Hulton-Deutsch Collection/CORBIS; **203** TNA ADM 38; **205** TNA ADM 188; **206** © Hulton-Deutsch Collection/CORBIS; **209** Private Collection, photo: Royal Exchange Art Gallery at Cork Street, London/BAL; **210** Private Collection, photo: The Stapleton Collection/BAL; **211** © Hulton-Deutsch Collection/CORBIS; **215** The Trustees of the Weston Park Foundation/BAL; **216** Abbot Hall Art Gallery, Kendal, Cumbria/BAL; **217** TNA E 179; **223** An Execution of Witches in England, English School (17th century)/Private Collection, photo: The Stapleton Collection/BAL; **225** © Bettmann/CORBIS; **229** House of Lords from Ackermann's *Microcosm of London* by T. Rowlandson & A.C. Pugin/Private Collection/BAL; **233** *Execution of John Thurtell at Hertford Jail in 1824*, Anonymous/Guildhall Library, Corporation of London/BAL; **234** Guildhall Art Gallery, Corporation of London/ BAL; **239** TNA HO 144; **247** Map of East Prussia. from *Le Theatre du Monde* or *Nouvel Atlas*, 1645, by Joan Blaeu/ Bibliotheque des Arts Decoratifs, Paris, France, photo: Archives Charmet/BAL; **253** *In the Land of Promise* by Charles Frederic Ulrich/ Corcoran Gallery of Art, Washington DC/BAL; **254** *A Government Jail Gang, Sydney, New South Wales*, 19th century by Augustus Earle/ Private Collection/BAL; **256** Private Collection, photo: Philip Mould, Historical Portraits Ltd, London/BAL; **259** Mallett & Son Antiques Ltd, London, UK/BAL; **264 left** *Portrait of George Fox*, engraving after Painting by Chinn. © Bettmann/CORBIS; **264 right** © Bettmann/CORBIS; **267** *Swarthmore Hall* by John Jewell Penstone/Newport Museum and Art Gallery, South Wales/BAL; **269** Private Collection, photo: Christie's Images/BAL; **270** © Archivo Iconografico, S.A./CORBIS; **271** © CORBIS SYGMA; **272** © Mike Laye/CORBIS; **273** © Lee Snider/CORBIS; **274–5** Smiling Young Family on doorstep. © Leland Bobbé/CORBIS; **276** © Digital Art/CORBIS; **279** Boats moored along fishing village, Iceland. © Layne Kennedy/CORBIS; **280** *Victoria at age two, with her mother, the duchess of Kent*, 1821, by Sir William Beechey. Mary Evans Picture Library; © Bettmann/CORBIS; **282 above** © Hulton-Deutsch Collection/CORBIS; **282 below** Ms.3066 fol.42 v Bibliotheque Municipale, Rouen, France/BAL; **284** San Michele in Isola, Venice, Italy/BAL; **287** *Clans of Scotland* by W. Eagle, no date (c.1850); **288** Sign at St. Patrick's Quay, Cork. © Richard Cummins/CORBIS; **290** Private Collection, photo: The Stapleton Collection/BAL; **291** Lord Lyon's Office, Edinburgh, Scotland, photo: Mark Fiennes/BAL; **294** © Tim Graham/CORBIS; **299** Harley 4205 f.37 British Library, London/BAL; **300 above** Stirling Castle, Scotland/BAL; **301** © Royal Hospital Chelsea, London/BAL.

ACKNOWLEDGEMENTS

AUTHOR'S THANKS

This book could not have been written without the help of many people – the expertise I have picked up over the years from a host of genealogists, professional and amateur, or the many clients and TV volunteers whose research cases first alerted me to some of the examples I have used in the text. My thanks go out to all of them in proportion to the kindness they have shown me. I would particularly like to thank those colleagues in the profession who have been of direct help in providing facts used in the text: Marie Louise Backhurst, Judith Batchelor, Mrs Nancy Bedwell, Sarah Bulson, Mark Bonthrone, Rosemary Byatt, Philip Coverdale, Veronica Craig Mair, Paul Dart, Patric Dickinson (Richmond Herald), Essex Record Office, Norman Fairfax, Simon Fowler (to whom especial thanks are due for his help with the chapter on armed forces), Michael Gandy, Joanna Guariglia, Mrs Josephine Harwood-Little, Reg Havers, Peter Horne, Mrs Dora Kneebone, Daphne Knott, Richard Lloyd-Roberts, Justin Martin, Sue Mendel, Peter Nutt, Jeremy Palmer, Tinka Paterson, Mark Pearsall, Dr Peter Pohl, Chris Schofield, Diana Spelman, Steve Thomas, Gerry Toop, Charles Tucker, Basil Twigg and Michael Watts. Especial thanks, too, go to my esteemed fellow writer James Essinger who gave me enormously valuable encouragement at the outset of my writing career; my agent, Michael Alcock of Johnson & Alcock Ltd, who calmly created the opportunity for me to write this book; Denise Bates of Collins, who had the wonderful prescience to conceive and commission it in the first place; Emma Callery for managing the project, Brian DeLeeuw for his help with the initial stages, Ruth Prentice for her handsome design, and Kate Parker for her meticulous proofreading.

My thanks also go to those who gave me their kind permission to use their stories in this book, including those that space did not, ultimately, permit us to use: Mrs Deorwyn Baker; Mrs Lorna Barbour; J. Blain Esq.; Mrs Claudia Brannback; I. Burns-Thompson Esq.; Mark Curtis Esq.; W. H.Galleway Esq.; Louisa Jenkins; Dr Terry Lacy; T. J. Lewis Esq.; A. P. Lingen-Stallard Esq.; P. J. Littlemore Esq.; M. A. Lowry Esq.; Messrs M. S. and U. Mehta; Major P. Mercer; Simon Mountenay Esq., W. C. Nichols Esq; Major R. D. Seals; D. P. Stewart Esq.; F. J. Tourlamain Esq.; R. V. Upton Esq.; Vice Admiral D. B. H.Wildish CB; L. A. Wilmshurst Esq.; M. Wilson Esq.; to Ms Petra Barberini; Ms Benhilda Chisveto and Ms Naomi Jalil, whom I was unable to locate, I send my thanks for alerting me to their wonderful family stories through *Extraordinary Ancestors*.

It has been commonplace to say that we live in a dislocated society, in which people do not feel they belong, and do not understand where they come from. Yet, thanks to genealogy (amongst other things), we are becoming much better informed. More and more people tracing family trees means more and more people are aware of the plethora of connections that bind us together and which make nonsense of religious and ethnic divides. If society is becoming a little fairer, less prejudiced and more cohesive, then genealogy can take its share of the credit and, the more popular it becomes, the greater too – I hope – will be its positive effects. But, above all, enjoy it.

...r Erfindung verschwunden war." ...

...nisch. „Nun, glücklicherweise war...
...e eine Hälfte davon, die andere...
...versehrt zwischen meinen Stiefeln...
...o ich sie vorsichtshalber versteckt hatte.
...reude werden die Beefsteaksesser...
...aub nicht erlebt haben — und ihnen...
...te Schurkerei mit Zinsen zurückzahlen...
...o hier."

„Kommen Sie endlich zur Sache!"

„Mein Mittel, ein Stickstoffpräparat...
...at, ist im Grunde harmlos, doch sobald...
...sobald Sie wollen, den Engländern...
...flotte und ihre Schlachtstellung...
Sie werden wollen! — Ich habe mich Ap...
...rat konstruiert, der mittels...